ON BEING A TEACHER

ONE OF THE FOREMOST SOCIAL writers in the USA, Jonathan Kozol—Harvard educated, a Rhodes Scholar, and a teacher—has written passionately on poverty, homelessness, illiteracy and education. *Death at an Early Age*, his first book, won the National Book Award in Science, Philosophy and Religion, and has sold over 2 million copies. *Rachel and her Children* was awarded the Robert F. Kennedy Book Award for 1989 and the Conscience in Media Award of the American Society of Journalists and Authors. *Savage Inequalities* was a nominee for the 1992 National Book Critics Circle Award, was awarded the New England Book Award, and is a New York Times Bestseller. Mr Kozol has held two Guggenheim Fellowships, has twice been a fellow of the Rockefeller Foundation, and has received fellowships from the Field and Ford Foundations. He lives in Byfield, Massachusetts.

Books by Jonathan Kozol

ON BEING A TEACHER

JONATHAN KOZOL

ONEWORLD

OXFORD

A Oneworld Book

First published 1981
Revised edition first published by Oneworld Publications 1993
This paperback edition first published 2009
Reprinted 2009

ISBN 978–1–85168–631–5

Cover design by Mike Harpley
Printed and bound in Great Britain
by Bell & Bain, Glasgow

Oneworld Publications
185 Banbury Road
Oxford OX2 7AR
England
www.oneworld-publications.com

Acknowledgments

Tisha Graham has worked with me on every page and paragraph of this book. I have relied on her loyalty during endless hours of revision. She has helped me in attempting to make difficult decisions regarding classroom strategies. She has advised me concerning the terrible (but sometimes fascinating) challenges that are encountered every day by conscientious teachers. She has done her best to teach me to write with patience of those with whom I deeply disagree. She is a truthful, totally unselfish woman. I am deeply grateful.

I would also like to thank my fellow teacher Leonard Solo for his loyal support and my patient friends and allies Judith Arnold and Joyce Tatelman, who have typed this book through four revisions. Finally, I thank my mother and my father and my special co-worker Genise Schnitman.

It may be that there is no other way of educating people. Possibly, but I don't believe it. In the meantime it would be a help at least to describe things properly, to call things by their right names. Ideally, what should be said to every child, repeatedly, throughout his or her school life is something like this:

"You are in the process of being indoctrinated. We have not yet evolved a system of education that is not a system of indoctrination. We are sorry, but it is the best we can do. What you are being taught here is an amalgam of current prejudice and the choices of this particular culture. The slightest look at history will show how impermanent these must be. You are being taught by people who have been able to accommodate themselves to a regime of thought laid down by their predecessors. It is a self-perpetuating system. Those of you who are more robust and individual than others, will be encouraged to leave and find ways of educating yourself—educating your own judgment. Those that stay must remember, always and all the time, that they are being moulded and patterned to fit into the narrow and particular needs of this particular society."

The Golden Notebook[1]
Doris Lessing

For this, and all subsequent quotations, references, and items of documentation, see "Notes" in back of book.

Contents

Preface to the Second Edition

This book, which was first published thirty years ago in the United States, emerged from my sense of deep frustration at the ethical dilemmas faced by teachers, and sometimes their students, in the schools of the United States. Inevitably, as a result, certain references seem slightly dated and some passages convey a note of special anger at America that I no longer find quite logical or justifiable.

The writing grew out of an era when the Watergate scandal had discredited the honor of the U.S. government and when a right-wing political climate had begun to sweep the nation, canceling out the gains that had been made in civil rights and social justice in the age of John F. Kennedy and Martin Luther King. The bitterness of that climate forms the social context of this writing and may help explain some of the harshness of the tone.

If there is one aspect of the work that I especially deplore, it is my tendency to treat indoctrination in the public schools as if it were the unique property of education in one nation, rather than a tendency familiar to all nations. Surely there was far more indoctrination in the schools of the Soviet Union, for example, than in those of the United States; but one would never know this from the writing. I wish that I had made it far more clear.

Then, too, there is the curious assumption that only public schools indoctrinate their children and that private education is somehow intrinsically more generous and friendly to dissent. As we now know in the United States, this is by no means true. Private schools identified with fundamentalist Christian groups, with various ethnic sectors of the population and with conservative business interests are often even more overtly partisan, intolerant and narrow in their ideologies—and sometimes quite vicious in the suppression or exclusion of competing views.

The longing to indoctrinate the young in an accepted body of adult beliefs is neither uniquely North American nor solely characteristic of the public realm. It is a characteristic of societies of every kind, and to a troubling degree it limits the potential of young people everywhere to grow beyond the arid values and, too often, ardent bigotries of the preceding generation. It is for this reason that I welcome publication of this book for English-speaking people in all nations.

With the end of the Cold War and the break-up of the Stalinist regimes of Eastern Europe, we are facing for the first time in a century the prospect of a world no longer split into armed camps of overweening power. One might like to hope that such a world would find less need than in the past for the indoctrination of its youth. Unhappily, however, narrow biases and partisan distrusts seem almost to have grown more rampant in the past few years. Ethnic groups from Germany to Yugoslavia, from Africa to Russia, seem to have exploded into internecine frenzies of hostility and fear; ethnic and linguistic balkanization threatens Canada and the United States as well. In this climate, the desire to indoctrinate the young in fealty to one narrow loyalty—and in hostility to those who do not share it—may well grow more common than at any time in many years. So the need for teachers to develop strategies of ethical denunciation and dissent is all the greater and more urgent while the punishment for such dissent may be considerably more severe.

This little book presents a set of strategies for teachers to employ in classroom education. While the specific examples given here are, as I have said, somewhat outdated, the strategies themselves are not. They represent an arsenal of pedagogic independence that may be of use to teachers in all nations and all decades. I hope that they will be of help to serious educators as they join the worldwide struggle to release our children from the shadows of old demonologies and as they work to plant the seeds of an intelligent irreverence in their students' hearts and minds.

Jonathan Kozol
Boston, Massachusetts

Preface

This is a book for teachers and for those whose children are, for twelve consecutive years, entrusted to their care. In writing all that follows, I have drawn repreatedly upon my own six years in the classroom as a teacher of fourth and fifth grade children and as headmaster of a small and independent urban school, as well as upon a number of other teaching obligations that run the range from pre-college work in Upward Bound to a recent spring semester at South Boston High.

The deepest and most resonant portions of this book, however, depend upon many hundreds of late-night conversations with rank and file teachers. Again and again, at the weary tail-end of a conference, lecture or colloquium, four or five teachers will ask me to sit down and chat. They open up a bottle of wine, or a six-pack of beer, and quietly start to speak about the struggles, fears, dilemmas of a life's career.

Many of these teachers have labored for decades to confront the myths, the tedium and the repetitive humiliations of archaic textbooks and preposterous conventions long-embedded in the written or unwritten rule books of the schools in which they teach. As our late-night meetings continue, I listen to the voices of extraordinary people with a deep tradition of persistence in the face of system-wide timidity and intimidation—teachers who have worked from day to day, and year to year, with neither the glamour of book publication nor the short-lived glow of press or media attention, seldom rewarded in any way at all except perhaps in the one and only way that decent teachers ever find reward: in the gratification of a difficult job done well and in a very basic kind of private dignity courageously upheld.

They work hard, are paid little, but are obliged to contribute almost all their waking hours to the daily task for which they are employed. Virtually any of these teachers could earn more, at less expenditure of time and energy, in almost any other field of intellectual pursuit. Still, they persist.

This book, then, is not only intended for the use of classroom teachers. It is also, and to a very large degree, a compilation of their own views, strategies and ideals. In the long run, it is they—a good deal more than family or TV—who shape the values and establish the competence of the generation now in public school. Their obligation is, for this reason, all the greater—no matter how difficult the task, no matter how high the price or how bewildering the odds.

PART I

Brass Tacks
Strategies for Change

Why Are We Here?
What Is the Job That We
Are Being Asked To Do?

Conscientious teachers who have studied the origins of public
education are faced with a difficult and painful choice: If they
are honest with themselves and with each other, they cannot
help but look upon the public school today as an archaic and
dehumanizing institution. This is true not only for the students, but for their teachers also. Students reside within this
house of lies for only twelve years at a stretch. Their teachers
often are condemned to a life sentence.

Many teachers live and work, as a result, in somewhat the
same state of mind as intellectual guerrillas, determined somehow to awaken students, to spark their curiosity and to open
up their minds, yet no less determined to *remain* as teachers
in the schools. We live and work with a strong resolve to raise
some basic, challenging and perhaps subversive questions in
the consciousness of children. At the same time we have got
to keep in mind the needs of our families, health care, food
and mortgage and the rest.

How do we begin? How do we start to free ourselves from
impotence and from inertia—in order to be able to fight back?

One logical first step in this process is the effort to desanc-
tify the public school itself as a seemingly immutable sanctuary of some of the most conservative values of the social order.
There are dozens of ways to open up this subject in the full

view of the class. It can be done by quoting the words of various respected people, such as Horace Mann, who were unhesitant in giving voice to the real purposes of public school. It can be done by giving older students access to a wide array of contemporary books—excerpts, for example, from the words of Edgar Friedenberg, Jules Henry and Paul Goodman, as well as several others who have helped us, as adults, to demystify our own conception of the public schools. It can also be done (and this I believe is the most effective way of all) by sitting down and talking openly with students, in much the way that Doris Lessing recommends.

For those, however, who hesitate to start out with expression of their own opinions, and who prefer to take advantage of provocative quotations from authoritative sources in the present or the past, it is fortunate that some of the most intriguing and revelatory statements happen to derive from unimpeachable, or in any event unquestionably respectable, authorities.

The Board of Education of the state of Arizona, for example, lays it on the line in very brisk, explicit terms. "It is not the job of the schools," the Arizona Board explains, "to create a new social order . . ." The job is "to augment a child's love of country . . . ideals of the home . . . appreciation of traditional values . . ." In another statement, the Arizona Board goes on: "We are proposing a course of study for American children . . ." The document explains our obligation to enable children to appreciate "the nature of national power . . ." The consequence of this education, we are told, ought to be a recognition of those forces which could undermine our nation, in order that students "may recognize and . . . thwart such threats . . ." The final result which Arizona teachers are expected to achieve includes, above all else, a recognition that our nation is "the envy of the civilized world . . . the last best hope of mankind . . ."[2]

There is no pretense here of going to school to learn to be a sensitive, loving or compassionate person, nor one who is concerned in any way at all about those people who do not live in this nation but who, nonetheless, in the opinion of most teachers and their students, still may seem to hold some claims upon our loyalty as human beings.

However we do it, I believe it is our job to make quite clear to students that schools exist precisely in order to destroy such loyalty: to lead us to conceive an evil "differential" in the worth of human life, depending on whether that life is white, American, Nordic, Western European, or whether—in contrast—it is the life of someone black or brown, Third World or socialist, or, in any event, "not like our own."

Teachers who do no more than find and make available to pupils a number of forceful quotations on this subject, but do not choose to underline the fact that tragic actions (My Lai, for example) are the direct result of education of this kind, have got to face the fact that most of their students will protectively absorb these statements back into the undisturbing matrix of a lifetime of parental bias, TV pacification and eleven other years of public school indoctrination which either precede or follow those few months in which our pupils have a chance to look into our eyes and (sometimes) hear our views. We have no choice, therefore, if we should wish to make our point both unforgettable and clear, but to add something of our own conviction to the words we quote from others.

I spoke above of Massachusetts educator Horace Mann. Mann's views are in painful accord with those of the Arizona Board of Education, although his most disarming words speak less about political indoctrination than about another major function in our public schools: class stratification. In a report to the Massachusetts Board of Education in 1844, he made it all too clear: "Finally, in regard to those who possess the largest shares . . . of wordly goods, could there, in your opinion, be any police so vigilant and effective, for protection of all the rights of person, property and character, as such a . . .

system of common schools could be made to impart. . . .
Would not the payment of a sufficient tax to make such education and training universal, be the cheapest means of self-
protection and insurance?"[3]

Here again, I see no reason why a teacher ought to hesitate
to make quite sure that the children wholly understand what
Horace Mann has said. His name is carved in granite on the
front of schools all over the United States. His words (*protection* and *insurance*), therefore, are very much like precious
gems to those who wish to clarify this point. Students who are
only in the sixth or seventh grade, however, are likely to lose
themselves in his elaborate syntax. I don't believe that any
sensible person is going to accuse a teacher of manipulative
imposition if all we do is to make sure that children really get
the point of these extraordinary words.

Another man whom teachers might do well to quote (and
whom, of course, they would be able to quote with absolute
impunity from potential adversaries) is the twenty-eighth president of our nation, Woodrow Wilson. "We want one class of
people to have a liberal education, and we want one class of
persons, a very much larger class of persons, of necessity, to
forego the privileges of a liberal education and fit into specific
manual tasks."[4] How can a school board which professes to
respect American tradition plausibly seek to reprimand a
teacher who relies upon the words of Woodrow Wilson?

The reason for quoting educators such as Horace Mann—
still better, a distinguished president of the United States—is
in order to protect ourselves against malicious and destructive
criticism. A lot of other people, such as Upton Sinclair and
Jack London, say very much the same things Woodrow Wilson
did. But why go out and hunt up radical and angry writers
when the men who run this nation state it all so well themselves? Those who fight a battle of whatever kind against a
powerful foe often find that one of the most effective strategies
is to steal into the weapons warehouse of those who hold the

reins of power and obtain their ammunition there. The words of people such as Woodrow Wilson represent precisely the kind of ammunition that I have in mind.

If school, as Horace Mann insists, is meant to be "the cheapest means" of self-protection for the rich, then students ought to know this early in the game—while they are still in school—not once it is all over. John Kenneth Galbraith has observed that mass deception seldom works so well once people understand that it is taking place.

Another way to underline this point about the actual as opposed to the mythical objectives of our public schools is to draw the parallel to a "consumer fraud." Schools are the fourth biggest business in the nation. (Defense, "the readiness for war," comes first.) Like many other business enterprises in this nation—food producers, for example, and the supermarket chains—schools are guilty of most of the major facets of consumer fraud: false labels, dangerous content and half-empty boxes.

Schools advertise a lot of sweet and optimistic things: truth and beauty, the pursuit of greater insight into our own soul, "a search for humane values in a troubled time"—along with a couple of good old-fashioned things like basic skills. That, at least, is what the label says. Inside the box, too often, what we find is just exactly what the founders of our public education system said that we would find: class stratification and political indoctrination. For many teachers, the example of consumer fraud provides a very simple means by which to make a complicated point more clear: School advertises one thing, sells another. In any other realm of life, this would be castigated and forbidden.

Issues like these can be conveyed to students without the use of radical rhetoric—and also without the attribution of "conspiracy" to any sinister or demonic force. Rich men and women, school board members, textbook editors—and the people at the State Department and the C.I.A.—don't need to meet each other in a secret bunker beneath the mountains of Montana every year in order to decide the way to fry the brains of little kids and stamp a patriotic imprint in between their eyes. The reason they don't need to meet or to conspire is quite clear: They share most of the same self-serving values as the consequence of their own long period of years in public school. Those who have so much in common to defend by law-mandated lies do not need to meet in secret hiding places in Montana.

To make this point in front of students—and to try at the same time to steer away from ominous talk of "ruling-class oppression" and the like—seems to me a useful way to ward off criticism from those who otherwise may try to slot us, in a simpleminded way, as "troublemakers." In honest fact, we *might* be, but we are certainly not simpleminded or dogmatic. And we are a great deal more effective, I believe, as a direct result.

Whenever I have the chance to speak with pupils in the public schools, I do my best to emphasize a fact that schools do everything they can to lead us to forget: Public schools did not exist forever. They did not come out of the forehead of a Greek or Roman god. They were contrived by men and women—ordinary, sometimes clever, sometimes not so clever, men and women—and, for just this reason, they can be rebuilt or reconceived, dismantled or replaced, not by another set of gods, but by plain men and women too.

A teacher might speak to students in such simple words as these: "Anything that was first contrived by men and women can be taken apart or thrown away by men and women also. It isn't unchangeable. It isn't inexorable. You and I can leave school as it is, can change it slightly, or else we can turn it inside out and upside down."

If a teacher does say something of this sort to students, certain people will probably protest that children should not be compelled to hear this kind of talk when they are still so young. I disagree: Why should we wait until our students are as weary, weak and soul-broken as we, before we dare to tell them what it's all about?

It may be that school manipulation will no longer work once students have a chance to see it for exactly what it is. Those who tell us we should wait "another year or more" before we speak of matters of this kind are usually those who wish that we would wait forever.

Why should we delay in areas so basic to the truth we wish to live by—or the lies that presently degrade us and our pupils too?

First Person Singular—and Plural

In order to be able to achieve the sense of inner leverage to perceive the schools as institutions we have power to transform, students and teachers need to feel they have the right, the license and the sanction to speak out in the first person plural: "we." People, however, cannot easily say "we" if they do not first achieve the sense of self-possession to say "I."

Schools, by tradition, do all that they can to train us *not* to speak in the first person. In the classic situation in the elementary grades, if a child speaks in rude, impatient words to a school teacher, there is a stock response that comes out often in a kind of singsong. "Is that any way," the teacher asks, "to speak to me?" Instead of saying *me*, however, teachers often seem to step away and speak as if they had replaced themselves by someone else: "Is that any way to speak to . . . Miss O'Brien?"

It is, for just one moment, as if she were not "in presence" in the room, but locked up somehow in the closet with the chalk and chalk-erasers. In the universities and high schools, we hear the same thing—for example, in those "regulations for term papers" which instruct the students to avoid the sound of their own voice: "The paper should have a clearly indicated introduction, body and conclusion. Do not use the word *I* except in the conclusion . . ."

It is as if the students can't admit that they are *there* until they are about to leave the room. It is the ideal language for an alienated people in a mechanistic land. Those who do not know that they exist, and live, and breathe, in the first person are the perfect workers to press buttons on sophisticated instruments in vast and modern industries of war—or else to press those buttons that release the bombs and napalm on defenseless villages in foreign nations.

Pilots and presidents who live and breathe in the third person can make the gruesome choice to wipe out a whole continent, destroy a population or obliterate a city with a single weapon, then go to bed and sleep for eight good hours in uninterrupted peace. It isn't just a foolish English lesson, then. It is something far more frightening and more disturbing.

One of the ways by which a teacher can begin to fight this myth, right in the context of the public school, is by providing students with direct, exciting access to the words, the voices, the whole manner of self-presentation, of some of those men and women in our own or former times who have been able to transcend this inhibition and who do, as a direct result, feel power to speak out in their own words and to regain the sense of their own voice.

"In most books, the 'I', or first person, is omitted. In this [book,] it will be retained." These words are from the first page of *Walden* by Thoreau. That, he says, is "the main difference" between his own book and those of other writers.

There will be dozens of other examples of this willingness to speak out in first person pronouns in the later sections of this book. Merely to quote from famous people is, however, less effective, in my own belief, than another method which many teachers put into effect without a tactical intent, but pretty much by nature. This is—in a literal sense—to learn to speak out and to *be,* an open and at all times undisguised "first person," exemplified in the very ways that we behave with students and in the words we choose to speak in the course of conversations with them.

I do not mean simply that we ought to be prepared to state our own opinions within earshot of our pupils (although I do mean this, as well), but that we also need to be first persons in the eyes of children in the deeper sense of letting all our own complexities, our viewpoints, hesitations, dreams and passions—and our vulnerable aspects, too—become apparent to the class.

I think that many seasoned teachers will perceive in this a recommendation which is far more subversive than it may at first appear. It is subversive both of the age-old school tradition of professional behavior on the part of educators and also—sad to say—of many teachers' age-old concept of *themselves*. Few of us are encouraged, in the course of teacher preparation, to grant ourselves the luxury of being just plain human beings within the eyes of children.

The concept of professional behavior, as it has been defined for fifty years in public education, is devoid of almost all intensities. The teacher does not easily yield to indignation, weep for passion, rage at grief. All that we love in drama, all that we find breathtaking in a film, all that is tragic, comic, intense, extreme, remarkable, is filtered from the teacher's manner. If film and drama were restricted to the range of feelings present in this type of classroom, the theaters would quickly empty and the people would pour out on the streets. Only the schools command a captive box office, because attendance at their presentation is compulsory.

Sometimes, seeing the traditional grade-school teacher standing there within that room, blackboard behind her, chalk dust about her, one wonders what would happen if, for a terrible moment, she should lose control, forget herself—and swear. Swear right there, in front of the class, like ordinary people do, without the time to qualify her words. Would the children smile? Would she be smiling too? It seems at times as if the sky will break in pieces, the roof collapse and the walls come down in timbers if the teacher, walking across the room before the class, should bang her knee on the edge of a table and it should start to bleed. One wonders if, perhaps, it wouldn't even bleed—not like the knees of other people. If it did bleed, it would tell the children she was human.

The professional inhibition I have just described is one that was carefully molded and foisted upon us by successive generations. It is a pattern which self-respecting teachers will no longer tolerate today, and everyone who cares for kids *and* teachers—as well as for the future of American education— must rejoice as a result.

In making this statement, I do not intend to recommend, instead, the whimsical and irresponsible behavior which was identified with the counterculture of ten years ago. This sort of behavior (exemplified often in a slipshod manner and a disrespectful style of dress) seems to me, indeed, almost more dangerous than the style it was intended to replace. Moreover, it cannot conceivably win us allies where we need them most. It either alienates or, at least, disquiets many parents who might otherwise have given us support.

I do believe, however, that we ought not to be scared to let our real emotions show—to do so, moreover, every bit as openly with our students as we would with our adult friends, our families and (if we have children) our own kids.

There are certain instances, of course, when teachers have excellent reason to conceal particular aspects of their lives, not only from their pupils but from anyone at all; there is no reason on earth why teachers ought to feel compelled to share *all* of their private feelings with their pupils in ways they would not do even with adult friends. But teachers also have the right to laugh, the need to cry, to demonstrate anger, pain, anxiety or fear, right in the classroom just as openly as they might do in their own homes. We do not make ourselves professionals by rendering all our motions stiff and wooden—and our humor or exhilaration rigid and unreal. Teachers can weep when we are mourning someone we have loved, and we can tell our children we are feeling rotten if we just wake up one morning and feel sick. There is no reason why we have to tell the class we need to "wash our hands" or "freshen up" if what we really need to do is use the toilet; nor is there a reason why we cannot swear like hell if, by bad luck, we should fall down and twist our leg or bang our knee.

Teachers can bleed in every way, inside and out, and students should know it; they will not hate us as a consequence, because they bleed as well. They suffer too, and do not simply need to "freshen up" when they request permission to "go down the hall." They sweat also, often laugh, and sometimes need to weep.

This is, I think, the most important way of all by which we teach our pupils the power and license to speak out, and cry, and breathe, and live, and love—and someday struggle—in first person pronouns: first to say "I" and one day to say "we."

Extreme Ideas

Often, if a student tries to give expression to a strong belief, especially if that student states his views in terms that seem to lead in the direction of a real dispute, teachers tend, by an automatic reflex, to try to cool things off and to persuade the student to tone down his views: "Peter, isn't that a bit strong?"

If the student agrees to backtrack and retreat, then he often wins respect or even praise for self-control: "That sounds more sensible."

In actual fact, and by direct result, as there comes to be *less to believe*, the teacher says it sounds increasingly believable. The same thing happens with a strong opinion which has not been rounded off to fit the class consensus: "Okay . . . David says that black Americans are now fighting for their rights . . . and Susan says that we need law and order. . . . Well . . . there might be truth in *both* of these positions . . ." Long pause. At last the resolution: "Why don't we see if we can't find a *third* position?"

The teacher seldom comes right out and states the truth: "Look, we're going to have an easier time together if you'll just cut back on your convictions for a little while." Instead, there is the absolute suggestion that the third position is *more true* than either of the two extremes: that truth lives "closer to the middle."

One consequence of this idea is the viewpoint, reinforced by many modern school materials, even of the most sophisticated kind, that anger, conflict, confrontation of all kinds are nothing more than a perceptual mistake: "Nobody really disagrees with someone else once we have explained ourselves with proper care." Hence, the new and profitable field of bogus classroom ethics known as "conflict resolution" or as "clarification" of our values and our former points of view. The message of this new material is clear: Confrontation is perceived as if it were the consequence, in almost every case, of poorly chosen words or of inadequate perception: "We have to learn not just to talk, but also how to listen, how to understand . . ." The message here is that, if we learn to listen well, we will not hear things that we do not like. To hear things that we do not like is to hear incorrectly.

There are these words in the Bible: "Where there is no vision, the people perish." A vision is, by definition, both expansive and extreme. It is, precisely, the exclusion of the vision from the public classroom—and, in particular, from the inner-city school—which guarantees that apathetic mood, those arid and unstimulating class discussions, so easily mistaken by observers for "a lack of pupil motivation."

It is not simply a case of pedagogic styles that fail to elicit the intensities and emotions of our pupils. It is, rather, a case of school-mandated *absence of intensity* which has successfully *excluded* such emotion. The conventional wisdom of the U.S. public school is the virtue of the low-key, the cautious, the consensus view. Because a vision of justice is incompatible with such a preference, the students have learned, long years before the secondary grades, to leave their sense of passion at the classroom door.

The bias against extremes is paralyzing in its impact on the teacher and the student both. All intense ideas or radical views are treated as inherently suspect, while moderate statements ("notions," not "convictions") are given credence from the start. The term *radical* is universally described in textbooks as a sickly aberration of a healthy state of mind called *liberal*. In the same sense, *revolution* is defined as an unwholesome word, an agonized distortion of a healthy term: *reform*.

There is a phrase, consistent with this view, found often in the textbooks, press and magazines: "extremists on both sides." The purpose of this phrase is to make people believe that there is something evil, in all cases, in extreme ideas. This, clearly, is not so. Extreme devotion, for example, to the implementation of the details of annihilation of the Jews is not the same as an extreme determination to assassinate the Nazi leaders. "Extremists on both sides" is a deceptive phrase. It tries, once more, to get a student to believe that there is always more truth sitting someplace in the middle. It also tries to get a child to believe that there must *be* a genuine "middle" every time. This, too, is simply not the case.

A ruling principle, in many high school texts, goes somewhat in these terms: "All extremes of action or belief are equally unwise. Sooner or later, all will lead to self-betrayal, self-corruption or deceit."

The Soviet Union is the traditional example of the failure or inevitable distortion of extreme beliefs. The textbooks never speak of the extreme success of that most memorable revolution that took place two hundred years ago in the United States, nor of the extreme importance of the revolution which is, in a sense, still taking place today in Shanghai and Peking. Nor do they speak of the extreme ideas of Malcolm X, Saint Francis or Saint Joan.

The truth is that extreme reaction to extreme ordeal is not only healthy and intelligent at times, but also very often the sole ethical response of honorable people in the face of human pain. How can we begin to render this unpopular point of view both potent and persuasive to our students?

My own approach is to confront the issue head-on, in subjective terms, by stating some of these arguments to children outright, much as I have stated them right here, and as we all do with one another in the real world. Many teachers, how-ever, will probably react to this suggestion much as they have done before. They will ask why we must *state* such matters to the class when, instead, with richly assorted data scattered all around the room, the children can discover all of this them-selves? Although this is a method that I always find peculiarly circuitous, I see no reason to object to teachers who prefer this means of getting an idea across to children. I simply think that we are being far more candid if, at least at some point in the game, we state it in our own words, too.

The other approach, delineated above, is to make available a broad array of relevant quotations of a number of "extreme" ideas and points of view, stated by people like Tom Paine and Thomas Jefferson, for instance—people whom the textbooks have already taught the children to revere.

"The tree of liberty must be refreshed from time to time with the blood of patriots and tyrants."[5] Jefferson wrote these words in 1787. Many teachers nowadays discover that direct quota-tions of that kind—drawing on the real (extreme) beliefs of highly reputable and patriotic people—tend to stir up an ex-treme response in children, while simultaneously they leave the teacher partially protected from attack.

William Lloyd Garrison, the abolitionist who lived and wrote in Boston over a century ago, also spoke about the matter of extreme reactions in dramatic terms. Asked by a friend why he was "all on fire" with his rage, Garrison replied: "I have need to be all on fire, for I have mountains of ice about me to melt."[6]

Henry David Thoreau, whose quotations and convictions re-cur (and will recur) again and again within this book, is a man I take to be a model of straightforward talk and of unhesitant denunciation of whatever it was that passed for conventional wisdom in his time. He proved also to be indignant and re-markably unbridled in defense of a style of speech for which he would be graded very, very low in all too many of the U.S. public schools.

"I fear chiefly," Thoreau stated in 1854, "lest my expression may not be *extra-vagant* enough. . . . I desire to speak somewhere *without* bounds."[7]

Of all such expressions of conviction on this subject, the one I like the most is that of Martin Luther King. In "Letter from Birmingham Jail" (1963),[8] he wrote these words: "Was not Jesus an extremist for love? . . . The question is not whether we will be an extremist, but what kind of extremist we will be. Will we be extremists for hate or will we be extremists for love? Will we be extremists for the preservation of injustice or will we be extremists for the cause of justice?"

Apart from straight quotation, there are also many concrete and well-documented cases of extreme behavior, based upon extreme belief, which did not lead into a self-destructive or corrupting end result. What if, for instance, teachers were prepared to put aside the obvious betrayal of the dream within the U.S.S.R. and to speak instead of the extreme success of public education in post-revolutionary Cuba or of the extreme success of health care in post-revolutionary China? In order to do this, teachers need to have good—indeed, impeccable—data and resources. The rebel, here as in almost all other situations, must be an infinitely more careful scholar than the writer or speaker of innocuous and inoffensive views. I have tried to give a lot of leads for interesting and helpful source materials in the final pages of this book.

The ultimate approach in attacking this dilemma is not the lesson of "the right quotation," nor of "the right example" from the distant past. It is the power of the teacher to articulate a point of view in words of passion equal to the substance which those views convey. This alone provides a class of students with an inviolable precedent for honest exposition of their own intense beliefs. A teacher who reverts, in every case, to colorless understatement and to oblique expressions of belief cannot offer pupils any credible lessons in the virtues of outspoken, lucid or extreme ideas.

The hidden curriculum, as we have seen before, is the teacher's own integrity and lived conviction. The most memorable lesson is not what is written by the student on a sheet of yellow lined paper in the lesson pad; nor is it the clumsy sentence published (and "illustrated") in the standard and official text. It is the message which is written in a teacher's eyes throughout the course of his or her career.

It is the lesson which endures a lifetime.

Disobedience Instruction

One of the most effective inhibitions planted in the consciousness of students and teachers in our public schools is a sel-
dom-stated yet remorseless sense of terror at the possibility of
saying no.

Textbooks achieve this goal by use of various time-honored
and, by now, almost unnoticed methods of dogmatic certitude
and condescension. They do it also by the use of small catch-
phrases which are contrived to frighten students into blind acceptance of an adult point of view. When, at times, a student
does break out in clear-cut condemnation of a text or an idea,
there is a stock response. Students are accused of being "negative"—or of "making unconstructive comments."

There is some paradox in this. Americans would not be the
citizens of a land called the United States at all if a number of
rebels such as Sam Adams, Thomas Jefferson, Tom Paine and
several thousand more had not been extremely "negative" in
their viewpoints on King George III—and offered to suggest
no "positive" alternatives.

Students in the early grades of school, if they are bright
enough to recognize the devious materials that fill their texts
and readers, and blunt enough to speak of it out loud, often
are contained or silenced by another familiar manner of
suppression: "Let's not be negative or hostile. Let's not indulge
in unconstructive criticism. Why don't we try to find the good
points in the story?" This litany of seductive affirmation leads,
too often, to another pattern of familiar words: "It isn't right to

knock things down unless we are prepared to put up *new* things in their place."

There are innumerable variations on these words: "A great many people worked for a long, long time to write these stories for us, and to draw these illustrations, and to print this book. . . . It's all very easy for a little boy or little girl to criticize the work of someone else without suggesting something better."

This is, of course, an unjust argument. All of us have the right to criticize what we detest, whether or not we have the skill to "make a better one" ourselves. Patients in the hospital have an unquestioned right to voice their protest if a surgeon seems about to make use of a rusty scalpel, even if those patients cannot claim to do the surgery themselves. In the same sense, students who do not know the way to write, to print, to illustrate and bind a polished substitute for the fourth-grade reader, should not let an adult take away their right to speak with anger of a book they feel to be dishonest—or just dull.

There is an unspoken agenda in these curious clichés: Whenever students are told they do not have the right to knock down an idea (or to attack a book) unless they are prepared to offer up an instantaneous replacement, there is the message, tucked between the lines, that there has got to *be* a "something better" every time. It is as if a builder were to put up a gigantic A & P right in the middle of a beautiful green valley in the state of Maine, then were to look his critics in the eyes and ask us if we think that we can build a better one ourselves.

Words like these lead people to forget that there was once a time when they could stand and look across unspoiled land and see the blue-green line of the horizon. Everything does not need an alternative suggestion. Some things need not to exist at all.

Many teachers, in frustration, have resorted to a number of ingenious methods to subvert this myth. Some teachers do it by the presentation of a simple line of logic: describing, for example, the imagined situation of the patient underneath a rusty scalpel, or of a small village of poor people in the face of a huge and irresponsible construction firm.

Other teachers have made extensive use of major news reports—those, for example, which were generated by the events at Watergate or Three Mile Island. Both are situations where the inability of well-trained American adults to *say no* to an ongoing process of deceit, or of progressive self-deceit, has led to tragic consequences, not just for those who were the victims, but also (in one way or another) for themselves. Events in the more distant past (the bombing of Hiroshima, for example) provide a teacher with even stronger historical evidence to reinforce the point. Again, as before, there is no need to search for radical sources of reproach if the strongest evidence is already present in the daily press.

A teacher might line up, in opposite columns on a ditto sheet, certain statements published in their textbooks praising the virtues of acquiescence, of obedience and of "positive ideas" and, on the other side, the courtroom testimony of those ordinary but pathetic figures who went into Watergate to steal, into My Lai to kill—among other reasons, because they lacked the power to *say no*.

There is a verse which, up until recent years, was contained within the official curriculum of the Boston Public Schools: "Every day, in every way, / it is our duty to obey."[9] A teacher might take this rhyme and line it up, along with a number of comparable quotations, on the left side of a page. On the right side, we might display some of the words of American soldiers who (as we might carefully remind each student) were the products of a school "just like our own."

Many teachers—without suggestion from me or any other writer—have, for several years already, made highly effective and always upsetting use of quoted words from Adolf Eichmann, whose own preparation for obedient behavior was received in German public schools. Teachers might point out, as well, that our own schools were modeled on the German system more than a century ago and that both systems have quite similar objectives: the education of "good Germans," or "good citizens," as we in the United States would say.

"I was only obeying my orders," Eichmann said. What other lesson could he possibly have learned within a well-run public school?

Again, I believe it is our special obligation to make certain that the point at stake cannot conceivably be blurred. "Normal" American students, after all, already sufficiently socialized by their prior years in public school, have a powerful vested interest in attempting to avoid the real significance of our references to Eichmann or to Hiroshima.

"Do you get the point?"

I have often asked this question in the presence of a high school class. I do not pretend that there is *not* "a point." I do not pretend that I have no idea of what conclusion my pupils might possibly "discover." Nor do I pretend that every possible conclusion might be "equally correct." I do not turn the class into a preplanned guessing game ("discovery method") by which to direct students to my own conclusion. I do not renounce my adult judgment and pretend I have no serious objectives of my own.

"There *is* a point. Dumb, dangerous rhymes like those our school supplies to us have led a lot of people just like you into some tragic acts of theft or murder. Blueprints, alternatives and optional suggestions are all fine and good; but there are also moments when a well-planned act of straight refusal and denunciation proves to be a lot more useful and important to the preservation of the human race. I would like it very much if I could leave you, by the year's end, with the courage to say no, in spite of all the doubts and inhibitions which will always be within you."

There are, however, as we have seen, certain teachers who prefer to quote from others rather than to say these things themselves. Instead of speaking out in their own voice, such teachers prefer to make certain that the writings of many different kinds of moral and political rebels are available and constantly accessible to students. Moreover, they make certain that the relevant writings are displayed in such a way as to advertise themselves. The writings of distinguished social critics are spread out across the tables and display racks of the classroom, not crowded onto shelves or packed in cartons.

My own belief, repeated often in this book, is that a teacher's stated views—and, more important, the visible actions which that teacher takes during a year in public school—are infinitely more relentless in their impact on the students than a wealth of books of any possible variety. More powerful still is the degree to which a class of children comes to feel that it is safe to say no even to the teacher. Since students have learned for years that this, of all denunciations, is the one most to avoid and fear, it is also the one which is most difficult to batter down.

In trying to make this mode of thought and of denunciation even conceivable among the students I have taught, I have sometimes opened the semester by announcing to the class that we would be involved, for several days, in something that I call "Disobedience Instruction."

Grade-school children at times appear alarmed by the idea. It takes a bit of work to make it clear that I do not intend to urge them to go home and be malicious to their folks, nor do I hope that they will feel the urge to be malicious here in school. I draw a line, as well as I can, between two very different states of mind: the sheer vindictive malice of defiance and aggression on the one hand, and a vigorous note of ethical irreverence on the other. The first attacks the person, while the second concentrates on that person's viewpoints and beliefs.

There is another reason why the line has to be drawn between our criticism of another person's views and an attack upon that person's heart and soul. In order for a student to be able to believe that it is safe to say no to a teacher, it is important that the student feels that he or she will not be subject to retaliation. If there is not a clear distinction made between a person's words and his or her own inner self, then students often seem to feel that they cannot attack the words a teacher speaks without, in essence, striking at the teacher too.

Even worse, students will find it difficult to believe that teachers can do combat with a student's views without thereby reflecting a deep-seated anger at the student also.

To begin the class with a discussion about honest disagreement seems to me to be the logical way for us to start. It enables students to engage in sharp disputes that bring their thought and feeling to a strong insistent pitch, yet also enables them to feel entire safety at the hands of teachers—or the class itself.

Schools tend to steer away from heated disputations of the kind I have in mind, fearing (as one handbook[10] of the N.E.A. has put it) that emotion-charged issues "may lead to an argument so explosive that fighting can result." (We are so far from this eventuality today that teachers—plagued for ages with the undevoted apathy of mediocre class discussion— might very well get up and cheer if anyone in their class should ever care enough to throw a spitball in defense of an idea!) Students, in my experience, are wholly capable of learning to say no, with both control and dignity, not only to each other but to adults too, and to the teacher first of all, and to distinguish between anger at a person's point of view and hatred for the person who expressed it.

This, to me, seems an essential precondition in a classroom where the teacher plans to take a controversial stand on serious ideas. If the students can't say no (or think somehow that they'd better not for their own personal well-being), then the teachers find themselves in a restrictive situation. Their power, being irrefutable, is limitless. Their viewpoints, being past all disputation, come to be totalitarian.

Again—apart from all the words that we can speak in this regard, and even apart from all the various people we can quote to give our students precedent for courage and denunciation in the face of our own views—the very best lesson of all is *demonstration*. Teachers can demonstrate the point in obvious ways: by their own disobedience of a supervisor or a school board, for example. This, however, is an action that many teachers may well judge to be unwise for obvious reasons of survival, at least in the early years of their career. Another method, therefore, far less dangerous and more direct, is to invite another teacher into class, someone who disagrees with you on a dead-earnest issue, then do your best to start a heated disagreement with that teacher.

Students who have been taught to think, "The teacher's always right," are faced with a dilemma when two teachers disagree. The students know both people can't be right, yet both are teachers and both are adults. The lesson seems to set at least two useful precedents.

First, it shatters the idea that teachers can't be wrong, giving the students more reason to dissent with *either* teacher in the months and years ahead.

Second, it demonstrates that people can dissent with great intensity and still retain respect for one another.

The open disputation of two teachers, in the full view of the class, no matter how unconventional or unexpected, proves repeatedly to be a lively catalyst for students who are otherwise reluctant to come out with their own views. Once the students see their teachers in articulate dispute, the idea of infallibility is gone for good. From that point on, students are able to speak with full irreverence, but without the terror of retaliation. Teachers, as a result, are freed at last from arid imitations of neutrality.

Needless to say, this kind of work is seldom part of the traditional curriculum within the public schools. In the wake of the decade of Watergate, however—not even to speak of recent revelations of government-authorized and possibly organized duplicity, actions of cover-up and collusion in Miami by the courts and the police, the multiple and apparently unabated plottings of the C.I.A. (plottings which too many people now unhappily accept as part of our national self-interest) or the slow, unceasing radioactive leakage of contaminated wastes throughout our land, followed by the grotesque denial of such dangers by the very corporations that are most involved—it may well be that the courage of unabated indignation and denunciation is the most important single lesson that remains within our power to convey to children in the public schools.

It would be overly optimistic to predict that hundreds of thousands of teachers, in the next few years, are likely to adopt these strategies without grave hesitation. It is the truth, however, that hundreds of teachers in the past few years have already begun to seize upon this frank approach as the one most elemental lesson they can offer to their pupils in the first weeks of the year.

It calls for just as much work, in a nation like our own, to return to kids the license to *say no* as it required once, in an earlier age, to take that privilege away.

Women in History, but not in Public School: Some Ways of Fighting Back

For generations women have been treated with contempt, or else relegated wholly to oblivion, within the U.S. public schools.

In most textbooks it appears that great, heroic or courageous women don't exist at all. Those few who do are almost always dull and unexciting people, seldom important on their own, but famous only for their luck in being married to a famous man. Martha Washington and Mary Todd Lincoln are two obvious examples. The black leader Harriet Tubman receives a little better treatment than the rest, but even she tends to be drained or sanitized of nine-tenths of her most serious beliefs.

The one woman who appears in every textbook under her own steam is the patriotic seamstress, Betsy Ross. This choice, on the part of textbook authors, no longer comes to many teachers as a great surprise. Nothing could be more perfect, and predictable, than that the school boards should select as token woman of the U.S. public schools a person whose only competence falls squarely in that area of women's work known as "homemaking skills." Others of that era who were independently significant (Abigail Adams, for example) either are ignored completely or else given token mention at the most.

Even now, two centuries since the U.S. revolution, none of this has greatly changed. Most of the exciting women of the past one hundred years—Dorothy Day, Susan B. Anthony and Emma Goldman are just three examples—seldom are even named in public school. Teachers (above all, women teachers who have had to live with this bias for a lifetime) know very well the reason why the women I have named are bypassed totally in public school. Each of them represents a vigorous example of unfrightened women—liberated not just (as women) from manipulation by male leaders, but also (as passionate and indignant human beings) from the domination of a nation's lies and from the power of the major corporations.

Susan B. Anthony and Emma Goldman have been dead for many years—Dorothy Day only since the winter of 1980. Her death (on December 1st) came in her eightieth year. She was a devoutly religious woman who believed that the best way to be Christian is to practice Christ's ideals by standing up for those who are most poor and hungry.

In order to demonstrate her faith by visible witness, Dorothy Day participated in countless protest actions, fasted for weeks and even months, and went to prison many times. She also traveled to Cuba to learn first-hand about the Cuban revolution. When the migrant workers in the fields of California went on strike in 1973, merely for recognition of their right to have a union, Dorothy Day went out to join them on the picket lines, despite the fact that she was then well over seventy. When the police began to make arrests, she refused to step aside. She was arrested and later imprisoned with the workers.

For nearly fifty years, Dorothy Day, with the help of many friends of various religious views and political persuasions, edited and published a monthly paper called *The Catholic Worker*. The paper costs a penny a copy, as it did right from the start. It is a unique newspaper—independent in its views, full of a fascinating mix of political stories, personal diaries and reflections on (and sometimes by) the multitude of homeless people who were attracted to the house in which its editor lived and died.

Because the paper is never restricted by a single line or dogma, it does not automatically oppose all socialist ideas the way most other U.S. papers do. As a result, *The Catholic Worker* comes out with a number of well-documented stories that are seldom covered in the ordinary press: whether it is a story about a staff member's travels to a previously forbidden nation like Vietnam or else a purely impressionistic story of the life and death of men and women in the Lower East Side neighborhood of New York City where the staff of the paper has resolved to make its home.

Dorothy Day is viewed by many people as a saintly rebel. She never hesitated to speak in favorable terms of many revolutionary struggles in the Third World, even though she was a pacifist herself. Women with her unusual persistence are regarded as subversive people by the U.S. schools. Textbooks have managed to guarantee that students do not hear about a woman like Dorothy Day. Now that she is dead, and after fifty years go by, then perhaps she will receive her place in the curriculum—but, most likely, not for her authentic views. She will become another plastic heroine: empty of content, and scrubbed clean of real belief.

A standard question comes to mind as soon as we try to speak of people such as Dorothy Day: How can teachers possibly cope with areas of gross evasion that are both so sweeping and so vast—especially if they have no other materials at hand than what the school board gives them? It is for this reason that I have supplied a number of suggestions for additional reading in the end matter of this book. Many teachers also emphasize that the major lessons in regard to women ought to start, not with a list of famous people, but right in their own classroom in discussion of the ways that women, or young girls, learn to perceive their proper role within society and in the public school itself.

An additional point that receives a good deal less attention, even in the relatively innovative schools, is the causative connection between the rights of women in themselves (e.g., the ways that little girls relate to little boys right in the school) and the larger implications of political struggle on the part of women for the freedom of all people in conditions of oppression.

The problem that teachers face, in dealing with this issue, is how to speak of independent and irreverent women such as Dorothy Day, yet somehow manage to avoid dismissal or any of those other concomitant forms of vengeance that can be inflicted by a conservative and unforgiving school board. As in many other situations of this kind, teachers can often prove the point they need to make, yet simultaneously provide themselves with self-protection, just so long as they will choose, at least in the initial lessons, women who already have been canonized in public school but whose beliefs the children do not know and standard textbooks do not dare to tell. Out of a great many examples of such women, the one I find most vital, in the impact that her words can have, even on fifth-grade kids, is Helen Keller.

"Helen Keller," according to the standard text, "was a world-famous, deaf-blind lady who could read, write and speak."[11] The textbooks tell us also that she worked against "tremendous odds"—but with her, at all times, there stood "her trusted friend and teacher." Together, we learn, the two achieved things "all but past belief." Among the many famous people that she met were King George, Queen Mary, Lady Astor, Alexander Bell . . .

Most students encounter something similar to this at some point close to fifth or sixth grade. If, like many teachers, you have felt the sense of false narration I have just described, it might be of help to students to suggest this question: In the long run, does it matter a great deal how many famous people Helen Keller got to know? (Who really cares?) The one part of her work that seems to count the most is that she spent most of her life in fighting for the powerless and the poor.

"I have visited sweatshops, factories and crowded slums," she wrote. "If I could not see it, I could smell it. With my own hands, I could feel . . . dwarfed children tending their younger brothers and sisters while their mothers tended machines in nearby factories."[12]

She continues: "The foundation of society is laid upon a basis of . . . individualism, conquest and exploitation . . ." A social order such as this, "built upon such wrong [and] basic principles, is bound to retard the development of all."

The result, she says, is that the greed for money comes to be our major goal: "The output of a cotton mill or a coal mine is considered of greater importance than the production of healthy, happy-hearted and free human beings."

In regard to free elections, she has this to say: "We, the people, are not free. Our democracy is but a name. We vote? What does that mean? We choose between Tweedledum and Tweedledee."[13]

What would happen if a teacher were to put those words up on the wall under a photograph of Helen Keller? Or perhaps not the entire passage, but only the first line. "WE THE PEOPLE ARE NOT FREE."

To start with, it would certainly make a lot of people very angry. On the other hand, it's hard to know how teachers can be fired from a public school for putting up the words of Helen Keller on the wall. If the school system tried to fire a teacher on these grounds, they'd have a tough fight on their hands and, far more important from a pedagogic point of view, the public would receive a fascinating education.

Since the question will come up for sure, it seems important to establish here that all of these quotations come from the written works of Helen Keller. They come from either her speeches or her books. In order to make the basic point as powerful as we can, it might be of use to pose to students an explicit, loaded question of this kind: "How much of this material can you find—either in those books now present in the classrooms of the school or else in the school library? Do any of your textbooks offer even a little hint of these ideas?"

The follow-up question seems to be implicit: "If not, why not?" Obviously, the school officials know quite well that they might be in danger if their students start to hear the real ideas of some of those brave women who have fought so long and hard against injustice. Textbooks tell our students that Helen Keller learned to "see." They do not dare to tell them what she SAW. They tell our students that she learned to "speak," but do not dare to tell them what she SPOKE.

The textbooks are right, of course, that Helen Keller was a brave, heroic woman—but not for the reasons that the textbooks tell. She overcame at least two kinds of blindness: the blindness of the eyes (that blindness everybody knows) and then the blindness of the heart as well. Textbooks choose to talk about the first part only.

It is within our power to discuss the second, too.

The Hero in Jail:
"The Truth Will Make Us Free"

In trying to select historical examples of free-thinking men and women, teachers are forced to consider the question of their own protection in the face of potential critics on all sides. The ideal rebel, from a tactical point of view, is a person who has been already canonized by public school.

The area of black studies offers us an obvious example. I have always been fascinated by the life and work of Malcolm X. Nonetheless, in approaching the topic of racism with students, I think the words of Martin Luther King are bound to be much better starting points. They offer a conservative school board far less reason to give the teacher a hard time. King has already been credentialized by TV, press and public school—while Malcolm X has not. The point, however, once having made a tactical choice of biographical subject, is to refuse to accept the falsified version of Dr. King which school administrations will too frequently be asking us to sell.

Dr. King is regularly presented to our students as a noble, decent, but incredibly predictable and rather boring human being, who did a certain amount of "good" for his own people, adhered at all times to peaceful means, and never became impatient with white people.

Textbooks omit from the story of his life the only facts that make him genuinely great and worth our real respect. One of these facts, for instance, is that Dr. King, while peaceful in his tactics and devoted to the principles of Gandhi and Tolstoy, was nonetheless a militant and unyielding man who fought great battles and broke unjust laws, spent months in jail to dramatize the limits of conventional efforts carried out within the letter of the law—and urged the rest of us to find the willingness to do so also.

Dr. King spoke his mind freely, if perhaps somewhat too late, about the U.S. role in fostering needless and unjustifiable devastation in Vietnam and in other parts of Southeast Asia. He frequently expressed his outrage at the fact that Lyndon Johnson lied, first to the nation, then to the entire world, spoke of peace while dropping bombs on innocent civilians in Vietnam, leaving behind so many victims maimed, crippled or blind.

"America," said Dr. King, "is the greatest purveyor of violence in the world today."[14] He spoke these words on June 4, 1967. Ten months later, a sharpshooter in Memphis would prove his words correct by killing *him* as well. He was murdered on the terrace of a Memphis motel—a bullet fired through his throat.

Teachers can share with students the profound convictions that were honest reflections of the character of Dr. King, not the sanitized and prize-winning plastic preacher, but the man who spent so many days and nights in prison cells, lived with the constant threat of death and danger from the Ku Klux Klan, and also had to live with the blackmail of the F.B.I. Teachers can also extract, from straight respectable sources like *The Congressional Record* and *The Boston Globe,* a number of important stories on the ways that Dr. King was blackmailed by J. Edgar Hoover.[15]

None of this may please the local school board. As usual, however, the source of the material seems the key to our protection and survival. Any school that seeks to fire a teacher for the honest, undistorted use of documentation from the U.S. Senate and *The Boston Globe* is asking for considerable humiliation. In this way, teachers can with relative impunity make use of the life and words of Dr. King to pose some interesting questions to the students in their classes.

What is the reason for a man or woman to spend time in jail for his or her beliefs? What does it mean to be a "free" or "unfree" person in a nation that allows so little true and lasting freedom to its poorest citizens?

Are people free in any way that really counts if they are compelled to spend their lives within a prison made of lies? Dr. King once said that people who are not prepared to die for their beliefs aren't fit to live.[16] Teachers might provoke a startling debate even if they do nothing more than ask their students how they feel about such words. If the issue proves disturbing to the students, then the students might well bring it home to ask their parents, too.

Thoreau provides another dramatic example of a man who is included in the textbooks and curricula of public schools, but one who is denied most of those values and convictions that have given him a place in history. Ironically, with Thoreau, just as with Dr. King, the school boards have excluded from the acceptable life story virtually every item which compels them to include him in their textbooks in the first place. They are forced by his heroic and historic acts of civil disobedience to contain him in their province of consideration; but they are forced, by their alarm at this *same* power of disobedience, to delete or neutralize that very virtue. We might well wonder why they bother with him at all—if it were not for the obvious reply. They have to present him, respect him and defuse him, precisely in order that students will not meet him on their own. The dangers of disobedience, like those of sainthood, must be neutralized in warm, well-lighted rooms.

The purposes of the educational system would seem bizarre and self-defeating were they not so cleverly effective. It requires no conspiracy to bring about this intellectual emasculation. It is the natural behavior of well-educated and appropriately domesticated adults. All of us are complicit in these deeds, though many teachers have at last begun to learn the ways to free themselves from this complicity.

Like so many rebels of the past ten, twelve or fifteen years, Thoreau was thoroughly detested by a number of his fellow-citizens. Once he had been dead for many years, the schools and critics decreed that he had been a brilliant writer. It seems to be a rule of thumb in the United States, as in most other nations of the modern world, that the only acceptable rebel—certainly the one whose greatness is most certain and un-clouded—is a dead one.

If students could get an early look at some of the strongest political writings of Thoreau, they probably would find it much less difficult to understand why citizens of Massachusetts felt uneasy with his views. "How does it become a man to behave towards this American government today? I answer that he cannot without disgrace be associated with it."[17]

Thoreau was enraged by several attitudes and actions of the U.S. government, above all our toleration of the slave trade and the war with Mexico. Very few of the students that I meet in public schools today know anything at all about the war with Mexico. If they have even heard of it, I find it is the famous battles they remember. They do not remember either the purpose or the outcome. Few of them know that most of Arizona, all of California, Utah and Nevada, and a large part of Colorado and New Mexico, would not be parts of the United States at all if they had not been stolen wholesale by the U.S. Army. This, of course, is the real meaning of the war with Mexico.

One night, in 1846, Thoreau defied the U.S. government in the most dramatic way he knew. He spent a night in Concord jail as price of his refusal to pay taxes to support the Mexican war.

"When a sixth of the population of a nation which has un-dertaken to be the refuge of liberty are slaves, and a whole country [i.e., Mexico] is unjustly overrun and conquered by a foreign army and subjected to military law, I think that it is not too soon for honest men to rebel and revolutionize. . . . As for adopting the ways which the state has provided for dealing with the evil, I know not of such ways. They take too long and a man's life will be gone."

The heart of Thoreau's political opinion is contained within his essay *On the Duty of Civil Disobedience*. Curriculum guides generally make reference to this work but then divert our students to those sections of his longer books in which Thoreau speaks mainly about nature, woods and streams. These passages, of course, are beautiful and moving. This, however, is not the part of Thoreau's work that makes his name important in the history of ideas. Nor is it the part that renders him an influential moral force in almost every corner of the earth.

Teachers who care about Thoreau, and plan to speak of him at all, have it in their power to insist on going back to his essential work. School officials may perhaps inquire why it is that we do not restrict ourselves to his less controversial work—"the writing about nature."

Teachers can comfortably answer that it isn't writings about nature that have rendered Thoreau a central and seminal figure for so many of the world's nonviolent leaders. Why waste our students' time on aspects of the man that count the least?

I find that candid questions of that sort tend to disarm our interrogators. Many (hard as it may be for their potential victims to believe) have simply never thought of it before. Their tendency is less to be offended than bemused. It is experiences like these which lead me to withdraw my credence from various radical theories of "conspiracy." People pass on, often unknowingly, the lies their fathers and their mothers lived by. It seems to me that this statement comes much closer to the truth than any of the demonizing theories.

As in earlier chapters, what I am proposing here is the radical rediscovery of the innermost moral meanings of those heroines and heroes who have already been canonized by the public schools. Even when teachers choose their symbols and examples with great care, however, they still may be faced with serious trouble, inflicted by a hostile school board or a school official who is *not* "bemused" but, frankly, out to get them. It would be foolish, and misleading to young teachers, if I were to argue here that merely to invoke such names as Helen Keller and Thoreau and Dr. King, and then to defend them with a totally unexpected lack of guile, is going to serve as absolute protection against people who know very well exactly where their own self-interest lies and view our actions, therefore, as a threat.

Some administrators *are*, in truth, vindictive or afraid. Others are innocent of either malice or intelligence. And others still are highly intelligent, quietly grateful, and very much on our side. In this respect, as with most others raised within this book, there are, in short, no simple guarantees.

Postscript

Every distortion, every exclusion, every action of emasculation or denial of those men and women we have reason to revere, appears to find its curious counterpart in *another* body of American leaders who are clothed in the trappings of profundity and ethics which do not appropriately belong to them. While King is diminished, Lyndon Johnson is progressively transformed into an ardent activist for social justice. While Thoreau is appreciated as a sensitive man of nature, Emerson is exalted as the ethical and intellectual rebel he was not. While Garrison, Brown and Frederick Douglass are denied, and frequently forgotten altogether, Abraham Lincoln is given unwarranted praise and credit for the emancipation of the slaves.

The latter example is particularly disturbing to anyone who believes, as I do, that there are some genuine reasons to admire Lincoln. Abraham Lincoln was, unquestionably, one of our most distinguished presidents; we do not make him more distinguished, rather we tarnish him a bit, by attributing to him virtues he did not possess. The textbooks describe him as a "brave, heroic, kindly and generous man—famous, above all, as a fighter for the freedom of black people." The same books also speak of him as "Honest Abe." The second statement may very well be true. The first is not.

Lincoln signed the Emancipation Proclamation, as historians make clear, not because he was a partisan of equal privilege for all but—as ample evidence attests—because he was advised by friends that it would be to his political advantage to adopt this action. He did so, moreover, only after many years of desperate struggle by the real emancipators of black people. Those real emancipators of the blacks were, in large numbers, black themselves. Those who were not black were predominately the northern abolitionists. If it were not for the long and often dangerous struggle undertaken by these activists and constant agitators, Lincoln would not have been under pressure to emancipate black people.

This version of the truth is seldom stated in the books that school officials order for our classroom use. We can ascertain the truth, however, in any number of scholarly books which give an accurate history of the United States in the 1800s. Lincoln assigned to the black race a secondary role in our society. His attitude, indeed, is difficult to distinguish from that of the most committed segregationists of the 1980s. He did not simply *believe* that blacks deserved a separate and unequal role. He *said* so—and he did it in a speech which ought to be part of every U.S. text.

"I am not," he told his audience, "nor ever have been, in favor of bringing about in any way the social or political equality of the white and black races. . . . I will say in addition that there is a physical difference between the white and black races which, I suppose, will forever forbid the two races living together upon terms of social and political equality; and in as much as they cannot so live, that while they do remain together there must be a position of the superiors and the inferiors; and that I, as much as any other man, am in favor of the superior being assigned to the white man."[18]

Lincoln was, in many respects, an honest man. We should be honest, in turn, about *his* honesty. He was honest in describing his profoundly racist views. This is perhaps one reason why so many black men and women do not particularly like to see his photograph posted on the walls inside their schools.

We need to treasure the relatively small number of distinguished people who have risen to high office in our nation. One of the ways to do this, I believe, is to praise these people for their genuine and unquestioned virtues—while we concede, without a bit of hesitation, these prejudices, that narrowness of outlook, which they held in common with their generation. Lincoln will not appear to our students to be a lesser man for his deficiencies. He will appear to be more interesting, and more human, and more real—and therefore a person with whom both black and white kids can identify and grapple, or else struggle to confront.

The truth, here as in all ways, makes us free.

Secret Records

One of the most persistent instruments of class stratification, indoctrination and repression in the U.S. public schools is the "cumulative record." Academic, personal and psychological records of this nature exist for virtually all of the forty-three million students in our education system.[19] Much of the data in the cumulative record is of purely practical importance: height and weight, color of eyes, date of polio, typhoid and tetanus antitoxins, telephone number and address of parents. Other sections of the record are a lot *less* harmless and can frequently portend considerable danger to a student in the years ahead.

The sections which are probably most harmful are those that deal with reading scores, math levels, science aptitudes and other test results—especially those that have to do (or which are said to have to do) with matters such as I.Q. The latter items represent an area of ever-present danger to a student who has not succeeded in attracting the affection of his former teachers or his school administrators, but rather *has* succeeded in attracting their hostility and condemnation.

In many schools—especially in cases where, during the past ten years, there may have been racial tensions between teachers and the class—these folders often hold some truly painful commentaries. Often they are worded as advisories from one year's teacher to the next: "Benjamin is a potential rebel. Jennifer is very good at satirizing teachers. . . . Watch out for

Olivia and Susan. Either one can make the school day hopeless if she gets most of the children on her side . . ."

Few of the teachers who have entered public classrooms in the past few years have any reason to defend or justify these cumulative records. It is, indeed, their own suggestions and ideas that constitute the remainder of this chapter.

There is, first of all, a parallel to be drawn between the status of the students in battling against their lifelong supervision by the public schools and that of a very large number of adults in battling against surveillance by the government. Thousands of American citizens in the past five years have come to recognize the increasing dangers represented by the F.B.I., an agency set up initially (as we are told) for patriotic purposes, but used too often, in the years since 1965, to maintain records on political dissenters of all kinds. As we have seen, the former Director J. Edgar Hoover used the power of the F.B.I. not simply to gather documentation on important protest leaders but, in one notable case, in order to intimidate and blackmail Martin Luther King.

The cumulative folder is the school board's version of the secret records kept on citizens by the F.B.I. It holds the same potential danger for all students. That danger lies in one inevitable fact: It grants a great deal too much power to a small number of people to affect the present lives and future hopes of far too many. At its worst, it gives unscrupulous or misguided school officials (those who see a possible danger in a particular pupil's ethical intentions or political ideas) an almost limitless power to destroy that individual's career. Cumulative records have been used throughout the past ten years, for instance, to warn colleges, to which a student has applied, of possible threats that are implicit in the student's independent views.

The truth, too often, is that someone in the school administration does not *share* that student's views (or sometimes just dislikes him) and takes only enough data from his file to destroy his chances for admission to the college he is hoping to attend. Evidence shared with me in recent years confirms the fact that one of the nation's most prestigious universities has made occasional use of warnings of "potential rebels" during the process of selection, in order to be certain that the student body of the present period would be less troublesome and less political than the students of the 1960s and the early 1970s.

The consequence of political selection of this kind is bitterly frustrating: First the colleges learn the way to filter out potentially indignant or devoutly political applicants for entrance. Four years later, the press reports that "students on campus appear to be growing less political and more quiet and self-centered . . ." A carefully and methodically constructed lethargy is subsequently portrayed by gratified political leaders, careless sociologists and delighted college deans as if it were a curious but fortunate change of weather, perhaps "a cyclical phenomenon—ten years on and ten years off . . ." They describe as an objective phenomenon a situation which they have, themselves, unforgivably and in repeated breach of law and confidence, brought into being. Clearly, this is not the only reason for apparent quietude and student acquiescence in the academic world. Economic panic has a lot to do with it as well. So also does the media's distortion. But it is one obvious and initial cause.

Much of this would not happen, none of it could be done with so much ease, if it were not for the student dossiers provided by the cumulative records.

In view of the large number of cases of this kind, and especially in view of the well-noted fact that the right of access has already been won by adult citizens in coping with the records of the F.B.I., it seems to me a reasonable approach for teachers to initiate a similar policy of "open folders" with the pupils in their own class. Once a policy like this has been established, teachers in other classrooms will, of course, be far more careful as to what they dare to put into a cumulative folder in the first place. Once teachers know the folder will be read, not just by higher officials or by other teachers, but by the students too, those teachers will be a lot more cautious not to be sarcastic about someone that they simply do not like.

Even in schools and educational systems where opinion is divided, teachers at last are beginning to debate the pros and cons of open records with their students. Frequently, one of the other teachers in the school will grow uneasy, merely at the thought that students are even considering such issues, and especially under the aegis of another teacher in the school. Even those teachers who would, by personal preference, like to see an end to record-keeping of this kind cannot transcend an overriding fear that any rebellious action might be viewed as gross disloyalty by fellow educators.

There probably is no way to get around the fact that considerable anguish and a genuine "choice of sides" (on the part of teachers) are at stake. The truth is that—in good traditional terms—it *is* an act of breaking rank and taking sides with those (the pupils) who have often, in previous times, been viewed as adversaries by the staff. In terms of building teacher-pupil loyalty, however, it is an inescapable act. The price we pay is that some teachers may, at first, feel less at ease with certain colleagues than they did before. In the long run, I do not think that anyone we could possibly respect is going to suffer by reason of the fact that we are being honest with the pupils in our class. Among such teachers, I do not believe that a sense of tension or distrust is likely to persist for long. Soon enough, decent educators will discover that they have no reason for alarm. Those very few who do would not be valuable allies anyway.

The ideal resolution of the question—in all cases where this course of action is realistic, plausible and has some chance of amiable success—is first to discuss the matter with the principal and with all other teachers in the school, invite their willingness to rethink the whole issue about cumulative folders and, at the very least, to fight for a uniform respect for student privacy.

In such a way, the interests of the students are significantly advanced, if not yet totally protected, while the sense of solidarity among a good number of teachers will remain strong. Teachers who anticipate a lifetime of additional (and many more intimidating) struggles, will thereby have adhered to principle on the issue of the cumulative folder, yet they will have managed at the same time to maintain the loyalties of two groups—both students and their fellow teachers—who may be of strength and help to them in years ahead.

There is another solution which some schools have seized upon—but it is neither an honest nor attractive one. It is to keep two *complete sets of records for each pupil.* One set is relatively harmless and routine and remains, therefore, within the teacher's desk or filing drawer. The other one is not routine at all. It contains all sorts of personal and subjective comments, along with I.Q. scores, predictive opinions from psychologists and such—and stays, therefore, within the principal's locked files. Parents and students who do not know of the existence of a second set of files will not, of course, have any way to ask to see its contents. Only a helpful friend within the system—the student's teacher, for example—has a chance to help those students and their parents to discover all the things they have a right to know.

School boards cannot easily—or legally—suspend us or dismiss us for an action of this kind. Parents and children now have theoretical right of access to virtually all records in every state and city in the nation.[20] Clearly, however, school administrations have other ways than those which are official to retaliate against a teacher for his or her behavior or beliefs. If we have already done some work to build a groundwork of strong loyalties and friendships with the parents and their children, then principals and school boards will at least think twice before they try to use such methods of revenge.*

Much of my emphasis, up to now, has been upon the ways in which we might be able to maintain the loyalties of teachers, yet at the same time build a sense of solidarity with the students in the school. As the efforts we make to stand up for the rights of students grow more serious and sustained, it seems almost inevitable that some of our fellow teachers will begin to draw away from us—if not for good, at least for a limited period of time.

In the past year, in the course of a seminar that I did with classroom teachers, many of the teachers would reiterate the point that, sooner or later, you could not be loyal to your conscience, loyal to your students, open with their parents, and still remain totally trusted and accepted by all of the other teachers in the school. I am sure that this is true; yet I also believe that really good teachers will continue to remain our friends and allies in these difficult situations, just so long as it is clear that our behavior is entirely conscientious and responsible.

Malicious teachers who attempt to curry favor among students and their parents out of a quiet sense of satisfaction or delight at the power to subvert the lives of others often end up losing everybody's trust.

Immature teachers sometimes fall into this trap; but these are not the kinds of rebel teachers who will change the public schools. A gentle rebel often moves more slowly, agrees to bypass some of the small battles, tries very hard to avoid the needless suffering of others—and ends up winning the real war. This is the kind of ally we can only hope for.

---

*The Family Education Rights and Privacy Act, also known as the Buckley Amendment (1974), would appear to provide an absolute resolution of this problem if it could be conscientiously and consistently enforced. Unhappily, for the sake of many children, this is—as of the present writing—not the case. (See note 20 on p. 175.)

"Lead Children to the Following Six Points…"

Those who do not know the inner mysteries of public school may not be familiar with a curious classroom institution known as the "teacher's guide."

A teacher's guide provides instructions for the teacher as to certain methods guaranteed to help us lead our students to a set of seemingly inevitable conclusions, yet simultaneously to get the students to believe that it is *they* who have arrived at these conclusions on their own. There is a separate guide for each commercial line of standard texts. The publisher prepares the guide as one of the means by which to win the teacher, or school system, to the newest history, math, geography or English series.

The guide appears to serve two obvious objectives:

(1) to help the teacher put across the lessons without needing to devote a vast amount of time to preparation;

(2) to render the teacher something of a captive to a single series. Unfortunately, while seeming to make the teacher's job more simple, the teacher's guides are also taking away the satisfaction of all independent and creative labor in the preparation of the daily work. The guidebook seems to be the teacher's friend. Insidiously, it also robs the teacher of the only intellectual dignity which our profession still allows us: the individual, passionate or whimsical exhilaration of *invention*. We cease to be the

architects even of one reading period each morning—or of one English lesson every afternoon.

We obtain a set of neat, swift, "classroom-tested" lesson plans to sell these mediocre texts to children. The guidebook sells the series to the teacher, and the teacher sells the textbook to the class: a progression of increasingly well-planned seductions. In the end, we are the pitiful addicts of the little red annotations printed in the margins of our book, suggested by an invisible expert in a distant city. The expert is rarely a person we recognize by reputation. The preparation of these guidebooks is the special province of the second-rate and the seldom seen.

But this is only a small part of the problem: the insult to the teacher. There is, above all, the insult—and the injury—to our students. I have joined with other teachers in long and exhaustive studies of these guidebooks in the past five years. Some of the more obnoxious are published and distributed by the massive textbook factory, Scott Foresman, a company which is sufficiently adaptable to its potential market to have distributed two parallel editions at the time that I was teaching school: one with multiracial illustrations, one with no black people in the book at all. I am told that the latter edition has since been phased out of existence.

Most of the guidebooks offer confident predictions on the way that students will react (or "ought to") in the face of certain stories, poems, ideas. ("Children can be easily led to recognize and understand the special beauty of the image *heart like cracked gravel,* line six, stanza three. Point out, if the opportunity occurs, that this is a simile.")

The passage above does not do serious damage to a student's heart and mind. It falls into the category, rather, of a foolish, somewhat boring and dishonest waste of time. (What if a student happens to be bright enough to understand, for instance, that this is not a "beautiful image" after all, but an impossible image in a very, very sorrowful piece of verse?) The guidebooks that are truly dangerous, however, are those which try to tell us how to lead a class of students to a "logical" conclusion in the areas of politics and current issues. Most of these logical conclusions, as we know too well, have to do with jingoistic loyalties, the recognition of the merits of the U.S. economic system, and the power, prestige and importance of the United States as compared to those of nations which adhere to socialist ideals.

Many teachers no longer will deny their own intelligence and taste by using books like these. Others, however, find themselves in situations where they have no choice. Either they use the guidebook and make lesson plans according to the rules, or else they risk the likelihood of condemnation by their supervisors, charges of stubborn and recalcitrant behavior leading at last either to demotion or else to suspension or expulsion. Imaginative teachers who are in this situation, and who clearly recognize the devious behavior in which they are invited to participate, now and then have used their ingenuity and skill in order to arrive at a way out. In fewest words, what they have managed to achieve is to make certain that the guidebook cannot lead their students to those preplanned conclusions at which its authors confidently predict they will "arrive." In order to do this, teachers simply figure out a tactful way to get a copy of the guidebook into the hands of children.

School officials who hear of this may well condemn our action as the very essence of unprofessional behavior. Teachers, however, seem to be on solid ground with the straightforward answer that their students have a very high stake in recognition of the details of the way by which the process of indoctrination works.

Obviously, teachers are likely to run into a good deal less resistance if they are able to address potential critics in a noncombative tone which more or less anticipates agreement. The manner of the teacher is, more often than not, the crucial factor in obtaining a satisfactory outcome to these altercations.

The assumption of a hostile answer can pretty well guarantee that we will come across as adversaries in the eyes of our superiors. On the other hand, a gentle sense of "presupposed agreement among sensitive co-workers" is a very appealing way to cope with those whom we are eager to win over. It is my own misfortune that I was often, in my first year as a teacher, more eager to "take a stand" than to achieve a goal. If the objective is to demythologize some of the worst of these expensive texts and readers, it does not help to let our principal believe we view him as a fool.

Once students have had a chance to see one of these teacher's guides, they frequently will ask their teacher how to get their hands on multiple copies of the book. One teacher in Nebraska told me that she sends these students to the principal. If the principal answers that he has no power to consent, the teacher sends them to the school committee. It is hard to see how school committees can refuse a student who requests the right to buy one of these books. If the school committee does refuse, however, it is simple enough for us to tell our students how to write off to the publisher and order a few of these documents themselves. (We can, of course, always lend them several copies of our own.) Once they have a couple of guidebooks in their own possession, it is an easy matter to assist them in examination of particular pages, then Xerox and distribute copies to their classmates.

Sometimes, as with guidebooks for the literature texts, the consequence is merely comical. In other subject areas such as history and government, the end results are genuinely explosive. It isn't pleasant to discover that a book, or a school system, that appears to have been urging you to think, reflect and shape your own view of the world, is, in fact, by clear intention, leading you by clever stages to a set of inescapable conclusions. It is even more unpleasant when these logical conclusions manage, almost every time, to demonstrate the failure—or, more tastefully stated, "the disappointing aspects"—of all other ways of life, in contrast, of course, to the way that we live here in the United States.

The various approaches that I have suggested here, relatively gentle in their flavor and quite certainly within the limits of the law, have nonetheless led, in several cases, to intense reactions on the part of students. A teacher's guide appears to be about as dull and nonsubversive as the stories of George Washington and Betsy Ross. Yet, turned around for uses such as those I have proposed, it can be a quite effective means by which to undercut at least one instrument of student indoctrination and control.

The knowledge that a class of students has been able to examine various sections of the teacher's guide, even before a teacher has had the chance to put those sections into use, will sometimes cause a certain amount of anguish in some of the other teachers in the school. It is like the issue of the cumulative folders. For most teachers, however, this is not the case at all. Teachers are by no means such predictable and uniform cowards as the public likes to think. Many teachers, frankly, find the revelation (to their pupils) of the teacher's guide, and similar manipulative materials, a great source of relief. Very few teachers get much satisfaction out of doing lessons where they know that they will have no possible chance of learning something new, because they are advised well in advance exactly what the class is going to "ask"—and also what the class is going to "discover."

Teachers, for decades, have been denied, thereby, not only the satisfaction of creative and imaginative planning of their own day's labor but also almost every opportunity for intellectual discovery, surprise—the unexpected. They write down in advance, on Sunday afternoons, in lesson books, the tedious ideas their students will discover Wednesday mornings in their English or their social studies class.

The tragedy in all of this is twofold.

The teacher's professional value is reduced, by the foregoing process, to that of a technical go-between. In political respects, the teacher is reduced to pimping for the textbook authors— those, in turn, who have already offered the little talent they possess to satisfy the political intentions of the powers that be.

I once looked over a teacher's guide in California which gave the teacher of social studies the following directions: "Lead students, by free and open discussion, to the following six reasons for the failure of socialism in Red China . . ."

The wording reflects the knee-jerk acquiescence of the textbook writers to the current political jargon of the nation. A decade later, they would not have said "Red China." Ever since Richard Nixon set foot on the tarmac in Shanghai, China has come to be labeled by its real name. Today, the very same teacher's guide, in search of suitable demons, would doubtless shift its animus to another Marxist nation. There, too, our students would be led to discover the seven, eight—or eighteen—reasons for the failure of an ideological system that our government views with disapproval.

The pejorative adjective, however, represents the least of evils. It is the manipulative teaching process which degrades the teacher most. What do we do with the disagreeable child who *refuses* to discover "the six reasons"? What of the child, for example, who comes up with only four or who insists that there are only three? What of the unhappy child, for that matter, who decides, by some calamitous mistake, that socialism is not failing in "Red China" after all?

The student who breaks the predictive pattern that has been laid out for the teacher who must use the teacher's guide becomes all at once a positive threat to the uninterrupted presentation of the daily lesson. The teacher, having once subscribed to this inane procedure, is left in an unenviable position. The uncooperative student becomes an adversary of that teacher, even indeed of the teacher who never believed in the procedure in the first place. The teacher's guide has erected a wall between the teacher and the student—perhaps the very student who was most likely to have given the class a moment of the unexpected.

One of the greatest satisfactions of teaching, in my own belief, is the ever-present possibility of "taking the imagination by surprise"—our own imagination or that of the children in our midst. Once we consent to conduct our class in accordance with the orders of Scott Foresman, we forfeit entirely the gratification of being taken by surprise. It is one of those factors that contributes rapidly to teacher burn-out, to tedium, to weariness, to a loss of day-to-day exhilaration.

Equally disheartening is the loss of anything that resembles dialogue between the teacher and the class. There cannot be dialogue in a situation that has been so carefully stage-managed. At best, one achieves the bizarre phenomenon of "divided monologue." The teacher asks, and the teacher replies—even though the replies appear to be coming from the mouths of children. In reality, the script that has been provided by the guidebook, adapted perhaps by the teacher who prepared the lesson plan, is subsequently read in two part harmony by the teacher and the class. *It is all, however, being spoken by one person.*

A preplanned nationally standardized monologue disguises itself as the dialogue of authentic education. It is an offense against all parties who must play the game; but the offense is greatest against the one who knows that the outcome has been "fixed" and still must play it with a smile. It is no wonder, then, that so many teachers either disregard these standard readers and their guidebooks altogether or else resort to such methods of subversion as the one I have proposed.

Once our students have a copy, or at least some sections, of the teacher's guide right on their desks, we find all at once that the use of that guide begins to serve a totally new function. Instead of the skilled manipulation of the students to arrive at predetermined places, it allows teachers and students together to study the very process of manipulation. A method intended to be used in service of aesthetic or ideological control serves us instead as a means of tearing the wrappings from the system altogether. The teacher's guide becomes the object of an "ideological dig." Teacher and pupil, like eager anthropologists, interpret a strange society (that of the public school) by close examination of a precious, whole, undamaged piece of clay. Humor abounds—but so, too, do ethical uproar and enlightened scrutiny. The sense of relief for many teachers is, if possible, even greater than that which will be afforded to their students.

In spite of all that I have said above, many teachers who have been using books like these for several years are going to feel threatened. Those who are least willing to smile at some of the absurdities with which we have, for too long, been obliged to live may even attempt to charge us with disloyalty.

If this should happen, although it does mean trouble for somebody (or, at very least, bad feelings), it can also spark some fascinating and unprecedented class discussions, as well as some helpful discussions among teachers, on the ethics of the whole idea of standardized deception in the public schools. Certainly, between the textbook publisher, school board and the class, there *has* been very serious and real deception.

The question is this: Which of the three—school board, publisher or students—should we call dishonest?

History from the Bottom Up

As we have seen, the child who dares to criticize the books provided by the public school can often expect to hear a certain familiar and predictable reply: "If you don't like this book that we gave you, let's see if you can write a better one yourself."

In the past few years, a number of teachers have had the sense of mischief and imagination to take up this challenge— but to turn it around in ways most principals and school boards don't expect.

In itself, a student-written text is nothing new. It is something that's been done before, but generally only in a time of crisis and also most frequently in a manner that did not distinguish it greatly from the textbooks that we had already. The content was better; but the format was pretty much unchanged. Civil rights workers in the 1960s put together something of this sort for students in the hundreds of "Freedom Schools" that were begun in Georgia, Alabama, Mississippi. It was a book for teaching kids to read—not by telling tales of Dick and Jane, but by direct use of the stories of the struggles and rebellions of black people. Its title, not surprisingly, was *The Freedom Reader*. Labor union organizers have also done counter-textbooks of their own for many years. More recently, a group of high school students in Wisconsin have begun to work on a similar idea.

Teachers who intend to set out with their students on a project of this sort sometimes find it helpful to examine first the special categories of distortion that seem to be predominant within the standard texts. It isn't just the obvious lies that publishers put *in*, but also the essential truths which they leave *out*, that constitute the ultimate deception. The point, then, is to do a lot more than to fix that which is present. The point is also to replace what has been lost.

History, as students almost always learn it, is not really history at all. It is the history of privilege, the history of those who have the power, cash and pleasure, not of those who do the work, who undergo the hardship and absorb the blows. In many cases, history—as it is made available in public school—is not a great deal more than endless tabulations of the actions and the attitudes of famous people: kings and commissars, builders and brokers, bankers, scientists, artists, authors and inventors, sometimes conquerors and killers.

Narratives of war are almost always stories of the bold and clever tactical ideas of generals and admirals. Seldom do we read about the lives and deaths of twenty million soldiers in the front lines. "International relations," by the same evasion, have always been described as confrontations and negotiations by the rulers or the representatives of rulers (such people as Von Ribbentrop, Molotov, John Foster Dulles), seldom as the lives and struggles undergone by those nine hundred million human beings who were organizers, soldiers, carpenters, coal carriers, day laborers—or children and school teachers—within the nations which these men controlled. U.S. history, too many times, is little more than rather dry, uninteresting and repetitive descriptions of quadrennial elections, followed by the so-called "Major Contributions" of each president, no matter how unoriginal, dishonest or inept.

As an initial act of independence, therefore, many of the student textbook writers reject for good those four-year spans that separate elections. By this decision, they subvert, right from the start, the semblance of importance which is otherwise assigned to those unreal and insubstantial choices between two affluent candidates—or those who have been hand-picked by the affluent—then to be sold as plausible and legitimate alternatives to a public which has had no input from the start. (Even the outcome of a primary election is determined by the campaign staff and budget of the candidate with the largest bank account.) The students win themselves, at the same time, a lot of space in which to speak of people and events that seem to them to count a great deal more: to draw, for instance, on the voices of those people whom the scholars used to call "the silent poor." Thus, from the start, they are prepared to tell these tales not from the "top" down but from the "bottom" up.

History not of a heroic westward drive on part of the United States, but history as murder and exploitation of the only native residents of North America.

History not of Waltham watches, but of Waltham women, history also of the international workers of the world, of the steel, coal, railroad workers' union, of the International Ladies' Garment Workers' Union.

History not of well-paid generals and their heroic deeds, but history of the frontline soldiers who lay down their lives in battle while the generals held expensive banquets at headquarters.

History of transportation, medicine and law, not in terms of high-speed turbotrains, of "milestone" decisions in the federal courts, epoch-making "breakthroughs" in the clinics of the rich, but documentation of high ghetto death rates, overcrowded clinics in Los Angeles, Chicago, the South Bronx.

History of legal process as dispensed not by distinguished jurists on the federal bench, but by the circuit judges of the Alabama courts. Travel not by Eastern Airlines but by Greyhound, Trailways and by thumb. History of business, profit and production not in terms of handsome photographs of Andrew Carnegie, John Rockefeller, Henry Ford, but industry in terms of labor, cash and its real sources: where it comes from, who creates it, who possesses it and who enjoys it.

The challenge here is not just one of refutation of a history of lies. It is a matter also of the textbook's point of observation—or, as photographers say, "the angle of vision." Even the most innovative texts of recent years speak of slave days still from the untroubled point of view of those who were *not* slaves but were either southern scholars or else northern commentators. Unjust customs viewed from universities, from libraries or from the hotel balconies of those who were their instigators, planners, profiteers, cannot be described in voices of necessity, of urgency and rage—but only, at the best, of kindliness, of pity, of amelioration. (A few books have been published in the past ten years which constitute significant exceptions; but all of these books are highly selective in their subject area—and these are not the books, in any case, that are selected or "adopted" by the public schools.)

History, as taught in public school, is history as seen from the top down. It is history as ordinary people would not feel it, did not live it and would not describe it. This is all the greater reason, then, why teachers who intend to help their students in the composition and production of a truly interesting book need to do an awful lot of work to help those students find the voices, documents and stories of the struggles of the poor.

One of the most obvious ways to help to free our students from the limitations of the textbooks and encyclopedias which are already on the shelf is by urging them to make use of a major library. If our students don't have time or travel money to do research of this kind, older friends in nearby universities will often do it for them. If they can't, the list of leads in the back section of this book ought to be of use in helping students to discover and obtain a lot of rich and interesting information on their own.

If the student-written text is to go beyond the stories about generals and millionaires and queens and kings, teachers have to help their students, in one way or other, to discover and record the voices of the common men and women who reflect the real life out of which all history is made. This is especially the case in writing about minorities, as well as about women. Our tendency is to attempt to make up for the errors of the past by listing (and praising) as many notable blacks, or women, as we can possibly "collect"—in order, it seems, to struggle back *in kind* against all of those white male Anglo-Saxon figures who now dominate the school curricula. We continue, however, to write about important people, prize-winning people, blacks of grandeur, women of great fire, fame or wit. We do not write about ordinary people.

For women especially, an authentic reclamation of history seems to demand that we examine those who worked in the sweatshops, those who were the backbone of the cottage industries, those who were midwives and ran schools for *other* midwives, those who operated little-known (and once-forbidden) "underground schools" for runaway slaves during the 1800s.

These are not women who were invited to the White House, led massive protest movements or delivered fiery, famous and exciting speeches. They are the women, however, without whom none of their leaders would have come to our attention because they would not have had anyone to lead. Their lives and words are an elemental part of what I mean by history "from the bottom up." I do not mean "bottom" in a condescending way—like "pitiful but decent." I mean those women who were workers, farmers, fighters, organizers and front-runners in the struggles of their times. Many of those elderly men and women still alive today can tell the stories of their mothers and grandmothers. Students can record and then transcribe and edit stories of this kind.

Another early stage within the struggle to demystify the standard texts is to involve our pupils in a close examination of the *language* that is used in many of these books, in order to begin to understand the power of a loaded word or phrase. Once students start to recognize the way that traditional textbooks load their words, then they can begin to figure out the way to do it on their own—but from a different point of view.

Teachers must often go to some extremes to demonstrate to students that there is no way to write "unloaded" language. Every word conveys some kind of bias, even if it is just the bias of those people who have given up so much of their own selves that they no longer have strong feelings about anything. (Theirs is the bias of surrender.) If students in the class wish to dispute this point, it might be of interest to invite them to attempt to make a statement in the subject area of politics or social change which is not loaded in one way or other.

An obvious example of a loaded word—one which was discussed, in passing, earlier in this book—is the modifier *radical*. The adjective is used in school as if it were a dangerous deviation from a healthy modifier: *liberal*. It is within the power of the students, if they so desire, to turn this right around. I have heard at least one high school teacher, obviously a little more audacious than most others, who spoke of liberals as "people who say that they agree with things the radicals have done—but don't intend to do those things themselves."

As we have seen, there are many teachers who do not choose to talk in terms like these. Teachers who hesitate to talk too much in class, but recognize that they cannot help but demonstrate a bias anyway, often try to work around their hesitation by resorting to a method that I have described above: setting out a broad, diverse, but still (inevitably) weighted set of offerings—both ideological and historical materials—a selection which will elicit many of the issues that are being mentioned here. Other teachers see no reason why they should not speak out bluntly for themselves. I see no reason why a teacher needs to "choose," or why we ought not to invite (and to expect) a mixture of both methods. The point, in either case, is to bestir the minds of students to perceive large areas of possible distortion and deception in familiar language use which they have not previously considered, and would have no opportunity to think of, without lots of outside help.

The same teacher I quoted above speaks to his class in terms somewhat like these: "Again and again, in history, whenever crisis comes, you'll find that liberals tend to turn against their former radical co-workers." If the students doubt this (as many do), he says: "Why don't you do some research and find out? Look a little into liberal behavior inside Germany during Hitler's rise to power."

If the students still feel skeptical, then he suggests they do the same thing also in regard to liberal behavior here in the United States during the time that Joe McCarthy came to power. "Several prominent newsmen that you hear today on national TV turned in their radical friends to save their jobs." After a sharp, non-neutral, controversial statement of that kind, the class at least has something of real interest to debate. Whatever the repercussions, class discussion won't be dull.

Another first step for a class that plans to write a counter-textbook of its own is to examine not only lies, omissions, loaded words, but format also—the entire manner of presentation of familiar texts. Most students are so well trained, for instance, to the use of sections and divisions, "units" and "sub-units," that it begins to be extremely hard to figure out the way to bypass all this complicated scaffold. Some of the structure of a standard textbook is, I suppose, essential. Most often it's of use to print an index. It also makes some sense to publish footnotes, especially in order to protect the class against the charge of reckless, overstated views. These, however, are quite different matters from the "units" and "sub-units" of the standard text.

Teachers can open up this issue with their students in a pretty direct and uninhibited way. (There's nothing about the subject which should threaten anyone in public school or in the F.B.I.) We ought to let our students know that they don't need to lock up all of their best ideas in boxes and containers. We ought to let them know that items can drift—and sometimes overlap. We ought to let them know they can repeat a point that seems important ten or fifteen times—maybe only for the sake of causing us to wonder why. We ought to let them know they do not need to print an illustration every two and a half pages. They might allow five pages with *no* illustrations—then, all at once, explode with fold-out photos, cartoons and other designs.

All of the above is based upon the supposition that the class and teacher have in mind the composition only of a single text. There is no reason why this need be so. Hundreds of other variations come to mind: multiple books on separate topics, for example, radical comic books for students of younger ages than those in your class, books on HOW TO WRITE A BOOK FROM SCRATCH, books which aim exclusively at local issues, books which do not try to match the national appeal of standard texts but which instead are aimed at one place and one season only.

One final thought: A lot of students, even in the preparation of their own text, hesitate to advertise their own beliefs in clear and passionate words. This inhibition is a natural carry-over from the inhibitions which so many of their teachers feel as well. Other students, however, have been able to get past this hesitation. They flood their work with totally wide-open statements (sometimes bitter, sometimes biting and sometimes satiric) of their own point of view. They also advertise the bias of their views by two-inch titles or by comical and unconventional headlines.

The sole purpose of such headlines is to challenge, sidestep, and even satirize, the standard textbook pretense of a neutral point of view. Thus, if another teacher looks at what the class has done and tells the students that it seems to tell "only one side," they can be candid and can answer that he or she is absolutely right. Those who wish can get the other side from TV, from the press or from the texts that still are lined against the wall. Honest bias is the best defense against such accusations later on.

"Of course it tells our side. That's why we wrote it."

Issues That Start to Send Our Students Home in Tears

Each example I have given, in the last three sections, remains within the precincts of the school itself: cumulative records, teacher's guides and student-written texts. The idea of action, growing out of a period of reflection, becomes a great deal more exciting and a whole lot more important when the process leads both class and teacher outside of the school into the world beyond.

It is one thing, however, to encourage students to take action on their own beliefs. It is quite another to encourage our pupils to go out and to take action on those ethical convictions which we have identified already as our own. It would, no doubt, be far less troublesome for teachers if we could feel content to state no more than this: "Students should be faithful to their own intense beliefs and feel the power to turn ethical intentions into lived convictions." It *would* be more convenient, but it would be totally dishonest.

The truth is that teachers do not think of "lived conviction" as an abstract virtue, but rather of conviction in the context of particular moral mandates and specific human needs. Many are needs and mandates that are likely to disturb our students and, perhaps, create in them a state of ethical upheaval that might sometimes send them home in fury or in tears. Whenever this happens, teachers need to be prepared for parent complaints, neighborhood concern and heightened anxiety levels within the administration of the school.

On the other hand, if teachers have engaged in prior and extensive groundwork with the parents of the pupils (groundwork of the kind that will be indicated in the second section of this book), then I think that it is worth the risk to raise such issues in the presence of the class, and I suspect that many of our principals and fellow teachers will support us. There are, certainly, large numbers of unfrightened educators who have been introducing issues of considerable provocation into public schools and urging their students to "get up and do something about it"—yet do not appear to have been beaten down by critics from inside or from outside of the schools.

One of the most familiar objections that is likely to occur is the question of the wisdom of creating "dangerous guilt feelings" in young people. A conventional viewpoint that repeatedly appears to win support from conventional physicians —especially conventional psychiatrists—advises us that all straightforward guilt, undecorated conscience and bad dreams are both unsound and (probably) symptoms of neurosis. The teacher who inspires such uncomfortable feelings is, of course, regarded by the social system as the most neurotic one of all.

The sinister part of all of this, of course—and certainly, in long-range terms, the most alarming—is that our logic rapidly leads us very quickly to believe that there are not *some* situations to which guilt might well be the only sane response. It also leads us to forget the sane and practical distinction to be drawn between two very different kinds of guilt which share, unfortunately, a single name: the guilt that simply binds up individuals within a tight and frightened knot of shame and fear, and—in striking contrast—that experience of pain and outrage, followed by a sense of individual self-liberation, which functions not as a neurotic bind but rather as a threshold into energetic and reflective action. It is a feeling which does not act to constrain but proves, rather, catalytic in its power to provoke us to enormous personal growth and new perceptions.

Of all potentially disturbing issues (those which might indeed be threatening to the children of rich people) the one most painful is the question of our own responsibility for the physical and psychological ordeal of those who live in our own social system but whose existence we are somehow able to perceive as disconnected from our own.

Many times students will begin, in class discussions on this subject, by taking an exceedingly defensive stand: "What does the life or death of children in the South Bronx have to do with you or me?" If they sit and talk a while longer with their teachers, it might become uncomfortably clear exactly what it has to do with all of us.

The children of white landlords who own rental units in a nearby urban slum often live well, eat good food and attend superior schools, at the direct expense of very poor people who live in neglected and unwholesome tenements which have been rented to them by *our* parents. The children of prosperous doctors in the northern cities often can afford to wear expensive clothes, travel to Europe in the summer, practice their tennis in exclusive clubs, because their fathers or mothers choose to care for people who can pay them high fees, leaving poor people—largely blacks and Spanish-speaking—to wait in line at poorly staffed health clinics where medical care is marginal at best. The children of rich, sometimes aristocratic owners of large farms and cattle ranches often live in pleasant, rich and elegant homes because their fathers hire, at low wages, illiterate farm workers, offer them no health protection, house them in filthy overcrowded shacks and make no effort to provide them with that bit of education that might lead them to protest against such desperate conditions.

All prosperous white students aren't the children of rich doctors, avaricious lawyers, predatory slumlords. Nor are all white middle-class young people really "prosperous" at all. (Many, although we think of them as middle class, often live in economic hardship which the national statistics do not honestly reflect.) It seems important to emphasize this point because I do not like to reinforce the crippling and simplistic view that every student whom we teach in school is either a victim or else the victimizer. Millions of students live in something of an economic limbo. Nonetheless, for a very large number of the affluent students in our schools, pleasure and well-being *are* obtained, in large degree, at the direct expense of many millions of others who live very close to the survival margin. It is this relatively privileged group that I now have in mind.

Once children from this background start to talk and think of poverty and excess in the meticulous way that I propose, and with the conscious and unhesitant participation of their teachers, they rapidly discover that there *are* some real and obvious connections between their own lives and those of the very poor people with whom they might already identify and with whom they sometimes even work as volunteers, but up to now only in a charitable or paternalistic state of mind. All at once, an unanticipated factor enters their consideration. It is not just that some folks have a little—and some others have a lot. One thing, rather *depends* upon the other.

Textbook publishers do their best to dodge this possibility altogether. They try very hard to choose a type of language that will manage to obscure the whole idea of causes and connections between rich and poor. School books seldom use a gritty word like *exploitation* or *oppression*. Instead, in writing of black people, for example, they speak in terms of *deprivation*. Deprivation sounds like something that "just happens" (a thunderstorm, a case of hiccoughs or the flu), rather than something that one person does to someone else. "Too little" can be said (about one social class)—but not "too much" (about the other). To say "too little" and "too much" in the same sentence is to make clear that we live, not simply in a land of pain, but also in a nation of injustice.

Troublesome or not, this is a subject which an earnest and

persistent teacher cannot easily pass by. Exploitation is not carried out by no one, but by someone. That someone—doctor, landlord, or landowner—no matter how careful we may try to be, is going to prove to be somebody's rich father. If we teach in an especially rich neighborhood, or even just a well-off neighborhood, there is an excellent chance that many of the children whom we teach are rich because some other folks are poor.

To deal with matters that come so close to home is not an easy business—especially for a teacher who has warm and affectionate feelings for the pupils in his class. It often means anger. Sometimes it means tears. There is no way, however, by which teachers of privileged children can avoid this point if we believe those children should receive the chance to grow up, not just smart and slick, but also ethical and strong.

If the teacher needs to postpone matters of this sort on tactical grounds—if the teacher, for instance, has good reason to anticipate a far more serious confrontation later on, perhaps with conservative groups that have already made it clear that they are watching his behavior—that is an unassailable reason to move gently in the area I have suggested. If, on the other hand, a teacher chooses to step back from any discussion of the causative connections which make poverty a fact of life in the United States, and if that teacher's only reason is a hesitation to face up to repercussions of his own beliefs, then I should think that teacher would perceive himself as working in collusion with the lies the textbooks teach. I cannot imagine any other way that we could understand such hesitation.

It is probably correct that teachers cannot easily raise these issues with the pupils of the first or second grade. On the other hand, from fifth or sixth grade on, it is difficult to justify a teacher's circumvention of these basic truths. It would be a relief to me, as to most teachers, if we could somehow always find a reason to sidestep these difficult dilemmas. I don't think that we *can,* however; and I don't think that we *should.*

In every neighborhood, in almost every generation, certain privileged children of the affluent members of society do find the courage to break away from many traditional ideas in order to work instead beside the victims of their social order. To make that choice, as many teachers know from their own life and work, is very hard. There is no reason, therefore, why students ought to suffer twice: once for sadness at the loss of all those things that once were easy and familiar, then a second time for guilt at being born the children of rich people.

If some of our students honestly should resolve to take a stand beside a victimized minority, they may not leave their homes in any drastic physical respect. In moral terms, however, they do make the choice to take sides with the victims of a world their folks, with rare exceptions, have either helped to shape or, at the least, accepted without protest. Students who come to this decision often suffer deeply for the distance it creates between themselves and their old friends and other teachers.

If students start to learn of pain and exploitation in their midst, their city, state or nation, and if they choose to disregard that pain (as many normal people do), then they have reason to feel guilty. If, however, they have begun to act upon their sense of what is just and true, and then have taken sides as well, and put their energies to work for weeks on end within a day-care center, or a clinic, or learned how to churn out leaflets from a ditto master for a strong street organization (like those many groups which do in fact exist throughout the country), then I see no reason why—from that point on—they ought to live with either guilt or any other form of inappropriate self-accusation.

In dealing with this issue, unlike many others treated in this book, it seems self-evident that there is only modest value in the act of exhortation in itself, since even the most ardent words of teachers still remain within the inert limitations that contain almost all other processes of public education. Only the teacher's actual participation in specific actions of his or her own personal determination (in keeping with those values that the teacher, and not necessarily the teacher's pupils, might hold dear) is likely to establish a persuasive precedent for pupils to take independent action of their own.

It is, of course, all the more exciting—and more deeply moving to everyone concerned—if, at some stage, the teacher's struggle and that of the pupils should turn out to be the same.

Postscript

I have distinguished in these chapters between two different kinds of guilt. Many students find themselves caught up in a neurotic and entangling labyrinth of self-accusation. Others are able to move forward from this state of mind into a vigorous process of self-liberation.

One of the ways by which the teacher can assist a student who is caught up in the former state of mind is to attempt to help to break down large and overwhelming socioeconomic problems into manageable items which are small enough for students first to pinpoint, then to attack head-on. So long as a problem appears to be too grandiose to be approached by ordinary, isolated and youthful human beings, students respond by stepping away and giving up the effort altogether: "The problem is too big."

I do not propose that we ignore realistic recognition of those many surrounding forces that control the schools, the banks, the neighborhoods, the hospitals or the police. I do suggest, however, that each teacher and each student need to find the willingness to enter into piecemeal battle, even in the face of larger issues, of whatever shape or size.

Struggles that we and our students hope to undertake ought to be measured by their value, on the one hand, and real chances for completion on the other: BATTLES LARGE ENOUGH TO MATTER, SMALL ENOUGH TO WIN.

The object is to break down overwhelming condemnations

into a number of small isolable items of potential action: to speak, if we must, of vast and sometimes circular causes of injustice and oppression, yet to encourage kids to go out anyway and open up a neighborhood day-care center, begin a picket line before the doorway of a racist banking corporation, organize a sit-down on the front steps of the landlord of a family of poor people in distress.

More clearly stated: The place to jam the gears of an unjust machine is where we stand, with quiet recognition of "the larger situation" in all cases, but with determination also to effect real changes *here and now* by means which are, in fact, within our range of dream and action.

I believe that we can spare our students a vast amount of needless grief by emphasizing an approach like this. The beginning of even the smallest move in the effort to undo a larger evil is the first step in a course of action that releases a person from self-accusation to begin the satisfying and rewarding struggle to make less the pain and the unfairness of the world.

It marks the difference between guilt and freedom.

It Is Evil to Tell Lies to Children

Many teachers, while irreverent in a number of other ways, appear to regard discussion of the flag pledge as too controversial for their taste. In justification of their own behavior, they often present an interesting but, I think, unpersuasive explanation. In the long run, they say, the content of the curriculum is not really so influential in the minds of children as are "the ways in which the student and the teacher can relate." For this reason, they believe, a matter as blunt and simple as the verbal content of a daily recitation need not be regarded as an issue of much import either way.

Very large numbers of entirely scrupulous teachers appear to share this point of view. It does not seem reasonable to speak of their position as if it were a conscious and disreputable evasion. It *is* an evasion, I believe, but not a conscious one, and it does rest upon a certain area of the truth. The process counts. There is no argument about this. Changes in the mode and manner of the classroom, without question, can democratize and humanize relationships. They do not, however, render possible a real subversion of the ideological bias that protects *this* class (this school, this neighborhood, these children) against a realistic recognition of the world of men and women in despair that stands on every side around them.

Few teachers would doubt that a democratized relationship among their students can be therapeutic and benign, but therapy will never be a substitute for social change. Teachers know very well that they will not undo the damage that is being done today within the U.S. schools if we can do no more than to prepare more wholesome, even-spirited and mutually respectful members of a sheltered, well-protected and anesthetic isolation chamber.

The flag pledge, being the most obvious form of pure indoctrination in the public school, is just exactly the variety of intellectual "content" that is now regarded with the most disdain by those who view the process of the school day as the sole point worth discussion. It is precisely for this reason, I believe, that it deserves the strong, intelligent and well-planned scrutiny and condemnation of those teachers who intend to change the public schools.

The longer we look at it, the more apparent it becomes that this is a peculiar—and a peculiarly undemocratic—exercise in several ways. First, it seems, more lucidly than any other lesson that we learn in public school, to leave exposed the true historic purpose of the institution. The time-honored objectives of the school and school board, in most other areas of education, are indirect, obscured by multiple contradictions, and at times benign in their appearance. Teachers and students cannot often look so openly upon the naked purpose of the school day.

Perhaps, therefore, we should be grateful for the flag pledge. Instead of futile protest or complaint, we ought to exploit the opportunity it presents. It tells our pupils, better than any other symbol, sign or lesson, both the name and nature of their landlord—or their keeper—for the years in which they are to be contained within the physical and psychological parameters of public school.

There are, I know, a large number of teachers who feel that they are compromised, and their intelligence insulted, by the obligation to enforce the recitation of this pledge. They struggle, however, to convince themselves and one another that the whole thing is a foolish unimportant custom with no power and no impact that endures. "We don't always do it anyway," some of these teachers say. Or else: "It doesn't work. We do it, but the kids don't really understand the words." The second statement has always seemed to me an odd excuse: If the kids don't even understand the words, why should a teacher ask them to recite it in the first place?

Veteran teachers know the truth of this only too well. The flag pledge "works." That symbol does not hang above the door for decoration. It is in the classroom for a very real and urgent purpose. A school or class that flies the flag makes an important declaration of intent. It makes it clear, no matter what we say we plan to do (and often really do intend) concerning free and open disputation in the course of public education, that there will be strict limits on all sides of our debate. Those limits are the limits of essential U.S. power and self-interest.

Certainly, many schools and many teachers do, at times, attempt to undercut the power of the recitation. There are also public schools where rituals like the pledge are very rapidly passed over—since the schools are eager to seem liberal and free. Even in these situations, nonetheless, most of us are well aware that exercises like the pledge do not cease to hold power. There is a familiar saying that the man who pays the piper calls the tune. The presence of the flag is our reminder of exactly who it is who pays the piper in our public schools. If we ever hope to have an open conversation, one that will not be contained with invisible restraints, it may well be that we will have to start either by taking down the flag or else by making clear, in vivid terms, the travesty and the self-contradiction which the flag pledge represents.

I do not believe that the recitation of the Pledge of Allegiance—or refusal to participate in such a ritual—has any connection with our loyalty as U.S. citizens. It does not have to do with either radical or conservative beliefs. It has to do with only one essential point: the plain and honest definition of the public school. If the school exists to serve the child and to guarantee the freedom of that child's mind, the flag should not remain.

Even beyond the bind on free discussion which the flag pledge represents, there is the troublesome matter that it simply is untrue as a description of the U.S.A. We do not live within "one nation indivisible." We live in at least two nations, skillfully and consciously divided by the genius of our real estate advisors and the red-line patterns laid out by the mortgage departments of our major banks. Again, liberty and justice, all too clearly, do not prove to be "for all." Instead, there is real liberty for a precious few—and the certitude of justice only for those who can retain the most experienced or prestigious lawyers.

Few of the teachers that I meet, at conferences and workshops, would bother to dispute these points. Many, however, try to handle the dilemma by attempting to "explain" the flag pledge to their pupils as a "dream" or "hope," and not an absolute description of the way things are. This tentative solution does not deal with the real problem. If the pledge is just a dream, an aspiration, then the wording ought to be revised. ("We pledge ourselves to find the ways to turn this segregated and divided nation into a just and decent land before we die.") Since this wording would be more obnoxious to the school boards than the alternative choice of just not saying it at all, it doesn't seem to help a teacher very much to offer this as a solution to the problem.

So far as I can see, there are two plausible options. One alternative is for a teacher to adhere to the decision handed down by the Supreme Court in the test case brought to Washington (and won) by the Jehovah's Witnesses in 1943, which denied the right of public schools to force a child to repeat the pledge.[21] (A later decision, on the part of a Federal Appeals Court in 1973, granted the same exemption to school-teachers.) Another alternative, adopted by some teachers, is to recite the pledge but then to invite the class to analyze the issue and, in cases of general agreement that the pledge is just plain fraudulent and incorrect, to aid and counsel the students to bring their protests to the public eye by urging them to present their arguments before the school board.

Whenever students do obtain a chance to pose their questions to the school board members, face to face, teachers ought to help them in advance to figure out the way to ask productive questions. Too many students, in situations of this kind, become uncharacteristically polite and tend to ask the people that they visit rather timid questions of the sort that politicians can expect. If our students suddenly grow shy and do this also, it is probable that they will get answers that we can anticipate. If it appears that this will be the case, we should at least encourage the class to plan ahead—to move beyond the first and obvious questions that they ask—in order to get to others that the school board cannot possibly predict.

Millions of students every year go off on a couple of "field trips" to the school board or the city hall. They tend to ask the same respectful questions as intimidated reporters at the White House. They end up with the same replies they could have read in their newspapers. There is a special skill in asking tough and searching questions—then in forcing answers which are not the old familiar kind that certain politicians almost always seem to have at hand.

As television viewers know quite well, it often takes an impolite reporter to obtain an interesting answer. I doubt that many kids can summon up sufficient nerve to ask aggressive and persistent questions to a school board of important (or of self-important) adults if we do not give them some explicit and quite pointed recommendations in advance.

Either of these suggestions seems to represent an avenue of logical dissent in the face of a dishonest obligation. The only form of personal reaction to the pledge which, to me, seems just plain unacceptable is to sit back and to do nothing in the way of protest. Sensitive teachers, finding themselves in similar situations, often say they feel uneasy but will add that they can see no possible alternative—unless they are prepared to lose their jobs.

Teachers who are genuinely troubled by this contradiction ought to recognize, from this point on, that there are many more viable options than they knew.

Code Expressions

I have postponed, perhaps too long, the most insidious and most bewildering of all forms of political indoctrination. These are the ever-present, repetitive and somewhat hypnotic forms of jingoistic propaganda that are conveyed by certain long-respected and seemingly immutable code expressions—words and phrases which clutter our texts, mislead our pupils and waste hours of our time in refutation.

Some of the most annoying instances of code expressions are, by this point in time, notorious. Many are the targets of considerable humor and sarcasm. In spite of their notoriety, however, they continue to prevail, uninterrupted, in the public schools. (Many things in public school are like this. It doesn't seem to matter how many books have proven them wrong or how many courts have judged them to be unconstitutional and illegal. Still they continue, like a grotesque and indestructible organism feeding on its own unloved position in the world around it.)

"Manifest destiny" is one of the most embarrassing of these phrases, being as it is a coverall for processes so brutal and, for several hundred years, entirely undisguised: the demolition of the life and culture of the North American Indians under the onslaught of a racist European population. Another phrase which has a similar effect and goal (either to disguise or to obscure a grave historic truth) is the "Good Neighbor Policy," a term which still lives on today—in face of all the evidence that any child or scholar could require—as the emblem of our national benefaction to the Latin countries.[22]

Of all such code expressions, perhaps the most transparent is the phrase "Free World." It is a peculiar phrase—one that pops up often in the textbooks, in the press and on TV. To many people, it might seem that the word *free* ought to have to do with something fair and honest: open to all possible points of view. It might mean, also, free food for people who are hungry and free doctors for the sick. It would be a stroke of great good luck for millions of poor people in those nations that we call the "Free World" if some little piece of this were true.

For many years, the term "Free World" has been used as a political code expression. It informs us of the presence of a nation that will fight beside our own, or side with us in diplomatic struggles, against the socialist nations of the world—or, as the texts label them, "the Soviet camp."

If a teacher were to sit down with a class and make a list of the nations now described within their textbooks as the "Free World," I suspect that there would be only a modest number (Great Britain, France and Canada, perhaps a dozen more) where the words might be at least half honest. There are many other lands, however, which are labeled "free" and yet are not free in any way that can be viewed with serious respect. The term "Free World" is one which must be adjusted every two or three years to include one or two new members and exclude three or four more. At the moment of this writing, the term includes all of the following: Argentina, Brazil, Haiti, Guatemala, Peru, the Dominican Republic, Chile, Uruguay, South Korea, South Africa, Pakistan and the Philippines. (Textbooks which were published prior to 1979 also include Nicaragua and Iran. These will doubtless be removed by the time of the next printing—and placed perhaps in the "uncertain" category.)

There are probably twenty or thirty other nations of this kind which public schools still designate as parts of the "Free World," but those listed above should be enough to demonstrate the actual function and intention of the code expression. Most of these governments hold in common certain basic traits: They kill, exile or imprison people who attempt to write "free" books or try to issue a "free" press. They channel large parts of their national resources into the pockets of the rich and leave the poor to starve or else to suffer lifelong malnutrition. Usually, they do not offer even token medical service to the poor. They make convenient military deals with the United States, giving us land to set up air force bases, harbors to provide both fuel and safety to our submarines and other naval craft and—in some cases—lend us mercenary soldiers if we should need them in what we have come to know as "brush-fire" wars. They also make substantial business deals with U.S. corporations—companies like Polaroid, Gulf Oil, Xerox, General Motors, General Electric.

In plain terms, "Free World" ends up with three simple meanings: free opportunities for very large profits by the U.S. corporations; free use of land or harbors by the U.S. military; free opportunity for the uninhibited exploitation of the poor, carried out by the power of a self-serving upper class that operates in close collaboration with the military forces. These forces are often trained and almost always funded by the U.S. government.

If this is the case, why then do the textbooks still resort to such a devious code expression in discussion of these nations? Why do they use a phrase like "Free World" for a nation which is free in no regard—and does not wear even a mask of freedom? The answers to these questions are exactly the kinds of answers that lead students and teachers back into examination and re-examination of the reason for existence of the public school to start with.

The same scrutiny and the same objective (to raise essential issues of the function and the purpose of the public school) encourage many teachers also to examine certain other code expressions—"violent" and "peace-loving" are two—which the textbooks, press and politicians use with unabated fervor. Most of the textbooks state, with little hesitation, that the United States is a "peace-loving" nation. The president says it. The preachers repeat it. The majority of the population seems to feel at ease with the idea that this is really true. At the same time, it must be obvious to most adults that a very large part of our foreign policy depends entirely on the fact or threat of violent action to achieve our goals.

In recent years, teachers have sometimes been able to confront this very special set of loaded words by careful analysis and discussion with their pupils of the sale of arms by the United States to ninety-three foreign nations.[23] The sale of arms may not, in itself, be evidence of a nation's preference for a violent resolution of its problems. It is clearly evidence, however, that we do not find the handling of weapon sales distasteful or abhorrent.

Using the power of our weapons, governments in nations such as Guatemala, Chile and Brazil can kill off students who defend the poor, can exile, murder or imprison teachers who defend the students, and can murder innocent citizens who seek to stand up for their own rights and those of their teachers and professors. In view of our wistful tradition as a democratic nation which once fought a revolution of its own, teachers seem to me to be on firm and patriotic ground in asking students to address themselves to two specific, painful and uncomplicated questions: Why do we sell weapons to fascistic governments? Why do we sell weapons to a government that tortures its citizens and tramples on all shreds of human decency—in order to suppress all possibilities of democratic revolution?

If teachers succeed in pressing issues of this kind, leading to the point at which their students start to look into the profits that are made from sale of weapons to some of the most dehumanizing and oppressive nations in the world, it seems quite probable that many of those students will also begin to look with skepticism on the total spectrum of school-generated code expressions.

In situations of extreme distortion or self-contradiction on the part of text materials supplied to us by school officials, teachers do not need to stand up and declaim, denounce, exhort, before the children in the class. Instead, they only need to make available the facts and figures and, wherever possible (as always), to draw those figures from such reputable sources as UNESCO or the major TV networks or the established European and American press. With careful, detailed and responsible preparation, teachers can offer their pupils access to all data and documentation they could conceivably require in order to recognize the unjust and unshakable self-interest of the U.S. government in joining in commerce with those nations which we arbitrarily assign to the "Free World" in order to protect our economic power and our military strength.

It is self-evident that the moment at which a teacher begins to deal with issues quite so precious, quite so desperate and sacred to the mainstream of America, is also the moment at which that teacher, in all likelihood, arrives at the extreme and outer limits of all possible toleration on the part of even the most generous and progressive school officials. Whether or not the principal of the school should truly wish to extend protective power to a teacher in this situation, there is no way in which the teacher can expect that higher officials—members of the school board, for example—are going to accept such unconventional and, literally, subversive actions. Wherever else we might arrive at a point of no return, we surely will reach it once we have started to play havoc with those sanctified code expressions that defend the adult world from thinking.

It is at this point that politics and education come together in the most explicit, inextricable and provocative respect. This, then, will be the subject of the next two chapters.

13

Indoctrination vs.
the Free Market of Ideas

Why must education be confused with politics at all?

Many teachers, even in the aftermath of all that they already know, still would like to tell themselves that education can be nonpolitical and neutral. It is not now. It has not been before. It will not be after we have finished with the struggles of our times. Teachers never can be neutral in the eyes of children. We are non-neutral by the clothes we wear. We are non-neutral by the kind of car we drive. We are non-neutral by the kinds of friends we choose, the books we read, the neighborhood in which we make our home. We are non-neutral, most of all, by the message of conviction or self-exile which is written in our eyes.

Since the teacher can't be neutral in the eyes of students, what then is the teacher's ethical answer to the propaganda sold to children in the textbooks which we are assigned to teach?

It may seem to many teachers that the choice is relatively simple: We either collude, connive, collaborate or else articulately rebel. (The foregoing, in any case, was once my own belief.) In my present view, however, none of this is so simple as it first appeared. Unless we designate the final word (*rebel*) in rather careful terms, I am afraid that we will end up in a dangerous position: one in which we effectively repeat the worst ingredients of that process of manipulation and control that we so passionately oppose. The ethical response to "bad indoctrination" is not something known as "good indoctrination." The sole response is: *no indoctrination*. The answer is a free and open market of ideas.

Schools, I have said, comprise the fourth largest business in the nation. It's notable, however—in a nation that professes to believe in the advantages of free and uninhibited competition in most areas of economic life—suddenly that principle disappears right at the classroom door. We've never been permitted to teach and learn within a free and competitive market of ideas. It is within the power of most teachers to *create* that kind of market; but, in order to do so, we will be obliged to go at least ten thousand light-years past the false and fragile options of the so-called "open classroom," "open corridor" or "open school."

In order to create a genuine free market, we have to find the courage to bring radical options into the consciousness of children—options which our supervisors, principals and school boards seldom have even dreamed about in years gone by and cannot be expected to approve.

The question, therefore, is how to go about it. Which options do we select? How do we choose them? How do we present them? With what intelligent and sensitive restraints? With what ambitious and compelling exaltation and imagination?

Many highly politicized teachers that I know are ready and willing to bring into their schools a viewpoint which is clearly ideological but, unhappily, in no respect conducive to real competition—one, to the contrary, which is angry, aggressive and intolerant in its unadulterated imposition of a radical point of view. Although I am convinced that I have often taught my classes in ways that do not differ greatly from the manner of unqualified imposition which these teachers recommend, I do not believe that it is an adequate or thoroughgoing answer to the problem that we face.

There are a number of reasons why I emphasize this point.

First, as always, there is a basic tactical consideration here as to the teacher's need for self-protection in the face of a predictable attack. Teachers who do not choose to spend another year in selling the ten significant ideas of Henry Kissinger to their class, but then replace them by the ten major beliefs of Mao Tse-tung, rapidly find themselves in an untenable situation. Those of their colleagues who do not share their views (and, very often, even those who do) will hurl at them the obvious charge of acting by unequal standards.

Once teachers have condemned the public schools for irresponsible indoctrination of the minds of children, those teachers end up in a dangerous position if they subsequently set out to sell to children their own exclusive body of beliefs instead— no matter how convinced they have become of the correctness of these views.

This is one of several reasons why I think that teachers make a serious mistake if they choose to use their classroom not just to confront the bias of the school, but to convert the students to their own political religion. Even in the wake of many hours of intelligent and well-meant "Disobedience Instruction," students will have no means by which to disobey *in interesting ways* if they know nothing but the gospel of the school and the rebellion of the teacher.

There is another reason why the teacher makes an unwise choice if he or she decides to stand up in the class and to confront the pupils with a set of doctrinaire slogans and rhetorical denunciations of the values represented by the school. Students by now have come to be anesthetized to counter-sloganeering. The words grow wearisome to the students before long. The teacher's views, having no prompt and vigorous counterfoil (the textbook hardly qualifies as such), cease to be catalytic in their provocations and become instead a tedious catalogue of shopworn phrases which, at best, may hypnotize but, more frequently, serve only to sedate.

There is a final reason why I do not think "indoctrination

from the Left" can be accepted as a viable answer to the bias now prevailing in the public schools. It is not a tactical matter, but a matter of fair play. For most students, as I have said, it doesn't seem to work particularly well. For a few, however, it works entirely too well—and unwisely. Students have the right to some sort of exemption from totalitarian control. Even if we should speak here only of one season, one semester or one year, still there is a dangerous lesson to be learned by children if the sole response to the indoctrination of the state is nothing better than indoctrination-in-reverse.

This is not to argue (after all that I have said already) that teachers should try to mute their own beliefs. It *is* to say that teachers must work very hard, and strive with all the ingenuity that they possess, first to steer away from propaganda, tyranny and unfair domination, second to build up a whole series of combative tactics in the consciousness of students long before we start to voice our own most forthright views, finally to provide those students with real substantive data, resources of every possible kind, in order to guarantee that their potential for revolt against our own rebellion will be serious—not token.

At this stage, we no longer are participating in a process of indoctrination-in-reverse—but rather in an ongoing exercise of intellectual energies in vigorous cross fire. In order to create an atmosphere so vital and so strong, teachers need to make available a very broad spectrum of contradictory ideas, materials and leads to outside forms of information.

Teaching in this kind of classroom takes a lot more work than do traditional methods of instruction, but the rewards are greater—sometimes spectacular—and, so far as I can see, there is no other ethical option for a serious teacher in a time of torment and in an unjust and bewildered land.

Postscript: Insisting on the Real Thing

Once we determine, by whatever means, to create the sense of option that allows our students to dissent with us in competent and effective ways, we then must do the work it takes to build a situation where the choices are not superficial. The contrast here is between two wholly different terms: authentic "choice" and inauthentic "whim."

Even the most progressive and enlightened of our public schools opt for the second almost every time. Following the lead of the romantic school reformers of the 1960s, they argue that the vigorous and provocative information which a sensitive and irreverent child may require will come to the child through "natural processes" of totally spontaneous and organic generation. This point of view is innocent but naïve.

Significant political data of the kind that genuinely counts never spontaneously occurs to students in the public schools unless somebody takes some pains to let them know that it is "there." It is like the situation in an airport lounge. No one, of his own free will, is going to buy a ticket to fly to Rio de Janeiro if he does not first know it exists.

In most of the so-called "open" schools that flourished in the early 1970s, many of which still carry on today, children have their choice between a lot of nonpolitical and harmless options: gerbil cages, batteries and bulbs, balance scales and other gadget-oriented learning tools. In political and literary terms, the students in these classrooms have a similarly circumscribed frame of ethical decision. They "freely chose" between the latest "issue booklets," published by a branch of Xerox Corporation, little plug-in film-and-listening centers shipped into the school by I.B.M., or programmed reading kits produced by S.R.A. (a corporate affiliate of I.B.M.), and then, for conflict, search through photo-booklets produced by Time Incorporated or else by Little, Brown (a publishing company wholly owned by Time). For radical contrast, they can get the latest news out of *My Weekly Reader* (also owned by Xerox).

The point is not that school materials need to represent a full array of every possible point along the spectrum of political beliefs, but they must represent a *significant* array—or else we might as well give up the effort altogether.

One of the best ways to determine whether students have

been given an authentic set of choices, I suggest, is by demanding a response to one specific question: "Is there anything here within this room to keep a child wide awake at night with painful self-examination? Is there anything here which can compel the students to confront, not just the textbooks and not just their teacher, but *themselves* as well with questions that might warrant a legitimate debate?"

My own personal choice of classroom options runs the full range from political data on the struggles of poor people in Brazil and Chile, Paraguay, Guatemala, Haiti and Peru, to the intelligent (but, in my own view, inaccurate) refutations available in such right-wing publications as *The National Review* and *Business Week*. If there is not at least this limited degree of confrontation present and available to pupils, then I do not see how we can honestly pretend that students have had access to conflicting attitudes and information on a level that commands their serious respect.

Teachers do not need to go to the absurd degree of trying to bring all *possible* viewpoints into play within their public schools. Nor do teachers need to make an effort to pretend that all ideas are "equally correct" or "equally worthwhile." Quite to the contrary, my point of view insists that they are *not*. Teachers, instead, are asked to do their best to argue for the primacy of their own views within a free, yet fervent, field of competition.

I naturally assume that teachers with political positions very different from my own (including those of extreme conservative belief) will wish to enter the competition I propose. There is no way to avoid this competition, and I do not see why we should wish to do so. It would be a more exciting nation—and, I am convinced, a more enlightened one—if students were given the chance to grapple with a multiplicity of ideologies and points of view.

No one can possibly argue for a particular point of view as well as the man or woman who believes it. Those to the left of political center in this country often react with considerable alarm to this idea: especially if it means that people such as William Buckley were to be given the chance not just to "be heard" within our public schools, but rather to *persuade,* to *argue,* to *win over.* ("What kind of an education would it be if someone such as William Buckley were allowed to win the ears of high school students in the morning—and someone such as I. F. Stone or Dr. Spock during the afternoon?" My own reaction is to view this prospect with incredible excitement. At long last we might begin to teach our children how to think.)

As for the sense of danger that so many liberal-leftists seem to feel, I do not understand the reason for their fear. I have no doubt but that my own ideas will ultimately win out within the minds of children. But this is because I really do believe my viewpoints are correct and that truth has a power of its own. It is my own suspicion that a great many liberals really don't believe this. It is for this reason that they often settle for the boring kingdom of consensus, rather than to place their views in opposition to articulate adversaries. Like many conservatives, it seems that what they fear the most is not the potential power of another person's point of view, but rather the extreme fragility of their own. But that is just another excellent reason why we need to change the schools.

If, in the first six grades of school, the teacher's continuous contact with the class creates a situation that appears to make all dissident viewpoints seem ridiculous or unacceptable, not only due to the personal power of an individual teacher but also, and more likely, due to the affection which the children in the room will feel for their own teacher, then I suggest once more that other teachers in the school—or else community people—who definitively *do* dissent be given the chance to join the class, not once or twice, but on a routine basis.

It seems important to conclude this chapter by restatement of a dual point that I have made before. Indoctrination, in order to work, must be totalitarian; it must take place within a vacuum. We seek, instead, to achieve a high degree of moral and political democracy within the class. Teachers, as I have said, do not need to offer every point of view with equal force. Most of us—we might as well be frank—will offer our own as powerfully as we can, because we know that our pupils will be ready to fight back, that we have provided the weapons to fight back, and that there are other teachers who will fight back also. So there *is* bias. There *is* persuasion. It is not, however, indoctrination-in-reverse.)

Teachers have the right to say what they believe without the fear of accusation or self-accusation. No student, however, should be forced to suffer social ostracism, nor compelled to pay a price, beyond that of the moral anguish of the issue in itself, for taking a stance in opposition to that of the teacher. Both conditions can, and must, be realized by an ethical teacher in rebellion against all that is implied, inflicted or reflected by the standard dogmatism of the textbooks, the curricula and the time-embedded customs and conventions that prevail today within the U.S. public schools.

Patriots with Blinders

The argument is raised, in opposition to almost every sentence that has been written in this book, that every social order needs a certain amount of political indoctrination in order to maintain its own cohesive character. It is argued that, particularly in the context of the 1980s, with ominous signs of class and ethnic conflict that might splinter the nation in a dozen different ways, the last thing we can possibly afford is a disintegration of the uniform traditions represented by the standard textbooks and conventional schoolteachers.

Even those teachers who do not share this belief, and who do not see social disintegration as the danger which so many citizens perceive, must nonetheless be prepared to deal with this concern. Not everybody who will raise this issue is necessarily reactionary in political position. Some are alarmed that uncontrollable turmoil will result from presentation to young people of that spectrum of divergent and conflicting views that I propose. For all of these reasons, we must be ready to defend our own position with a number of reflective answers.

First of all, in trying to deal with opposition or anxiety concerning dangers of disintegration, the point can be made that school indoctrination of the kind we face today does not succeed, in ultimate terms, in reaching patriotic goals. The short-term victory is indisputable: little students standing to salute the U.S. flag, bigger students—sometimes only ten years older—marching to war beneath that flag, and singing patriotic songs. The long-term goal, however, is lost repeatedly, because we seldom do succeed in educating either rational or long-lasting patriots. The archaic methods that we use will not survive the test of either truth or time, except in the cases of those who have agreed to cordon off all access to new information and ideas that might enable them to grow in understanding as historical conditions change.

To those who are troubled by the possible risk of chaos and conformity in failing to forge a uniform consciousness of patriotic loyalty among our boys and girls, teachers can make the point that what we now produce—in terms of patriots or citizens—is something totally different from the sensible and democratic goals of those who helped to found the nation. Either we turn out mindless and unthinking soldiers for our predatory or (as we like to say) mistaken wars, or else we turn out numb and acquiescent people who experience, at most, a vague malaise about the actions of the rest but end up doing little more than to sit back before the TV screen and offer impotent remarks about it all. There is another frequent outcome, too. This is the situation of the man or woman who has been protected from the truth for twelve long years (or sixteen years, if he or she has been through college also), then goes to pieces at the first exposure to the fact that we, like almost every other major nation, do a vast amount of evil on this earth. A narrow-minded and protected patriotic dogmatism is both perilous and frail.

Shall we produce fake patriots with blinders—protected by well-fabricated lies—or honest patriots, prepared to live with knowledge of both good and evil in our land, restless to root out the second, passionate to reinforce the first?

This is a question that has at least a chance of winning listeners to our point of view. It is a blunt appeal to the self-interest of sophisticated and farsighted parents. If they love their children, they may be willing to think hard about the dangers of a sheltered nationalism and false patriotic pride that shatters at first contact with the truth.

The goal, as it is designated here, is not to undermine and to subvert ("deschool") society, but only to open up the windows and let in fresh air—along with a free market of ideas. If the traditional values of the nation can survive in contestation of this kind, then they will thrive and grow far more emphatic by the competition. If they cannot, then possibly they do not merit the devotion of our students in the first place.

Three hundred years ago, John Milton wrote these words: "Let [Truth] and Falsehood grapple. Who ever knew Truth put to the worse in a free and open encounter?"[24] If the more conservative parents of our school and neighborhood are alarmed at the idea of that encounter, there is a relevant question to be asked: How much can a citizen believe in those ideas which represent the heart and soul of an American tradition if he or she does not even dare to see those values stand the test of conflict from outside?

It is probably true that there can never be a totally free and open contest of ideas. It is quite possible, nonetheless—with a good, exciting mix of teachers from one level to the next—for an imaginative school to come extremely close. Most public schools do not even try to offer the free and open contest I propose. It is in the power of our teachers, nonetheless, not just to build that cross fire in the classroom, but to defend it on entirely reasonable grounds.

Those who treasure blind obedience, in their nation, in their children or in their own immediate subordinates in life, will doubtless continue to wonder whether an open competition of this kind will tend to undermine the selfish interests of the U.S. corporations or the U.S. government itself during the years to come. It seems to me these people ought to think a little more about the ways in which a nation does, or does not, win allegiance in the world beyond its own frontiers. There has been much talk in the United States of wishing to win the hearts and minds of people in the Third World. It ought to be apparent by this time that we will never win the hearts and minds of people who are victims of our corporate predation with bigger bombs and more expensive gifts of automatic rifles and jet planes. There is, however, at least an outside chance that we may win some badly needed friends if we can educate a generation of young people with an ethical sensitivity to the needs and aspirations of all human beings, whether they live in Boston, San Francisco or Bombay.

The breadth of compassion that can be implanted in our students during the early years of school ought to be valued for its own sake. But the same quality, the same compassion and the same capacity to open our minds to viewpoints, ideologies and longings that are different from our own, may also be viewed as the highest form of intelligent self-interest. The starving masses of the earth, who still must struggle daily for the bare necessities of life—for food, clean water, health care, housing, labor, literacy and the like—will choose their political allies and potential friends, at least in part, on the basis of the active ethics which those friends and allies seem to represent. Military strength and the calculating use of our capacity for economic benefaction seem to be losing value in the geopolitical world that is developing today. Small-minded citizens who cannot see beyond the dollar margin in our international relations or cannot conceive of foreign trade agreements other than those that bring us immediate military opportunities or possible inroads into profitable markets are no longer working in the long-term interests of our country as a whole.

If certain groups, leaders and entire populations in the Third World speak at times with admiration for the people and the symbolism of this nation, it is because of the spoken words, the writings and traditions represented by our poets and our prophets—not our dollars, not our color TV consoles, not our jet planes and our guns. This, then, is a selfish argument for the education of unselfish people. It is the best way we can arm ourselves for a world in which war will, before long, have been outdated by the longing for survival and efficacious human love.

American foreign policy, for several generations, has been solidly resting on a narrow definition of our military, economic and political self-interest. One of the direct results of this behavior is our willingness to export military weapons, or to grant funds for military aid, to nations which, by all humanitarian standards, have no claim upon our friendship or allegiance. We deal with these nations solely on a basis of cold-blooded, short-term and immediate self-interest.

The most conspicuous example of short-term interest is our sale of weapons to South Africa. In this situation, we have not only sold weapons to one of the outstanding racist governments on earth but have done so in the face of worldwide protest.

On August 7, 1963, then later the same year (December 4), the United Nations issued a request, known as a "solemn call," asking member nations not to sell more weapons to South Africa. The American government, however, did not choose to alienate a useful ally. Nor did we intend to let our corporations lose a favored trading partner. It was our decision, therefore, to defy the plea of the U.N. From 1962 to 1968, according to the Department of Defense, U.S. companies sold military goods worth twenty-five million dollars to South Africa. In 1969, according to the Pentagon, South Africa was the second largest customer for U.S. weapons on the continent of Africa. One of the attractions was the fact that South Africa could pay us for our guns in gold. Another was this: Sixteen percent of all uranium, at that time, came from South Africa.[25]

The U.S. government defended its sale of weapons to South Africa on the grounds that the U.N. did not forbid the sale of weapons. It issued only a solemn plea. Today our government would probably maintain that we no longer sell our military hardware to South Africa. Whether or not this is the case we have no way to know, since the C.I.A. has asserted in public its continued intention to do whatever it must in service of our national self-interest. Even if the present prohibition should be absolute, however, it is too late to make up for the damage we have done. Unlike the unsafe automobiles which seem to have become one of our major items of domestic sale, attack planes, automatic rifles and rocket launchers cannot be "recalled."

The weapons we sold to South Africa throughout the period of a decade past are used today as instruments of repression in the struggle of white rulers to contain insurgent blacks. Teachers might find it of interest to read to their pupils certain of the news-dispatches on this subject from various papers such as *The New York Times*. How can a school board fire a teacher for reading an article from a paper like *The Times*?

Those same weapons were also used in 1978 when the South African government chose to invade the newly independent nation of Angola. It was South Africa's heavily armed invasion of Angola which offered the Cuban government either a moral or, in any event, politically convincing pretext to send in tens of thousands of troops to help to defend Angola against a well-armed, white and racist government.

At a point in time when American policy toward African liberation had begun to undergo some modest reconsiderations, we found ourselves—whether we liked it or not—the objects of considerable contempt among the leaders of black Africa. Their enemy, after all, was armed with weapons manufactured in Ohio, Oregon, Texas and Connecticut—"made in the U.S.A." We found ourselves aligned in the eyes of the Third World with one of the two or three most hated governments in recent history. The Cubans today are demonized in the U.S. press, while the U.S. government is demonized throughout black Africa. Who can have gained from these series of transactions—except for the owners of certain U.S. corporations and the brutal and white-dominated government of South Africa?

Postscript

Many Americans, and too many of our students, have not yet had an opportunity to stop and understand how fast the world is changing. Sooner or later, teachers themselves have got to make up for the time lag represented by the textbooks and TV.

American citizens can afford no longer to place their conscience second and a patriotic banner first. Teachers cannot afford to yield to pressure from the school boards or the P.T.A. to place the lives of U.S. citizens above the lives of at least four billion other human beings. It is, in any case, a meaningless division. In the present age, national flags and patriotic slogans will not offer anyone protection from the nightmare of a nuclear war. Super-American patriots with blinders—and billions of men and women in all nations with their eyes wide open and uplifted to the sun—will die together in the holocaust of nuclear disaster.

The Pledge of Allegiance becomes a recitation of psychosis, the "Star Spangled Banner" becomes an anthem for the mad, in the wake of Hiroshima and the evolution of the hydrogen and neutron bombs. We were not hired to train our pupils for insanity.

This, then, is one additional reason for the argument I make within this chapter. There is the argument for honest and responsible patriots. There is the argument against the danger of false patriots who fall apart at their first glimpse of the real world. There is the argument for winning some small bits of loyalty or friendship on this earth, not because we can afford to *buy* it but because our national character might *deserve* it. With all of the rest, there is the question of survival. Surely there is ample ammunition here for any teachers who should speak out of their hearts and then discover that they must be ready to defend themselves, in face of community critics or their academic peers.

It is one of those ultimate issues about which a conscientious teacher simply has no choice.

A Time When Certain Things Are Not Allowed

There is a dangerous fashion gathering followers in the United States today. It began six or seven years ago, but it is only coming into its maturity today. It goes somewhat like this.

Social protest and active struggle against the kinds of societal injustice which are described throughout this book are permissible only under certain conditions, at certain stated periods of time and, above all, only in the decade (era, period) specifically assigned to social activism by the press and by TV.

The 1960s represented one of those periods in which protest and visible action on the various aspects of our protest were okay. They were okay because there were certain prominent black leaders at the helm. They were okay because the manifestations of struggle provided a fascinating light show for TV and an ongoing narrative for newspapers and magazines. They were okay especially (and this is the most insidious of all) because "people did such things at that time"—*at that time, in those years, in that decade, but not now.*

Sometimes, when I write or speak on a subject that troubles me and for which I am hoping to suggest a possible solution, somebody will observe in a critical review or essay: "It is amazing. He really sounds as if he thinks that he is living still in 1965."

I do not think that we are still living in 1965.

I think that we are living in the 1980s.

I refuse to accept the myth that somebody in a skyscraper penthouse in New York City, or in a newspaper office anywhere else in the United States, can abrogate the power to designate appropriate hours or decades for the moral or amoral purposes which *they* believe to be acceptable.

We write about social change—or, in this instance, about a plan to gather our forces to transform the public schools—not by asking permission from those people who presently live well (or perhaps not even well at all) in the wire mesh of economic avarice and despair which they have decreed to be the only proper moral texture for the 1980s.

We write, protest, struggle and make changes whenever we are moved, compelled or feel the personal energy to do so. Many teachers feel as I do on this subject and they do not intend to allow their actions to be orchestrated by those people who sell tennis gear, nostalgic movies, jogging shoes—or justice.

Editors will, I suppose, go right on attempting to control and manipulate each decade. If they must, they will also continue, in their innocence or cruelty, to assign each year to its appropriate activities: lethargy to one year, justice to the next year, roller-skating (greed or narcissism) to the next.

We have never consented to protest on assignment. We will speak of these matters—of each struggle, of each mandate, of each passion—when we must.

PART II

Grass Roots
Organizing Parents
and Teachers
for Collective Strength

Building a Base of Trust
and Friendship with the Parents

Nothing is possible unless we organize.

Teachers need to organize not just among themselves, but also with the parents of their students—and, in all possible cases, with the students too. This is the case, at least, if they have any hope to win the loyalty of friends for times of confrontation that will frequently result from almost any acts of conscience they may choose to undertake in order to transform the public schools.

The organizing sequence I am going to describe begins with parents, proceeds to fellow teachers and ends up in consideration of the ways that we can build a sense of mutual protection with the students in our schools.

In seeking support among the parents of the neighborhood and school, a teacher's initial actions ought to be informal and relaxed. The first goal is not to build a political structure, but rather to establish a sense of private loyalty and personal affection with even a limited number of parents and community leaders in the neighborhood nearby.

One of the most natural ways to go about this is to establish a regular habit of late-afternoon or early-evening visits to a student's home, ideally under circumstances which will not be sterilized and frozen by that atmosphere of falsified friendliness that undermines so may parent-teacher consultations. This is not, at first sight, either a radical or original prescription—nor does it appear particularly subversive. The truth, however, is that visits and informal relationships like these are seldom possible if we observe the orders of our principals or the dictates of our teacher education.

Teachers have been taught for generations to avoid such vulnerable liaisons with the parents of the children whom they teach. As a result, most of us have forever been restricted to the classic situation of the parent-teacher conference in the corner of our room at 2:15, after the class has been dismissed and nervous parents timidly appear. Neither the parents nor the teachers seem to like these meetings very much. The same is true of those mechanical home visits that some of the more progressive principals will now and then allow. The purpose and the situation are both awkward and unreal.

Few teachers feel at ease in making these professional visits: antiseptic sessions set up in advance in order to discuss the student's academic progress, peer relationships or learning difficulties. Most effective teachers who have built up good relations with the parents of their class tell me that they try to make a point to visit parents only under sociable conditions which can overcome these needless inhibitions.

The purposes of the type of visit I propose are totally different from those that lie behind conventional home visits. The goal, indeed, is not professional at all. Instead it is to begin to know our students and their folks not as our "clients," but as our allies and our friends. The best way that I know to bring about this goal is to time our visits to a student's home in such a way as to accord with certain normal social rituals—like dinner. Mothers and fathers seem to find it natural to chat, to offer us a beer or a glass of wine, and now and then will ask: "Have you had supper?"

If we have not, very few parents that I know will let us leave until we do.

If I had not spoken with so many teachers in the past few years, I would not feel so free to generalize from my own rewarding memory of many evenings of this kind. Other teachers speak to me repeatedly, however, of the same response. It is not long before the parents and the teachers begin to feel a sense of common cause.

This is, by intention, a modest way to start. It is only naive organizers, in my point of view, who think that they can jump right into massive organizing schemes, rally the neighborhood and pack the hall, without a long internship (as I think it properly might be called) in building up of natural loyalties, warm feelings of affection each for each, between at least some of the parents and at least some portion of the teachers in the school.

Parents who might deeply disagree with some of our professional or political ideals often find themselves our friends and allies long before they have a chance to think about our ideologies or pedagogic views. By this stage, they are likely to support us, if support is needed, on the grounds of plain affection and fair play. One week in the last part of September, we are having supper and discussing the World Series. Six months later, friendships made across that dinner table have been turned into a political allegiance in the sort of confrontation that explodes, at times we least expect, into the public eye.

I know a small number of principals who actually encourage their teachers to build up these easy and informal friendships; but these men and women are unusual. Most principals do not approve of social get-togethers of this kind. As a young teacher, I was seriously reprimanded by my principal for stopping in each morning before class to buy myself a little cream-filled cupcake, called a "Twinkie," at the corner grocery. She told me that informal access on the part of neighborhood people would diminish my position as a "school professional."

The reasons for administrative opposition to these natural forms of parent-teacher contact are diverse. Sometimes they are innocent and well intended. The principal wants to protect us from imagined dangers. More often, the reasons are devious and self-serving. Many principals seem to live in constant terror that the direct friendships which evolve from normal behavior of this kind will undermine their power over parents (a power that depends upon the parents' lack of detailed information in regard to the real status of their kids) and over the teachers (power which is based on an implanted fear of an unknown community). As a result, a principal will often take considerable pains to frighten teachers with the dangers of informal social contacts: "Don't go out of your way to visit with the parents. Let the parents come to *you*. If you are obliged to visit for some reason, then at least be certain that you don't lose sight of your professional behavior."

The term *professional,* by this rigid definition, comes very close to meaning a false smile and a frozen jaw: a kind of Maginot Line of artifice and ice. The same principal who warned me of the dangers of a visit to the corner store carried her warnings even to the point of detailed dinner-table admonitions: "If you are asked if you would like a drink, try to say no. If there isn't any way to turn it down without offense, then at least be sure to limit it to one—and drink it very, very slowly."

Talk of this nature strikes some people as amusing. It is tragic, however, that attitudes like these are so familiar and pervasive. The principal's concern, as stated, is for the loss of our "professional" protection in the face of an imagined danger—and, in part, of course, this may well be the truth. The deeper motive is, too frequently, the principal's alarm concerning the extent of his or her unquestioned power to give orders, to manipulate and to control.

If certain principals could have it as they like, parents would never have a chance to meet the teacher other than by mediation of the school administration in itself. In such a way, administrators constantly restabilize their power. Once the parents get to know the teacher on their own, there is no longer any way for school officials to restrict parental access to unseemly data on the reading levels, cumulative records and the other inner workings of a public school. Nor is there any means by which to limit teacher access to the loyalty of parents in the case of later difficulties with the school system itself.

All the worst fears of the school administration prove time and again to be quite justified. Parents do begin to trust those teachers who join them, first for social reasons only, later to divulge some of those areas of previously forbidden data which would otherwise remain beyond their reach. Teachers, on the other hand, begin to understand that in the case of a real showdown later on they will have a lot of good friends right in the neighborhood to stand up at their side.

The sense of intimacy increases even more once teachers start to join in far more carefully organized meetings with the parents of their pupils in a local church or other meeting place. The stakes are raised again, and friendships with the parents grow more natural and deep, once teachers start to join in neighborhood projects—a weekend's renovation of an empty lot, for instance, technical aid in setting up a tenant's union or—if the need should lend itself to such behavior—in the presentation of a set of neighborhood demands to members of the city council or the mayor.

Teachers who are working in suburban schools sometimes observe that there are very few clear-cut opportunities to demonstrate a personal loyalty of this kind: not, at least, in a manner so explicit as would be the case within an urban ghetto or a rural slum. The issues that concern suburban neighborhoods tend to be less urgent and overt.

In every neighborhood, nonetheless, teachers discover, sooner or later, certain issues of immediate importance to the parents of their pupils. Most of these issues have to do with problems in the schools themselves. Here, too, teachers frequently observe that it inevitably helps to reinforce their own position if they are prepared to do some work to help to advance those issues that are most important to the people in the neighborhood.

In such a way, the teacher has a chance to be an equal and active member of the school community. In ceasing to be a professional artifact, the teacher does not become a condescending moralist nor an intrusive agitator, but simply an ally, a co-worker and a friend.

Beyond Friendship:
Teaching Basic Skills

The previous chapter speaks of winning friendship. This one speaks of ways to win respect.

No matter how much we may speak of larger issues; no matter how much we may wish to speak of racist patterns, policies, curricula, in talking to the parents in an inner-city school, parents need, above all else, to ascertain that we will listen carefully to *their* concerns—concerns which often have to do with nothing more elaborate or more lofty, at the start, than issues of the basic mental health of their own children, or the sane, sequential and effective teaching of essential skills. All the rent strikes, neighborhood meetings, nights of fun and friendship and the rest count for nothing if the parents live with an unspoken anguish about reading, writing, math and other bread-and-butter matters of this kind.

Teachers, however, who intend to offer reassurances to parents have got to be prepared to come across with the real goods. The "real goods"—reading, writing, math—are not so easy for all teachers to deliver. Many young teachers, indeed, are not at all convinced that matters so tedious and ordinary as "the basic skills" are nearly so important as the parents of their children ardently believe.

It is hard to say this and not seem to turn against some of my former friends. Nonetheless, I think that teachers who intend to win the loyalty of students, yet wish to do so at the least expenditure of their own energy and time, often make the serious mistake of thinking that a minimum of hard work and a maximum of whimsical diversion will prove the perfect formula for student adulation.

The quickest way to forfeit parent backing, even if it wins some short-term ego satisfaction in the friendliness of pupils, is to sail off on a Summerhillian journey of ecstatic and spontaneous adventures, at cost of all substantial day-to-day hard labor in the areas of basic skills.

It has become a commonplace, among too many idealistic converts to the cause of school reform, to speak of themselves as if they were not teachers any longer, but some sort of "incidental person" who just happens to be present among children in the school. Apart from the fact that sensible parents will react with great uneasiness in the face of meandering resource persons with this aimless point of view, there is also the fact that educational abdication of this kind rapidly drives the class into exhaustion—and the nation as a whole into a state of mind which now begins to rally under the banner: "BACK TO BASICS."

This kind of behavior, on the teacher's part, bores the pupils, denies the teacher's genuine superiority of accumulated knowledge and ruins any chance of realistic solidarity between a conscientious teacher, sensible students and responsible parents. In place of innovation, we end up with collective tedium, communal apathy, an innovative void.

In the course of a recent visit to an English class in "Modern Fiction" at a relatively innovative and expensive prep school in New England, I asked the students a casual question about the work that was in process that semester: "What novels have you read?"

There was a pause before one student told me that they hadn't yet "got into books" because they hadn't yet made up their minds on how they ought to settle on the prior issue of "which books to read" and "who should make the choice." If this process had consumed only two weeks, perhaps the student's voice would not have carried quite so much despair. Two months had passed, however, and they still were locked up in that hopeless trap of trying to decide how to proceed and by what rules they and their teacher ought to "settle" on which books they ought to read—and in what order!

One student, a bright and articulate young man, spoke up at last: "You know what I wish? I wish that on the first day of the term our teacher had come in, slammed down a book by William Faulkner on the table, told us that he thought it was a good book and asked us to take it home and read it in a week. If we didn't like it, then we could have come back in and told him so. Maybe we would have got fed up with Faulkner and gone off instead to find some other American writers—maybe Hemingway or F. Scott Fitzgerald. Or else we might have liked the book a lot and gone right on and read a dozen more by the same man. Either way, there would have been some food out on the table. At least we wouldn't have had to spend two months discussing how we felt about an empty plate."

This incident occurred in a twelfth-grade class. The same issues inevitably prevail for teachers at all levels. Whether within a rich suburban village or in the poorest urban slum, students grow weary, parents grow alarmed, if they begin to feel that we, as teachers, are benign and well intending, but that nothing serious is really going on.

In certain suburban situations, where pupils have already had some good skill training in the first six years of school, teachers of the kind I have described may find that there will be a longer interval of time before the parents start to demonstrate alarm. In a poor neighborhood, by contrast, teachers will be granted very little chance to make their case (or, simply to make friends) if they cannot first manage to put something that resembles "bread and butter"—reading, math and writing—on the tables of those arid and despairing schools.

Some responsibility for these recent inhibitions, on the part of decent but intimidated teachers, has to be placed upon the doorstep of romantic authors who have led such teachers to believe that there is no third option between old-time tyranny and innovative abdication. If this were so, if there were not something very important and very much worthwhile in between, we might as well give up the game right now.

Many beginning teachers who have had an overdose of those euphoric but unrealistic writings of the early 1970s—what has been designated as "the literature of pedagogic laissez faire"—often make a serious mistake in failing to respect the real concern of many parents that their children may no longer have the means to manage and to cope within a technologically complex society. If a teacher can possibly convey to parents from the start that he or she is solid, sober and prepared to live with the realistic incubus of being an adult (hence, knowing more than children about certain things and being prepared to share what we *do* know without infuriating rituals of indirection), from that point on we can begin to win the loyalty of very large numbers of the parents of our pupils—and we can do so in a relatively short time.

Certain teachers will argue and debate forever as to whether or not they ought to bother to teach reading—all of this because they are convinced that any pupil who "really wants to read" will somehow lose himself in *Moby Dick* or *War and Peace* "at the right moment"—and just "read it on his own." Talk of this sort strikes me as a colossal fraud. It happens like that maybe once out of a thousand times. Moreover, it is not difficult to teach a child to read: to do so, furthermore, by any one of the many diverse and nonmanipulative methods, several of which are listed in the last part of this book.

In view of these facts, a teacher who seeks the loyalty and future back-up of a community of parents ought to refuse to let the issue of hard skills grow into a serious divisive force between himself (herself) and those whom he (or she) intends to win as allies for the years ahead. If this recommendation were to mean the sacrifice of every principle and every dream within a teacher's heart and soul—if, in addition, it appeared that teaching kids to read would be a long, unending process that would take up the entire day, entire month, entire year— then there might be reason to debate this matter as a central issue for defiance or capitulation.

It *doesn't* take up the entire day, entire month, entire year, however, and it need not represent capitulation to all other goals and principles a teacher might hold dear. For this reason the easiest thing, it seems to me, is to get into it, get on with it and show some measurable progress in the course of several weeks.

It isn't long before the consequences of a teacher's work in basic skills become quite obvious to those outside the school. Parents start to pick up rapidly on news like this. Many have no idea at all of what the teacher's politics might be. It doesn't seem to matter much to anyone concerned, so long as certain *other* things seem to be right. Then, too, with rare exceptions, the school administration—faced with something which it cannot help but recognize as effective progress—tends to leave the class and teacher relatively alone. All the principal cares, for now, is that the room is quiet, the kids are working, they appear to be learning, and the parents aren't complaining anymore.

There surely are thousands of ways of going about the task of organizing parents. One of the most obvious of all must be apparent to the reader by this time: If the teacher teaches, and if the students learn, and if the parents and the principal begin to sense some genuine peace and continuity within the class from day to day, a plenitude of shocking statements or political provocations on the teacher's part seem to be forgivable or, at worst, beside the point. Getting something done that can be seen, tested or tasted—reading and writing—words and numbers coming to life, like so many jumping beans, within a child's mind—this, for sure, so far as teachers are concerned, is one of the very best starting points for any subsequent organizing goals.

Up to this point I've raised the issue of hard skills solely as a tactic, or a precondition, for the building of alliances with the parents of the pupils in our class. There is at least one other serious reason to argue for effective reading, writing and math skills among those boys and girls who we may hope to grow someday into the ethical rebels of a generation yet to come. This is the simple point of basic power, competence, survival in the student's navigation of a complicated and increasingly perplexing world. If, as teachers, we would like to think that we can take an active role in seeking to render less intense the pain, injustice, disproportion in the world, we cannot sensibly agree to educate our students to be the beautiful, bold, but useless warriors of social change.

The need is for a generation of hard-working, ethically motivated and effective rebels: people who do not choose to leave the skills of numbers and of scientific competence to the engineers of Westinghouse and I.B.M., who do not choose to leave the competence of words and word persuasion to the managers, scriptwriters and producers of the major television networks. If those young men and women who now are students in the public schools intend someday to write a powerful press release in order to argue for a moral cause which they uphold, I see no reason why it should be one bit less effective than those statements which their corporate adversaries will be writing in return.

Why should we leave the skills of basic competition and survival to the people in the banks, the big insurance companies and corporations, or else to those within the Pentagon and C.I.A.? We cannot afford to leave the skills of numbers to the corporations that control us, the skills of reading to the advertising corporations that deceive us, the skills of writing to those governmental agencies that issue orders to young people which they scarcely comprehend but do not dare to disobey.

This is just one of many reasons why responible teachers should no longer feel inhibited, or reluctant, to attempt, with all their energy and imagination, to deliver hard, combative and effective skills to those who may, before long, choose to carry on the struggles we have only managed to begin.

Building Loyalties
Among the Teachers

In the last two chapters I have spoken chiefly about building up liaisons with the parents of the students in our schools. This chapter and the next one will address the various ways of building loyalties among the teachers and the kids.

Any grass-roots organizing process among teachers ought to be distinguished, at the start, from organizing efforts that take place inside one or the other of the major unions. This does not mean that we should turn our backs on powerful and immensely influential organizations of this kind. I think that those who *can* should work, wherever possible, through vehicles like these but not as docile cogs within one or another of two vast and intricate machines. The role appropriate to those of rebel and irreverent disposition—who nonetheless decide to take their stand within the N.E.A. or A.F.T.—ought to be that of intelligent critics, companionable gadflies, a quiet conscience working always from within.

As a classroom teacher, I was a member of the N.E.A. for several years and have attempted to maintain a close liaison with that organization ever since. I have been, on occasion, both uplifted by courageous positions taken on particular issues by the N.E.A. and relatively disheartened by the lack of any stand at all on certain of the other burning issues of our times.

Like many other powerful lobby, a teacher's organization

can be an immensely valuable force for ethical and social change. The direction of the organization depends entirely upon the courage of its members. Rather than leaving the organization work to others, whom many of us then comfortably condemn, it seems to me it is our obligation to do our best to *shape* the tone and values of an organization that both protects and oftentimes befriends us.

It is not in the nature of a large, well-financed and politically established organization to set out to subvert or even to excoriate that larger social system of which it has come to be an instrumental and important part. Individual members of the unions, on the other hand, need not be restricted by these familiar institutional restraints. Free-thinking teachers, rank and file members of the N.E.A. and A.F.T., constantly rebel, stand up for moral and political issues and address such matters of conscience as the cumulative record, I.Q. testing, historical distortions and evasions, with all possible courage and integrity. It is precisely these free thinkers and iconoclastic souls (those who annoy and frequently infuriate their colleagues and administrators most) who will redeem the teacher unions in the eye of history.

There *is* a role for independent teachers in both of the teacher unions, but it is not the habitual function of the building representative or collector of the dues. Their role is one of counterfoil and voice of protest in the heart of the machine (at least where there is any chance at all to win the members over to a strong position on a matter of fair play) and, overall, the task of toiling always from within, not so much in order to win power or position, but rather in order to be able to exert some leverage on the ones who *do*.

In certain cities, states and national regions, the union leadership itself has been effectively and democratically won over by a number of strong and enterprising teachers of the kind who, in most other communities, are forever in the caucus that protests the policies and actions that the leadership supports. The situation often seems more fluid in the N.E.A., but this is not the same in every state and, on this score, my own view certainly is not impartial. Both groups now are changing far too fast to be able to predict two years ahead.

There is a different road, however, that many teachers have begun to take in recent years: one which relegates the large-scale national battles of the major unions to a second or third place. Thousands of embattled and impatient classroom teachers are beginning, more and more, to invest their energies at the local level—and to do so through the vehicle of entirely new varieties of organizing instruments. I have in mind the interesting phenomenon of "teacher centers" which have begun to spring up with extraordinary speed during the period from 1975 to 1980.[26]

I have visited approximately fifteen of these centers—in New Haven, New York City, Milwaukee, Minneapolis, Chicago, San Francisco, Portland and Seattle. Each center I have seen is slightly different from the next. Some place major emphasis on teachers helping teachers in the areas of specific classroom skills. Others place greater emphasis on politics and mutual support for teachers who are in embattled situations. Some of the centers are operated as commercial ventures, although on a very modest scale. Many have union backing. A few have government funds. Whatever their origin or sponsorship, almost all of the teacher centers I have seen are nourished, above all, by a political commitment that is neither bureaucratic nor commercial.

Everyone who works within a typical teacher center does not have the same objectives. Nonetheless, in almost every center, there is an undertone of ethical/political conviction which appears to have been able to survive even the most reactionary moments of the mid-1970s, using the cover of curriculum development and teacher training for what, in effect, were predominantly political, partisan and grass-roots struggles. Although I've seen less than two dozen of these centers, I believe that there must be at least two hundred teacher centers now in operation coast to coast.

How do these centers start? Some, as we have seen, are begun with government or union funds or else by charitable private groups. More frequently, a group of teachers on their own will find a storefront in a low-rent neighborhood, stock it with a coffee maker, telephone, ditto machine—then churn out leaflets to distribute at a union meeting or in front of local schools. Before long, thirty or forty teachers start to drop in after school, mainly to relax, sip coffee and exchange ideas. Sometimes teachers will put in an old refrigerator and fill it with a case of beer.

Teacher centers are often able to raise government or foundation funds by placing emphasis on purely pedagogic matters such as reading workshops. Nonetheless, their real significance, so far as organization is concerned, lies in the power of the group to take away the fear and isolation in which so many teachers are compelled to work and live. A number of those teacher centers which began with only forty-five or fifty teachers from a handful of adjacent schools have rapidly grown to several hundred members when the word began to spread to teachers in surrounding rural and suburban towns.

The centers can offer more than coffee, beer and solidarity to isolated teachers. They can also provide the base for a political defense, a legal battle on behalf of teachers who are threatened with retaliation for the views which they espouse, access to defense attorneys and fund-raising lists, in order to be able to provide (first) quick advice, then serious counsel in the case of a protracted fight.

When wisely planned, these centers reach out also, beyond the teachers, to the sympathetic parents whom some of those teachers have begun to know, then to older students who have also felt a sense of friendliness and trust. Several centers have made strenuous efforts to involve, as well, the school custodians and secretaries. Often ignored by teachers in their organizing efforts, these are people who can wield substantial power in a lot of public schools, especially those in which the principal is absent from the building a great deal—or where the principal is frequently distracted from the daily operations of the school.

In situations of this kind, a friendly secretary often is the sole determinant of whether the books a teacher orders for September are available when class begins—or else do not show up within the classroom until Christmas. School custodians who have made friends with the teachers, and who have been respected as their equal and responsible co-workers, often will come into a class at end of school, notice that we have had to do a painting workshop on makeshift materials since the year's allotment of manila paper has run out, will disappear into a basement closet and return with several reams of crisp but (up to now) well-hidden cardboard.

All of our co-workers, whether they are school custodians or the people who prepare and serve our students' lunch each day, ought to command respect for difficult and tedious work well done. There is also the fact that any teacher who is fighting to transform the schools, and to subvert a number of unfortunate attitudes that most of us have been indoctrinated to respect, will need to find all of the allies we can get. Here, as in all other situations of potential confrontation in the public schools, the goal of reaching out to people whom we frequently ignore, or just pass by, seems to me both ethical and self-protective.

When parents, students, secretaries, school custodians and teachers all begin to stop in at the same church basement on a Friday afternoon, or for a potluck supper Friday night, principals also may begin to feel a little discontent at having been left out. One center that I know begins the year by urging local principals to stop in for a beer. If the invitation has been made in earnest and good feeling, it is frequently accepted.

Neighborhoods differ so much in every city, and in every state, that no one can sensibly predict what kinds of coalitions will be possible in any given case. The organizational process needs to be adapted with intelligence and sophistication to every possibility of conceivable alliance. The purpose at all moments ought to be political. The goal is to win allies for a time of trouble—a time when people will discover the necessity of choosing sides.

If the teacher center limits itself to little more than cardboard carpentry and innovative games upon an innovative floor, then it will not be significant in forging allies for beleaguered teachers. If the center is political right from the start, however, it will almost automatically become the center of the rebel camp. Parents, teachers and other school employees will consider it their own home base.

It would be naive to argue that the teacher center represents an ideal, incorruptible—or even consistently ethical—center for the energies of teachers in rebellion. Ironically, indeed, the more they succeed, in terms of drawing larger and larger numbers, of forming links, liaisons and collaborations and obtaining government grants, the less they are likely to maintain their grass-roots flavor and their independent and indignant tone.

So I do not describe the teacher center here as if it were the sole solution or the best solution or the ultimate solution for those rebel teachers in pursuit of strength in numbers and collective power to uphold their aspirations and defend their dreams. I view these centers, rather, as one type of organization which, if faithful to their members and responsive to their own initial reason for existence, ought to be able to serve a special function at the local level which neither of the larger organizations can so easily uphold.

The teacher's job is dreadfully difficult, unprestigious, ill-rewarded. The lot of the rebel and independent-minded teacher is more difficult still. Perhaps the teacher center is a stage, a tendency, a clue to new directions, rather than a sufficient instrument for teacher action in itself.

Viewed in this spirit, and with these reservations, it is a cheerful and auspicious step on an uncharted road—one which, for thousands of American teachers, has been all too lonely, all too long.

Broadening Our Base: Building Loyalty Between the Teacher and the Class

A final stage in the creation of the coalition I propose is one which draws into its realm the students, along with the parents and the teachers, of the public schools.

In the situation of the parents, as opposed to that of their own children, there is seldom any real alternative to active organizing at a distance from the school itself. This is, in part, because of the limited time that parents have at their disposal, but also because the school mystique seems most impressive and imposing to those people (parents) who have been exposed to it only at erratic intervals—or only years before. The parents, therefore, tend to be least open to the process of demystification of the public school while they are making one of their infrequent visits.

The situation of their children is quite often the reverse. First of all, we do not need to search for them at home since we already find them in the classroom. More to the point, their daily participation in the rituals of public school enables them to scrutinize those rituals more critically than parents who come rarely to the school and, when they do, too often do so in a state of mind that is still clouded by the aura of a sanctified institution.

I do not mean by this that students come to the moment of desanctifying school by their own genius or good luck. With students as with parents, teachers need to take a conscious role in stripping away some of those tapestries of pretense and illusion that hang from the classroom walls.

Apart from the actions that have been described in the first section of this book, other specific actions on the part of teachers that will help to lessen and subvert the mystification of the school include a willingness to undercut the grading system and the tracking system, to confront head-on the multiple modes of sex discrimination in a public school, to join in plans contrived to win our students license to do independent work outside of school and in this way to undercut the school attendance rules. (Many teachers have succeeded in providing cover for well-motivated kids who have already mastered the essential areas of basic skills and obviously can profit from a semi-independent learning situation.)

In certain schools, the issues will be substantially different from the ones I have described: bilingual classes, test scores, improper use of psychiatric testing, child control by use of drugs without parent permission. In a ghetto neighborhood where the schools have often been most blatantly destructive, teachers do not need to struggle long to build a sense of solidarity with students. One teacher, for example, confronted with the common situation of a class of all-black children plagued with substitute teachers and with consequently hopeless reading scores for three years in a row, recounts the following sequence of events:

In one of the first days of her first week in the school, she speaks to the children of the situation in which they find themselves. She tells them, without hesitation, that they are in trouble. "Most students your age are just about three years ahead of you by now. Unless you work seriously and struggle hard to make up for the years that you have lost, you'll soon be pushing brooms—or pushing dope—or scrubbing floors for rich white people like the ones who run or who control these schools."

None of this, she says, has been their fault. They have been cheated by an unjust institution—one, she explains, which is not a mistake ("a slip-up") but which exists in order to create a class of powerless poor people.

She tells the students that they will never have a chance of getting out from under, so long as they wait for someone else to come and set them free. The teacher's objective, in her choice of words, is to begin, right from the first, to build a sense of just denunciation and, more than that, a *lever* of denunciation in each child's mind: something to fight for, a cause they can uphold, a visible enemy, and good reasons to support their teacher in a struggle to transcend enormous odds.

It is the truth that all of these kids have been mistreated by the public schools. They *are* at war. So, too, is every student in this nation, although—in the cosmetic setting of suburban schools—the war remains forever undeclared.

The teacher's primary goal, in this particular case, is to identify some drastic and dramatic means by which to rid the classroom of its deathlike mood. The room is morbid, full of chalk dust and stale air, intermingled with the smell of floor wax, gathered and accreted in the course of ninety years. The windows, for some reason, are nailed shut. She pulls the nails and flings the windows open. A smell of lilac from a nearby garden drifts into the room.

The students, if not universally elated, are all at least attentive to her words. She promises the class that she will soon bring in a lot of paint and posters to cheer up the walls. She promises, too, that she will bring her record player the next day.

It is at this point that she also starts to build the groundwork for her own professional protection. She tells the students of her serious concern regarding the risks and obstacles at stake, not only for them but for herself as well, especially in outside interference from the school administration: "We will be doing certain things that are not really wanted in this school. The reason we will do them is in order to fight back against a system that has been unfair."

Her goal, at this point, is to be certain that the students will play ball and will assist her in a multitude of ways that might be crucial for her own survival. She sets out on a brief discussion with the class, in order to establish some of the most important means by which a class is judged to be "unruly" or else "well-behaved."

The instant consensus of the class is stated in five simple words: *filing quietly in the stairs.*

If some of this appears a little crazy to the reader, especially the reader who is unfamiliar with the daily rituals of public school, few students will find it difficult to understand. There are certain items that are close to sacrosanct within a well-run public school. To file quietly ("just like little soldiers," as the saying goes) is the clearest evidence of a properly soul-broken class.

The day after the teacher speaks of this, her students line up elegantly beside the door, wait for her signal and then file to the stairs—with all the discipline of William Calley's soldiers marching to My Lai. Next day, the second-grade teacher makes a sudden appearance at the classroom door. The children jump to their feet, turn eyes right to the teacher and recite in unison: "Good morning, Miss McCall!"

A smile is fixed and frozen on her jaw: "What well-behaved and cultivated children!" She turns to the teacher to explain why she has come to pay a call. "I want you to know—your children are the talk of the whole school! Everyone is so well impressed. *The way they have been filing in the stairs!*"

The students stare straight at their teacher (the teacher stares right back) as Miss McCall goes out the door. From that day on, for six or seven weeks, there is not one intrusion from outside.

Even at this point, nonetheless, there is a still more challenging issue to confront. The most difficult job is not to win the solidarity of students, but to get across the message to the class that—lilac blossoms and fresh air aside—they soon will be asked to work at an incredibly hard pace.

She tells the pupils that hard work doesn't need to be unpleasant and might even be exciting if they feel the willingness and determination to collaborate with some of her ideas. She also says they will not need to bother with Scott Foresman readers, nor with that invidious orange box from S.R.A. After all of this, she says once more, they have to get themselves prepared to do some tough, consecutive lessons in the weeks ahead. If not, everything else that they have tried to do will probably be lost.

In view of the sense of common cause and of embattled struggle which she has constructed by this time, the students respect her words and do not try to play games with her confidence and trust. They study with devotion (students teaching one another in spare moments) in order to try to make up for so many lost years. The children are excited by the sense of shared conspiracy with one another, and with their teacher too, in order to guarantee their own survival. They work as if they now have joined together in some sort of pedagogic "forced march." There is a goal to reach, an evil system to undo, and any number of dragons to destroy. The sense of struggle and of concrete goals (math, reading and writing, ethics and the power to transform) soon becomes intense and credible. It is upon this recognition of dead-earnest combat that all the rest of what the children and the teacher soon will do is going to depend.

All of the above is based upon a situation of extreme and visible exploitation which the pupils recognize right from the start. Teachers in the suburbs often make the point that very little of the blatant chaos and overt discrimination of a ghetto school is present in a rich, relatively stable and superficially "successful" public school. The overriding function of political indoctrination is, however, virtually unchanged.

If teachers can establish this preliminary point, and if we then can demonstrate the multiple ways in which it takes effect, we are—from that point on—in a position to establish strong alliances with pupils, both in rich suburban neighborhoods and in the poorest rural neighborhoods or ghetto slums. All students in an unjust social order are the victims, though they are not equal victims, of a twelve-year sequence of oppression and deceit. They are all victims of a pedagogic structure built on lies.

Short-Term Goals and Long-Term Victories

The four preceding chapters place almost exclusive emphasis on the ways by which to reach those three essential groups that can create a viable coalition for a teacher's self-defense in time of crisis.

What is a plausible sequence of events that might lead up to a crisis of the kind I have in mind? Imagine a young and highly competent—but temporary—teacher who is offended by the political bias of the texts and other materials in the classrooms of the school. He starts to bring in a number of unauthorized books and other forms of documentation on his own. The principal hears about the teacher's actions, warns the teacher for the sake of his career to work more closely within acceptable bounds, but two months later is obliged by pressure from the school board to issue a more formal admonition. He also forbids the teacher to continue meeting with the people in the nearby neighborhood. The teacher refuses to give in—and is dismissed. The union refuses to intervene because the teacher has not yet become a member.

The teacher turns to the parents for support.

A logical scenario, from this point on, might start with something very simple and routine such as a letter to the principal and school board, signed by parents, a number of pupils, a handful of teachers—and requesting a public hearing in ten days.

If, by the date requested, there has been no answer, subsequent actions might include a sequence of this sort: (1) A modest delegation of parents and students pays a visit to the school board, asking in polite terms for a prompt, responsible hearing. (2) A larger delegation pays a *second* visit, stating in less gentle terms a firm demand for an immediate hearing. (3) If this demand should be ignored, or if the hearing is indefinitely postponed, then it is perhaps the moment for the group to find a lawyer and for the lawyer to proceed to file suit. The lawyer requests a hearing on the part of both of the teacher who has been dismissed and of those parents who, in recognition of the teacher's loyalty and hard work, feel defrauded of their children's rights to decent education. (4) Simultaneous with the filing of legal papers, there might be a formal presentation to the press. (5) At the same moment that the grievance of one teacher is addressed, parents might seize the chance to raise some of those other issues which this situation only symbolizes. (6) Before, during and pursuant to the court case, constant meetings might be held to galvanize and to extend support in order to exploit whatever public controversy is created. (7) Lawyers, in the presentation of this case, ought to be raising certain of the larger issues at every point where legal process or the judge's patience will allow. (8) Prior even to a final outcome in the courts, plans should be in process for the type of public actions which will capitalize, in every way conceivable, upon a legal victory—or else to plan for extralegal tactics in the event the case is lost and an appeal is lost as well.

It goes without saying that it takes a specific crisis of real drama and significance before the total sequence I've described here can begin. If there is no issue both substantial and dramatic in appeal, neither legal action nor attention from the press is of much worth. Many groups are able to *provoke* a crisis if they do not find one handed to them in advance. Most often, however, school boards or school principals, even if they do not dare to do something so extreme as to dismiss a popular teacher, will do at least a few things so irrational and so absurd as to present us with the cause, or causes, that inspire both a protest action and a legal case as well.

The challenge is seldom how to find an issue. It is to know the way to *use* one. This is not possible, to start with, if we cannot find a lawyer who is willing to collaborate with the interests of the coalition. This can often be a controversial point with certain lawyers. Those who feel we live in an essentially just and democratic social system will not wish to use the courtroom to advance a cause; their sole desire is to win the case. This is the kind of lawyer we must carefully avoid.

The lawyer we need is one who tries very hard to win the case on its own merits but also struggles to provide a legal, extra-legal and political education to the public through the process of the trial and through statements in the press.

Lawyers who refuse to do this often speak of the client's interest as their sole concern. Frequently, however, they are thinking mainly of their own, recognizing a potential loss of business or acceptance by their peers if they should manage to offend the court. These are the kinds of lawyers who will often warn a client that he or she is being "used" by agitators for extraneous objectives. ("You're being naive. You're being used by other people.") The goals appear extraneous, of course, only because this type of lawyer feels that saving one man's or one woman's job, as well as helping to advance his own career, is more important than assisting in the build-up of an organization for the long-term transformation of the schools.

Having been through this problem with a number of friends in several situations, I have learned how skillfully a basically conventional attorney can persuade a client to pursue his or her own selfish ends at the expense of those whose efforts won that person legal counsel in the first place.

Even beyond the sticky question of which lawyer to employ,

and once the type of lawyer that we need has been retained, a second challenge is the designation of two separate goals, both of which we must pursue at the same time, but by two parallel roads. One goal is to achieve a victory within the courts. (If we sacrifice this purpose altogether, then those critics who believe that we are only using someone for extraneous goals are possibly correct.) The long-term goal, however, is to build a sense of heightened strength among the parents, teachers, students—sometimes maverick school officials—who provide us with support and who, in turn, are counting on the public interest which this case elicits to broaden their numbers and to reinforce the sense of confidence within their ranks.

Attorneys who will fight a case, not just to win an immediate victory but also to create a forum for discussion of important issues, may very well offend the courtroom protocol of decorous and old-fashioned lawyers—but they are not the ones who are naive. It is the conventional lawyer (the one who turns us down) who proves himself naive. He is naive because he does not know the reason why we worked so hard to bring this case to trial from the start.

In the event that readers are uncertain as to what I have in mind in speaking of "specific" legal cases, I would like to offer four examples. In at least three of these four examples, plaintiffs have at times won landmark victories.

One of them concerns the issue of the flag pledge, mentioned earlier. As we have seen, the Supreme Court has already found the forcible imposition of the pledge to be unconstitutional. Since the pledge is seldom *viewed* as voluntary in the public schools, and almost never treated as a casual matter, it would appear that many principals and school boards have been operating in defiance of the law.

Teachers who intend to fight this issue in a state or federal court are protected by precedent, as well as by their civil rights, against all forms of top-down condemnation or abuse;

yet very few teachers, fewer parents and scarcely any student I have ever met in public school are cognizant of the precedents in question. This, then, is an ideal legal issue to fulfill both short-term purposes and long-term goals.

Another legal struggle—specific in its detail, long term in its results—is one that can be built upon another issue which has been discussed above: the release of test scores, records, teacher comments and psychological exams that fill the cumulative records of the public schools. Here again, although state laws may vary on the details of this point, federal law demands the full divulgence of such records.

In spite of the law, as we have seen, schools tend to employ a number of devices of intimidation to deny the parents full and open access to these records. Teachers who take the action I suggest—of opening such records to the parents and the students of their school—can fight a good strong battle in defense of their behavior if a school board should object.

A third area in which it seems possible, ethical and correct to launch a tough, aggressive public battle is the one, described above, of our approach to history. Any school board dumb enough to try to punish or suppress a teacher for the honest presentation of the views of Helen Keller or Thoreau, will find itself in an extremely weak position in a court of law. Here again, although the legal issue would be worth the courtroom battle in itself, the larger possibilities—in terms of public scrutiny of school-mandated lies—are more important still.

A fourth and final example is one that has already been attempted and, to some degree, proven successful. This is the matter of initiation of individual or class-action suits against school districts, or specific school boards, for consumer fraud. The central issues here are virtually the same as those that would be raised in any other suit based on consumer fraud. Those who fear that they cannot win this type of suit in terms such as those which have been raised in the first section of this book ("ethical deception" on the part of public schools) may use instead an issue which can far more easily be proven in a court of law: the school's default in areas of basic skills.

If less important in political respects than the larger point of school indoctrination, the issue of skills is easier to argue, since the case can be presented in the same terms that the school boards claim to value and respect: tests and test scores, reading skills, math levels and the like. Once the case is in the court and in the public eye, the deeper points about historical distortion and political indoctrination can be brought into the limelight as we like and in the ways we choose.

The issue of "school as a consumer fraud" has already caught the eye of high officials in the nation's capital—and, in particular, of George McGovern. A number of high school graduates, McGovern said in an interesting U.S. Senate speech delivered on September 8, 1978, "refuse to forget what they did not learn in school. Recently a high school student of normal intelligence sued his school in San Francisco for educational malpractice—he had been awarded a diploma even though he could read only at a fifth-grade level." Attorneys for various state Offices of Education, said McGovern, "agree that the number of such suits will increase, and that increasingly they will succeed."[27]

There is one point in all of this that seems sufficiently important to restate one final time: None of these legal battles is significant, in the long run, if we do not hold ourselves in readiness to move beyond the realm of law in the event that legal avenues should fail to work. This is the reason why most groups that are experienced in struggles of this kind do not restrict their efforts to the narrow parameters of legal issues, but work at all times to make preparations for more passionate forms of struggle later on.

These forms of extra-legal struggle, and the ways that we make use of press and public information to advance our cause, are highly controversial even within the ranks of strong, political and unintimidated people. The reason for controversy is the fact that public actions which transcend the limits of the law will often lose us significant portions of our earlier support. There are times, however, when a teacher or a group of parents and teachers have no option but to forfeit a certain portion of their backing in order to invest their faith and energy in an action that affords some chance of victory.

Nothing is won without the risk of payment of a price, even if it is no more than the loss of friendships in pursuit of ethical ideals. Nothing that counts as much as this is ever won for free.

Creating a Crisis—
or Awaiting One

A legal case is a crisis in itself. Often, however, there is no single issue so specific as to justify legal action. In situations like these, many parent-and-teacher groups are likely to sit, complain, and wait for months—or even years—before an incident occurs to constitute a crisis.

People with a just cause, but no concrete and dramatic issue, need not wait forever if they have the willingness to force the issue on their own. It remains, at almost all times, within the power of a group of serious and determined people to provoke a crisis of the kind they need, and at the time they want, so long as they know the issue is for real and so long as the crisis—though "provoked"—is not "contrived."

In one respect, our customary inclination not to force an issue, but to sit and wait for an important issue to occur, is very much in keeping with the passive sense of those who view themselves as objects of historic process, never the progenitors of change. Teachers who grew addicted to the catchcries of the 1960s often speak, in perfect jargon, of "awaiting the correct conditions" or "objective situation" for an action or a protest of whatever kind. If, by this, they mean no more than to make realistic surveys of the power they possess, in proportion to the goals that they pursue, there is no question but that this would be a sane and proper caution.

If, however, as too often is the case, they simply are waiting for the school board or the school administration to provide them with the issues (the "conditions") to inspire an important struggle, then it seems to me that they have abdicated too much power and have permitted those whom they oppose to set the terms, and even choose the time, when they will be allowed to fight.

In many situations in the past few years, parents have known, long in advance, that a dismissal or a non-renewal was quite clearly in the air for one of the outspoken teachers in their school. The school board, as of June, however, had not yet discussed the teacher's case. As a result, no one spoke up in his or her defense. Two months later, in the deep heat of August, a summary dismissal of the teacher went through school committee session in ten minutes on a quiet Tuesday night. Students were gone. The teacher centers had been closed down for vacation. Half of the vocal parents did not even hear of the dismissal until after Labor Day.

The ritual of midsummer non-renewal occurs so frequently nowadays that we should take it as a challenge to ourselves to sniff out serious issues long before the hour is too late and to force these issues at a time when we have power to respond. Those who wait for "the correct conditions" to initiate a just and ethical demand will often wait forever.

If it takes a catalytic action of a certain reasonable kind in order to incite a school board to commit a reckless and precipitous deed, then it seems to me it is for us to choose with care the day we act, how many or how few should be involved, in just which schools, and at what grades or in which neighborhoods.

This is not an invitation to cause needless trouble in a relatively decent school which has the luck to work beneath the supervision of a loyal and protective principal. It is rather common, in the course of struggles that take place in public schools, that people tend to turn the soonest against those school officials who appear most vulnerable and open: vulnerable not because they have been stupidly oppressive, but rather because they have been candid with us and have tried their best to be our friends. (Blacks, in anger, will sometimes strike, in the first burst of fury, at those whites who work in close companionship right at their sides, solely because they are the only representatives of the white race within easy reach.)

Whatever the context, common sense ought to direct us to attempt to spare a sympathetic principal or other school official, especially when we know that almost every educational system in this nation has in its employ so many other individuals who do deserve and oftentimes invite a knock-down struggle. As an overall rule, it seems to me that practical rebels ought to do their best to treat with great respect even half-hearted allies.

One other point might possibly be misconstrued unless I clarify my words a bit. The purpose that I have in mind is not to see if we can cause a fellow teacher, or ourselves, to get thrown out—purely for the sake of offering our friends and allies a dramatic cause. Any behavior of this sort is, at the least, perverse and self-defeating. A decent teacher who survives for fifteen years is fifteen times more useful than a decent but impatient martyr who survives for only one. Our purpose is not to court dismissal but to be sufficiently alert to recognize a moment when dismissal is most likely to occur. If that moment is so timed as to deny us power to defend ourselves, then I believe that teachers are employing excellent sense by making certain that they are the ones to force the school board to take action. If it's certain to happen, and we know it's going to happen, why should we sit and wait when we can be the ones who *make* it happen, and can do so at a time of our own choice, when we are in a good position to fight back?

In the heat of struggle, as we have seen, many people tend to recognize no other goal than a specific victory in the immediate case at hand. Others understand that there are larger purposes as well. All of this brings us back to an idea discussed in the preceding chapter: the tactical distinction between a short-term purpose and a long-term goal.

The short-term goal will be essential to provoke discussion and to gather followers for a particular struggle. The long-term goal is crucial if the struggle is not going to be over once that single issue has been won. A coalition, for example, that intends to fight the issue of renewal of a teacher's contract may, if it likes, speak only of the teacher under fire or it can focus instead on hiring practices as a whole. In the same sense, in a rent strike, organizers can fight hard against the landlord to see immediate needs relieved within one building for one year; but if they do not emphasize as well, and finally demand, a written promise of a set of concrete follow-ups for all the buildings owned by this one landlord, and with guarantees for several years to come, they will be forced to undergo the same ordeal one winter later.

In all of these cases, the battle can be fought on the short-term issue only. A clear reiteration of the larger problem guarantees instead that no one will be silenced by a single court decision or a single calculated instance of capitulation from the school administration. The moment of victory, in situations which are carefully prepared, leads us instantly to resurrect the larger point which this one situation only symbolizes. Instead of ending an important effort, it helps to lay the groundwork for the next one.

If we do not keep in mind considerations of this kind, then it remains, for those who like, to let us think that we have won a victory when they know well that they will win the war. The point is that, without extravagant rhetoric but with some definite connections being drawn between immediate issues and large over-arching goals, we can both win the victory *and* launch the war.

It is hard enough to organize and to construct a coalition. It is harder still to reconstruct one from the ground up. It is not so hard to keep a cause in motion, once it has begun. The strategy of the school board is most frequently to give us enough, in one particular case, to send us home with the idea that we have won all that we hoped for. If we are wise, we will not let our adversaries send us home to bed "right after supper." Instead, we will be putting our heads together to anticipate the next ten battles that will lead not just to our own personal vindication but to a victory for every child and for every teacher in the system.

Confronting the Press and TV: Dissemination of the Facts

Nothing we do will have much impact on the consciousness of other people if we do not work out certain methods of dissemination of the facts themselves. This process runs the full range of promotion and publicity, from production and distribution of a neighborhood newsletter to the composition of a press release.

For many people, the following information may appear self-evident. For those who have never had any dealings with the press, some of this may prove to be of help. An initial consideration, in most cases, is to attempt to isolate a single journalist whom we believe to be open, or most likely to be open, to the cause that we uphold. Even in states or cities where the press appears to be alarmingly conservative, teachers are often able to pin down a handful of reporters who are sympathetic to their goals.

The best example is one that I recall from the Southwest. Here, a city editor and good reporter have been able to turn out and get into print so much first-rate material which, apart from all else, is well-written copy as to place the owners of the paper in a difficult position. It would hurt the circulation of the paper to dismiss them. Political organizers, liberal readers, poor folks in the Spanish-speaking and Mestizo barrios, learn to be quite certain to give all releases, stories and exclusives only to this writer. She, in turn, is careful to submit her story only on the nights when her co-worker is on duty.

This is, however, an exceptional situation. The usual method of dissemination of a story is through the preparation of a press release. One familiar format for a press release starts out with a short phrase which describes the content, then is followed by a date, identification of those who have released the story, and "phone for further contact." The statement itself, which might not get a great deal of attention if it's longer than two pages, should (like the headline) represent an effort on our part to write the story for the journalist or for the editor. If it's done well, even a very good reporter sometimes does no more than to revise its sequence, cut it to size, insert some extra data (comments from the opposition, for example) and then send it to the press.

No news release, no matter how well written, is likely to make it into print if it is not real news. No item is news if it does not have time value of some sort. A general story of the poor conditions in an urban public school is not considered news—except perhaps for an essay in a Sunday magazine or in a weekly feature section. If, however, the abysmal situation of one public school can be described, in vivid terms, as part and parcel of a genuine news story ("Students Close Down High School Cafeteria: Protest Unsanitary Preparation"), then it is possible to offer to reporters an ideal package of real news and of important background at the same time.

Even the most responsive journalists are likely to lose interest right away if what they see appears to them as "just the same old story" about ineffective public schools. If they can write instead that a group of fifty high school students, joined by kitchen volunteers, five teachers and two dozen parents, have forced the school board to agree to schedule hearings on health dangers in the school, then the details cease to be mere repetition but an item of good reading—what some editors, however hostile, may identify as a story that belongs on the front page.

Just as important as the production of a press release is its effective distribution. First we must find a handful of reliable co-workers who will keep their automobiles available, especially when the group is working frantically against the clock, ready to deliver the release to each newspaper and to every radio and TV station. (The delivery ought to be in early evening if we hope to make the morning papers, 11 A.M. or thereabouts to make the evening paper and the TV news.)

Assuming that there are no particular writers whom we know and trust, the best alternative is to get hold of the names of certain liberal or open-minded contact people at each TV station or newspaper. The least effective method is simply to leave a press release to sit and gather cobwebs in a crowded press-room, in a shallow metal basket on a messy desk, a few feet from the editor's left elbow. It is likely to remain there all night long.

Of all conventional methods to get out the news, a press conference is certainly the most dramatic. In this situation, an effort first is made to hook reporters on the story, whether by phone or by a "tentative release," thereby to get them all together in a single room and, at a single moment, to give out the details of the story to everyone at once.

Two documents are needed in advance of a press conference. One is a brief, intriguing statement that provides no details other than the place, the time and possibly one or two important high-points of the story. (To deliver the statement with all possible details spelled out in advance is to be reasonably certain that there will be no one present at the conference.) The second necessary document is, of course, the press release itself, which is to be read at the press conference.

Another detail, often helpful in creating a good press conference, is to settle on two or three people to present the case for the entire group. This way, journalists cannot resort to a device they otherwise may use to great effect: namely, to ask a lot of members of our group a similar question and then to make a major point out of the slight divergences between our answers.

Once a press release is read, and once the basic point has been presented clearly for the TV cameras, many people emphasize that we should take care not to let reporters lead us off in ten or twenty new directions of their own. Those who do this can quote exclusively the answers to their questions—and ignore all that we had hoped to say. The strategy, on our side, is to answer an irrelevant question with a statement that, in fact, does little more than to repeat the gist of what we said before.

A final approach, used frequently by politicians at all levels, is to give a "leak"—or an "exclusive"—just before a major paper goes to press, soon enough so they can get it into print, late enough so that other reporters still will feel impelled to come to the press conference and not regard the story as outdated matter. The sole reason to do this is, of course, to get a special favor in return—the likelihood of sympathetic treatment, for example, or a promise of conspicuous attention.

A last-minute conversation with one major paper in my city, five years back, was instrumental in achieving an effective front-page story, yet its release was so close to the time of the press conference that this did not keep the other media representatives away. Often, moreover, a conspicuous story in the written press provides the bait for better attention in the TV news. News, in this respect, repeatedly "creates news."

So much of this chapter deals with the large picture—press relations and TV—that I would like to conclude by coming back to the grass roots. In the long run, all the press, TV and radio attention in the city, state or nation will prove to be useless if we do not build a strong and loyal core of parents, kids and teachers at the start. There is no substitute for hard, exhausting organization of this kind.

The use of door-to-door approaches to entire strangers by a paired team (parent and teacher, if possible), accumulation and continual updating of a set of contact cards with numbers and addresses for both work and home, the use of fliers and newsletters mailed to parents or just handed out to kids (not by a teacher) at the end of school, the endless use of phone calls for last-minute checks so people won't forget a crucial meeting they have planned and promised to attend, the evolution of an instant "telephone tree" by which one person calls three others, and those others each call three—all of these efforts constitute the only possible basis for the long-term loyalty and mutual confidence that can endure beyond a single week, or month, or year.

None of this, I'm sure, will lead us to a pedagogic revolution. Nor, to use a term that I first used in chapter one, will it turn the system upside down or inside out. What it will do, however, is to give us the first taste of battle and the confidence that, in the last event, determined people, working together, can do more than merely to join their hands in struggle, but can labor long with tact and skill, and persevere in face of problems of all kinds, and now and then can even overcome these obstacles and struggle on a little more—and ultimately know the taste of vctory.

8

Fear of Victory:
Dangers of the Numbers Game

Various obstacles to any real success in organizing appear so vivid and so obvious as to constitute almost a set of incantations, neon lights and admonitions to remind us of the pitfalls in our way.

Most obvious is the inclination of many energetic organizers to exhaust themselves through internecine quarrels long before we ever come to grips with our real opposition. Often it seems that we forget the very name and nature of the unjust apparatus that we labor to transform, long hours before we ever get to anything like head-on confrontation—because we have expended so much of our energy in combat with each other.

Another inheritance from many misguided struggles of the past is an inclination to distrust our leaders, and to do our best (when we do make the tentative choice to trust some leaders for a time) to do what it takes to break them down as fast as possible—and then to drive them out. This is the case today in many parent-teacher coalitions. Natural leaders, as they gradually emerge, have been compelled to undergo intense harassment, seldom for their failures but more often for their most effective actions and their most audacious dreams. The label "ego trip" appears repeatedly within those fearful sessions of recrimination that so often represent the final chapter in the story of a once-vital coalition.

Teachers and parents—all of us, I think—have got to learn to separate the fear of domination from the fear of excellence. If any group I know, or one with which I work, is able to discover or to move up through its ranks a leader with the power, first to stand, and then to speak in the first person present, unafraid, both to denounce that system of deception and injustice which a public school now represents, then to announce a dream of justice he or she has both the will and the determination to make real, I hope we will have brains enough not to attempt to undercut the passion and the strength that person offers us.

All of the above seem to be symptoms of a single problem which is far too common in the effort to create long-lasting coalitions. I am thinking of an attitude—a mood—which I have heard described by one of my old friends as "a radical inclination toward the insufficient."

I think of it sometimes as the "Cult of Incompletion." It is that sort of laid-back state of mind that looks with scorn upon the need for strong, consistent and uninterrupted processes of work and aspiration, but makes a virtue rather of the interrupted venture, of the unsuccessful fight.

It is time for us to face this problem of our own inherent fear of strength head-on. I think that we should be prepared to strive with all our hearts to be strong teachers, efficacious adults, unintimidated leaders and strong-minded provocations in the consciousness of parents and within the lives of children too.

There are some authors who, for several years, have sought to make a virtue of the capability to start and stop things in response to sudden impulse. There is, with this, the strange phenomenon of those who undergo a kind of anguish at the likelihood of real success—as if effectiveness itself must henceforth (by association with the Pentagon or I.B.M.) carry the copyright of evil men. I see no reason why we need to choose between a contaminated sense of competence on the one hand and a benign sense of ineptitude on the other. Those who struggle to transform the public schools cannot afford the presence in their midst of people who choose to tamper with the lives of children, not for the sake of the children or the teachers, but rather to satisfy their own unconscious need for self-defeat.

A final point may be of use in organizing teachers, students, parents—or all three.

Imagine the situation of the teacher who has worked for weeks to get to know the parents in the neighborhood around the school, has worked hard with pupils in the class, and has made a number of efforts to build up a sense of solidarity with teachers—then finds, when an initial meeting has been called within the basement of a local church, that seven people finally appear. Teachers often tell me stories of this nature and, of course, they speak of their enormous disappointment every time.

Whenever groups of parents and teachers grow depressed at situations of this kind, it might be of use to give each other brief and optimistic history reminders. In 1955, Martin Luther King and Rosa Parks began the struggle for desegregation of an urban transportation system with no more than a few hundred trusted friends and organizers. Within five years, they had created a dynamic and effective movement that involved at least five hundred thousand people.

Another point, in reference to the anguish at low numbers which so many people feel, is that it simply doesn't take one hundred or two hundred people to prepare the groundwork for a grass-roots coalition. Often all it requires is a close and loyal few to build a core of people that is capable, when need demands, of reaching out to hundreds more. If a teacher with a grade-school class of twenty-eight or thirty-two is able to win the strong allegiance of no more than seven parents, and perhaps of no more than three teachers in a faculty of twenty-five, those numbers offer all it takes to galvanize another twenty teachers and two hundred parents more in serious struggle on behalf of any worthwhile and dramatic cause.

It is easy to forget, when counting heads, that a very small number of the parents in a neighborhood will ever have time to take a burning interest in on-going matters of this kind. If, then, in our number panic, we can quietly subtract ten or more who will not really care (or, more precisely, don't have time to care), then we can see that a substantial core of seven allies already starts to constitute almost one half of the committed parents in the class.

If, in addition to these, a teacher should also receive the backing of a larger organization like the chain of teacher centers I've described, and if (at least within the high schools) we can manage to build up some active and responsible support from even half-a-dozen students in the class, then right away that early core of only six or eight begins to represent the dedicated center of much larger numbers of committed people who already know each other from a series of suppers, seminars and such.

I often undergo a sudden sense of hopelessness at walking into a room and finding only half-a-dozen heads to count, in contrast to the thousands of people who appear at rallies on TV. Mass rallies serve a useful function at particular times and for quite special goals. One of these goals is *not* to organize the parents on the block, students in the classroom, teachers in the halls. Small steps, meticulously and consciously contrived, leading to small but loyal coalitions, appear to me to be the only means by which to organize the grass-roots basis for those long-term struggles which so many teachers seem prepared to undertake.

One revolution started with an unprepared tea party. Others start in mountain sanctuaries with the preparation of a military plan and with painstaking lessons in the way to oil and repair a gun. The revolution that we need to bring about within our public schools is one that will begin with someone—parent or teacher, child or adolescent, well-to-do or poor—quietly summoning up the nerve, then softly knocking on a neighbor's door.

Postscript:
"Written Under Protest"

William R. Tysseling
Attorney at Law
401 Clark Avenue
Ames, Iowa 50010

May 18, 1976

Mr. Don Carlson
Welch Junior High School
321 State Street
Ames, Iowa 50010

Dear Mr. Carlson:

Suzanne Chaplik and her parents have contacted me regarding Suzanne's participation in the Pledge of Allegiance at assemblies.

Suzanne relates that it has been required that she either:

1. stand during the Pledge of Allegiance at assemblies, or
2. bring a note from her parents requesting that this requirement be waived, this note to be maintained in her permanent record, or
3. that she author and submit a statement of her convictions, also to be included in a permanent record.

In an effort to resolve this matter, I would request two things. First, that you notify me of any inaccuracies in Suzanne's perceptions of these requirements and second, that you provide copies of the system or school policies with regard to the Pledge of Allegiance and the inclusion of such information in the permanent record.

Due to the time constraints of the end of the term. I would also request some response by Friday, May 21, 1976 in order that Suzanne might have this information before the assemblies scheduled for May 26 and May 27, 1976.

Thank you for your assistance and consideration in this matter.

Very truly yours,
William R. Tysseling

Mr. Don Carlson
Welch Junior High School
32 State Street
Ames, Iowa 50010

May 24, 1976

William R. Tysseling
Attorney at Law
401 Clark Avenue
Ames, Iowa 50010

Dear Mr. Tysseling:

I have received your letter requesting information about your client, Suzanne Chaplik, and her parents, participating in the Pledge of Allegiance at the Welch Junior High School assemblies.

We have followed the practice of opening the assemblies at Welch Junior High School with the Pledge of Allegiance for the past twelve years. All students are required to stand for this activity unless they have a written excuse from their parents requesting permission to remain seated during the Pledge of Allegiance. Students may also write a request for permission to remain quietly seated during this activity. However, their parents must sign this request.

It is accurate that these requests are maintained in the student's cumulative folder until the student changes his/her desire to participate in the Pledge of Allegiance or leaves junior high school, either by three years of completion or moves out of the district. At this time the note is removed and the fact of action that this student does not stand for the Pledge of Allegiance may be recorded.

Welch Junior High School does not have a written policy on the governance of the students participating in the Pledge of Allegiance. It is an activity that we use to help students gain a greater respect for the freedom and privileges we have in America and a sense of allegiance for which it stands. However, a written note requesting permission, signed by the student's parents, will exclude the students from the activity. We ask the parents to assume the responsibility for the junior high students, their children, in such a decision. We don't feel this type of decision should be based on a daily whim of a junior high student.

If you have other questions, please feel free to ask me. Hopefully this issue can be resolved by Suzanne and her parents working with the school.

Sincerely,
Don Carlson
Principal

William R. Tysseling
Attorney at Law
401 Clark Avenue
Ames, Iowa 50010

June 16, 1976

Ames School Board
and
Mr. David Moorhead
Superintendent of Schools
120 South Kellogg Avenue
Ames, Iowa 50010

Ladies and Gentlemen:

Suzanne Chaplik and her parents have asked me to pursue the issue of Suzanne's participation in the Pledge of Allegiance at Welch Junior High School assemblies.

Attached you will find correspondence including a letter dated May 18, 1976 to Don Carlson, Principal of Welch Junior High School, and a letter dated May 24, 1976 from Mr. Carlson in response, together with a statement of convictions submitted by Suzanne to Welch Junior High School.

In summary, Suzanne has been required to submit a statement of convictions together with a note from her parents which is to be maintained in her permanent file for the purpose of "excusing" her from standing for the Pledge of Allegiance.

Suzanne's position is twofold:

1. She cannot be required to stand for the Pledge of Allegiance.
2. Even if she could be required to do so, inclusion of any "excuse" from such activity cannot be maintained in her permanent record.

I believe these are both sound legal positions.

I believe this is a symbolic gesture protected by the First

Amendment and that inclusion in a permanent record of any materials relating to a student's refusal to participate in the Pledge of Allegiance can only be found to be an unconstitutional deterrent to the exercise of free speech. I believe that the inclusion of any such notation also falls within the purview of the "loyalty oath" cases of the Supreme Court, and would also be found unconstitutional on these grounds.

I also question the appropriateness of such a requirement. It seems anomalous that in attempting to teach students ". . . a greater respect for the freedom and privileges we have in America . . ." the schools should choose to abridge the First Amendment freedoms and privileges guaranteed by the Constitution.

I am also concerned with the teaching process in which the parents of a junior high school student are asked to assume responsibility for the student's decision making. The taking of a student's right to self-determination over so symbolic an issue seems not to reflect a respect for freedom or to encourage a sense of allegiance to a political and social nation but rather to demonstrate the lack of such freedom and to unnecessarily create a distaste and anger for political and social governance.

It is our request of the board and school administration that no students be required to stand for the Pledge of Allegiance and that no sanction, discrimination nor special treatment be imposed upon those choosing not to stand.

Very truly yours,
William R. Tysseling

P.S. As a result of Suzanne's involvement in this matter it has come to her attention that there are two separate files kept at Welch Junior High School, one on curricular matters and another on discipline matters. While we do not resist the orderly administration of such paperwork, it is a concern that upon requesting to see their children's junior high school files, Suzanne's parents were not informed of the existence of the discipline folder.

While this may have been an oversight or previous to the creation of such files, we would ask that the matter be explored administratively and that in the future any parent or child requesting access to the files be informed of the existence of both.

WRT

Written Under Protest

This is a list of my convictions.
  It is written under protest.

I don't believe I need someone to
  write my words for my feeling.

I also believe that God is the only
  thing I can pledge myself to.

I strongly believe that standing for
  the pledge is also saying it.

If you were mute, you wouldn't say it
  by speaking but by standing.

I believe the pledge is truly contradictory
  to the actual state of the U.S.A.

Submitted by
Suzanne Chaplik
May 25, 1976

LIES

Telling lies to the young is wrong.
Proving to them that lies are true is wrong.
Telling them that God's in his heaven
and all's well with the world is wrong.
The young know what you mean. The young are people.
Tell them the difficulties can't be counted,
and let them see not only what will be
but see with clarity these present times.
Say obstacles exist they must encounter
Sorrow happens, hardship happens.
The hell with it. Who never knew
the price of happiness will not be happy.
Forgive no error you recognize,
it will repeat itself, increase,
and afterwards our pupils
will not forgive in us what we forgave.

Yevgeny Yevtushenko[28]

Appendix

Leads, Contacts, Publications

Education Groups and Publications devoted to Social and Pedagogic Change

Alternative Schools Network
1105 West Lawrence Avenue,
   Room 211
Chicago, Illinois 60604

The Center for Teaching and
   Learning
Box 8158, University Station
The University of North Dakota
Grand Forks, North Dakota
   58202

Community Education
275 Nineteenth Avenue
San Francisco, California, 94109

Council on Interracial Books
   for Children
1841 Broadway
New York, New York 10023

Education Exploration Center
P.O. Box 7339
Powderhorn Station
Minneapolis, Minnesota 55407

The Learning Center
2000 North Wells Street
Fort Wayne, Indiana 46808

Literacy Volunteers of America,
   Inc.
Midtown Plaza, Sixth floor
700 East Water Street
Syracuse, New York 13210

Laubach Literacy International,
   Inc.
1320 Jamesville Ave.
Box 131
Syracuse, NY 13210

National Coalition of
   Alternative Community Schools
1289 Jewett Street
Ann Arbor, Michigan 48104

National Institute of Education
Brown Building
Nineteenth and M Streets, N.W.
Washington, D.C. 20208

Pacific Region Association of
  Alternative Schools
1119 Geary Boulevard
San Francisco, California 94109

Public Education Association
20 West Fortieth Street
New York, New York 10018

Reading Reform Foundation
7054 East Indian School Road
Scottsdale, Arizona 85251

Rio Grande Education
  Association
P.O. Box 2241
Santa Fe, New Mexico 87501

World Education
1414 Sixth Avenue
New York, New York 10019

Hucksters in the Classroom (A study by Sheila Harty which reviews industry propaganda in schools). Published and distributed by the Center for Responsive Law, P.O. Box 19367, Washington, D.C., 20036. $20.00/year for corporations/$10.00/year for educators.

Inequality in Education. Published and distributed by The Center for Law and Education, Harvard University, 6 Appian Way, Cambridge, Massachusetts, 02139. Quarterly.$6.00/year.

Integrateducation: Race and Schools, Room 2220, University Library, University of Massachusetts, Amherst, Massachusetts, 01003. Bi-monthly. $15.00/year.

Interracial Books for Children Bulletin. Published and distributed by the Council on Interracial Books for Children, C.I.B.C. Resource Center, 1841 Broadway, New York, New York, 10023. $15.00/year.

Politics and Education, Wesleyan Station, Fisk Hall, Middletown, Connecticut, 06457. Quarterly.$5.00/year.

Radical Teacher, published and distributed by the Center for the Study of Education and Politics, 285 Court Street, Middletown, Connecticut, 06457. Quarterly.$8.00/year.

TABS: Aides for Ending Sexism in School (Contains lesson plans, swap sections, posters, feature articles and reviews). 744 Carroll Street, Brooklyn, New York, 11215. Quarterly.$8.50/year.

The Testing Digest (A publication of The Project to DE-Mystify the Established Standardized Tests), 1129 Twenty-first Street, N.W., Washington, D.C., 20036. Quarterly.$4.00/year for students/ $12.00/year for institutions.

Working Teacher, c/o Working Teacher Educational Society, Box 46534, Postal Station G, 3760 West Tenth Avenue, Vancouver, B.C., V6R 4G8. Quarterly.$5.00/year.

*Civil Rights Organizations, Anti-war, Peace-action Groups/
Related Publications*

American Friends Service
  Committee
1501 Cherry Street
Philadelphia, Pennsylvania 19102

American Indian Movement
  (A.I.M.)
Information Office
Box 175
Porcupine, South Dakota 57772

Amnesty International, U.S.A.
12 Parker Street
Cambridge, Massachusetts 02138

Black Hills Alliance
Box 2508
Rapid City, South Dakota 57701

Campaign for Economic
  Democracy
304 South Broadway, Room 224
Los Angeles, California 90013

The Catholic Worker
36 East First Street
New York, New York 10003

Central Committee for
  Conscientious Objectors
2208 South Street
Philadelphia, Pennsylvania 19146

Children's Defense Fund
1520 New Hampshire Ave. N.W.
Washington, D.C. 20036

Citizens Against Nuclear Power
711 South Dearborn
Chicago, Illinois 60605

Citizens Against Nuclear Threats
106 Girard Street, S.E.
Albuquerque, New Mexico 87106

Clergy and Laity Concerned
198 Broadway
New York, New York 10038

Coalition for a New Foreign
  and Military Policy
120 Maryland Avenue, N.E.
Washington, D.C. 20002

Committee Against Registration
  and the Draft
245 Second Street, N.E.
Washington, D.C. 20002

The Fellowship of Reconciliation
Box 271
Nyack, New York 10960

Mobilization for Survival
East Coast:
3601 Locust Walk
Philadelphia, Pennsylvania 19104
West Coast:
944 Market Street, Room 808
San Francisco, California 94102

Movement for a New Society
4722 Baltimore Avenue
Philadelphia, Pennsylvania 19143

Musicians United for Safe
Energy (M.U.S.E.)
72 Fifth Avenue
New York, New York 10011

National Association for the
Advancement of Colored
People (NAACP)
National Office
1790 Broadway
New York, New York 10019

National Urban League
500 East Sixty-second Street
New York, New York 10021

Science for the People
897 Main Street
Cambridge, Massachusetts 02139

Union of Concerned Scientists
1384 Massachusetts Avenue
Cambridge, Massachusetts 02138

United Farmworkers of America
P.O. Box 62
Keene, California 93531

VISTA (Volunteers in Service to
America)
806 Connecticut Avenue
Washington, D.C. 20525

Vocations for Social Change
P.O. Box 211, Essex Station
Boston, Massachusetts 02112

War Resisters League
319 Lafayette Street
New York, New York 10012

Akwesasne Notes (Coverage of the struggles of Native American peo-
ples), Mohawk Nation, via Rooseveltown, New York, 13683. No set
subscription rate; send contribution. Monthly.
The Black Scholar (A monthly journal of black studies), Black World
Foundation, P.O. Box 908, Sausalito, California, 94965. $12.00/
year.
The Catholic Worker Newspaper (A publication of The Catholic
Worker House), 36 East First Street, New York, New York, 10003.
Monthly.25¢/year.
*A Citizen's Guide on How to Use the Freedom of Information Act and
the Privacy Act in Requesting Government Documents* (*Thirteenth
Report by the Committee on Government Operations*), 1977. Avail-
able from the Superintendent of Documents, U.S. Government
Printing Office, Washington, D.C., 20402. $3.50.
Facing History and Ourselves: A Curriculum (Assists students and
teachers in dealing with the Nazi Holocaust, and with their own
moral decisions). Facing History, Brookline Public Schools, 25
Kennard Road, Brookline, MA 02146. 9 volumes/$15.00.

Feed, Need, Greed—Food Resources and Population: A High School Curriculum (Published by Science for the People, this curriculum encourages critical thinking and awareness in students and teachers regarding the corporate interests of the food distribution system and its relationship to hunger, population and resources.), $5.00.

"We Interrupt this Program": A Citizen's Guide to Using the Media for Social Change, by Robbie Gordon. Distributed by Volunteer Readership, P.O. Box 1807, Boulder, Colorado, 80306. $5.00.

Fellowship (A publication of the Fellowship of Reconciliation), Box 271, Nyack, New York, 10960. $6.00/year.

Freedomways (A quarterly review of the Freedom Movement), 799 Broadway, New York, New York, 10003. $4.50/year.

F.P.S.: A Magazine of Young People's Liberation, published and distributed by Youth Liberation, 2007 Washtenaw Avenue, Ann Arbor, Michigan, 48104. $10.00/6 issues.

In These Times (A weekly independent newspaper), published and distributed by the Institute for Policy Studies, 1509 North Milwaukee Avenue, Chicago, Illinois, 60622. $10.95/6 months; $19.50/year.

Peace Studies Institute Bulletin, % Peace Studies Institute, Manchester College, North Manchester, Indiana, 46962. Bi-annually. $3.00/year.

Science for the People (With special issues on "Science Teaching"), 897 Main Street, Cambridge, Massachusetts, 02139. Bi-monthly. $7.00/year.

Southern Exposure (Periodical of Southern struggles), published and distributed by the Institute for Southern Studies, P.O. Box 531, Durham, North Carolina, 27702. Quarterly.$10.00/year.

Win Magazine, Inc. (A weekly magazine dedicated to change through nonviolent action), 503 Atlantic Avenue, Fifth floor, Brooklyn, New York, 11217. $11.00/year.

Youth Alternatives (Advocates social change in youth services and focuses on issues that affect young people specifically), published and distributed by the National Youth Alternatives Project, 1346 Connecticut Avenue, N.W., Washington, D.C., 20036. Monthly. $10.00/individual; $20.00/institutions.

Third World Organizations/International Publications

American Committee on Africa
305 East Forty-sixth Street
New York, New York 10017

Indochina Resource Center
P.O. Box 4000 D
Berkeley, California 94704

Community Action on Latin
America (CALA)
731 State Street
Madison, Wisconsin 53703

Nicaraguan Solidarity Committee
National Office
1322 Eighteenth Street
Washington, D.C. 20036

Center for Cuban Studies
220 East Twenty-third Street
New York, New York 10010

U.S. China People's Friendship
Association
50 Oak Street, Room 502
San Francisco, California 94102

Cuba Resource Center
11 John Street, Room 506
New York, New York 10038

Washington Office on Latin
America
110 Maryland Avenue, N.E.
Washington, D.C., 20002

Bulletin of Committee of Concerned Asian Scholars, P.O. Box W, Charlemont, Massachusetts 01139. $8.00/year; $6.00/students.

Chile Newsletter: NICH—Non Intervention in Chile (A bi-monthly publication with updated information on Chile), Box 800, Berkeley, California, 94701. $5.00/individual; $10.00/institution.

China Books and Periodicals (National agency for publications in English from the People's Republic of China), 125 Fifth Avenue, New York, New York, 10003; 2929 Twenty-fourth Street, San Francisco, California, 94110. Send for free catalogue.

Cuba Times (A publication of the Cuba Resource Center), 11 John Street, Room 506, New York, New York, 10038

Cuba Update (A publication of the Center for Cuban Studies), 220 East Twenty-third Street, New York, New York, 10010

Dollars and Sense (Reviews the national and international economic situation from a socialist perspective), 324 Somerville Avenue, Somerville, Massachusetts, 02143. Monthly. $5.00/yr.

Latin American Perspectives, % CSMI, P.O. Box 792, Riverside, California, 92502. $10.00/year.

Middle East Research and Information Project Bulletin (MERIP) (A journal which focuses on the role of the United States in the political economies of Middle Eastern countries), P.O. Box 48, Harvard Square Station, Cambridge, Massachusetts, 02138. Monthly. $6.00/ year.

North American Congress on Latin America (NACLA Report), Box 57, Cathedral Park Station, New York, New York, 10025. Write for free literature.

People Acting for Change Together (PACT) (Provides resource material on Third World issues, women's issues and racism), 163 Madison, Detroit, Michigan, 48226. $10.00/10 packets.

UNESCO Publications, % The United Nations, New York, New York, 10017.

Bibliography

This is a selected bibliography. Many of the books listed here have been referred to in the text. Other books are listed because of their relevance to the issues raised in the text and therefore should be of special interest to teachers, students and parents.

General Interest

Adoff, Arnold ed. *Black on Black: Commentaries by Black Americans from Frederick Douglas to Malcolm X.* New York: The Macmillan Company, 1968.

Board of Education, City of New York. *Regulations Governing the Collection, Maintenance and Dissemination of Student Records.* 1973.

Bowles, Samuel and Gintis, Herbert. *Schooling in Capitalist America.* New York: Basic Books, Inc., 1976.

Braun, Robert. *Teachers and Power.* New York: Simon and Schuster, 1972.

Carnoy, Martin. *Education as Cultural Imperialism.* New York: McKay Publishers, 1974.

Channon, Gloria. *Homework.* New York: Outerbridge and Dienstfrey, 1970.

Clark, Kenneth. *Dark Ghetto.* New York: Harper and Row, 1965.

Coles, Robert and Berrigan, Daniel. *The Geography of Faith.* Boston: Beacon Press, 1970.

Cremin, Lawrence. *The Transformation of the School.* New York: Vintage Books, 1964.

Counts, George. *Dare the School Build a New Social Order?* New York: John Day Company, 1968.

Dewey, John. *Democracy and Education.* New York: The Free Press, 1968.

Fantini, Mario. *Public Schools of Choice.* New York: Simon and Schuster, Inc., 1974.

Freire, Paulo. *Pedagogy of the Oppressed.* New York: Seabury Press, 1970.

Freire, Paulo. *Education for Critical Consciousness.* New York: Continuum Books, 1980.

Freire, Paulo. *Pedagogy in Process.* New York: Seabury Press, 1978.

Friedenberg, Edgar. *The Dignity of Youth.* Boston: Beacon Press, 1966.

Gerassi, John. *The Great Fear in Latin America.* New York: Macmillan Company, 1963.

Glasser, William, M.D. *Schools Without Failure.* New York: Harper and Row, Publishers, 1969.

Goodman, Paul. *Compulsory Mis-Education.* New York: Vintage Books, 1966.

Goodman, Paul. *Growing Up Absurd.* New York: Vintage Books, 1970.

Greer, Colin. *The Great School Legend.* New York: Basic Books, Inc., 1970.

Greer, Colin, ed. *The Solution as Part of the Problem.* New York: Harper and Row, 1973.

Gross, Ronald and Osterman, Paul, eds. *High School.* New York: Simon and Schuster, 1971.

Holt, John. *The Under-Achieving School.* New York: Dell Publishing Company, 1969.

Henry, Jules. *Culture Against Man.* New York: Vintage Books, 1965.

Jencks, Christopher. *Inequality.* New York: Basic Books, Inc., 1972.

Katz, Michael. *The Irony of Early School Reform.* Boston: Beacon Press, 1968.

Katz, Michael. *Class, Bureaucracy and Schools.* New York: Praeger Publishing Company, 1975.

Keniston, Kenneth. *The Uncommitted.* New York: Harcourt, Brace and World, Inc., 1965.

Keniston, Kenneth. *Young Radicals.* New York: Harcourt, Brace and World, Inc., 1968.

Kozol, Jonathan. *Death at an Early Age.* New York: Bantam Books, 1968.

Kozol, Jonathan. *The Night Is Dark and I Am Far From Home.* New York: Continuum Books, 1980.

Lessing, Doris. *The Golden Notebook.* New York: Bantam Books, 1973.

Levine, Alan H., with Carey, Eve and Divocky, Diane. *The Rights of Students*. New York: Avon Books, 1973.

Lurie, Ellen. How to Change the Schools: *A Parent's Action Handbook on How to Fight the System*. New York: Vintage Books, 1970.

Marciano, John and Griffin, William L. *Teaching the Vietnam War*. New Jersey: Allanheld, Osmun & Company, 1980.

Merrill, Walter and Ruchames, Louis. *The Letters of William Lloyd Garrison*. 5 volumes. Massachusetts: Harvard University Press, 1971–1979.

Nelson, Truman. *The Old Man*. New York: Holt, Rinehart and Winston, 1973.

Nelson, Truman. *The Right of Revolution*. Boston: Beacon Press, 1968.

Nelson, Truman. *The Sin of the Prophet*. Boston: Little, Brown and Company, 1952.

Petras, James. *Politics and Social Structure in Latin America*. New York: Monthly Review Press, 1970.

Ravitch, Diane. *The Great School Wars*. New York: Harper and Row, 1974.

Rubin, David. *The Rights of Teachers*. New York: Avon Books, 1971.

Scribner, Harvey B. and Stevens, Leonard B. *Make Your Schools Work*. New York: Simon and Schuster Publishing Company, 1975.

Shor, Ira. *Critical Teaching and Everyday Life*. Boston: South End Press, 1980.

Spring, Joel. *Education and the Rise of the Corporate State*. Boston: Beacon Press, 1972.

Spring, Joel. *A Primer on Libertarian Education*. New York: Free Life Publishers, 1975.

Thoreau, Henry David. *Walden* and *On the Duty of Civil Disobedience*. New York: Holt, Rinehart and Winston, Inc., 1948.

Wasserman, Miriam. *Demystifying School*. New York: Praeger Publishers, 1973.

Wasserman, Miriam and Hutchinson, Linda. *Teaching Human Dignity*. Minneapolis: The Education Exploration Center, 1978.

Wynia, Gary W. *The Politics of Latin American Development*. New York: Cambridge University Press, 1978.

Women in History

Ahlum, Carol and Fralley, Jacqueline. *High School Feminist Studies: A Curriculum*. New York: The Feminist Press, 1977.

Ashbaugh, Carol. *Lucy Parsons: American Revolutionary*. Chicago: Charles H. Kerr Publishing Company, 1976.

Bradford, Sarah. *Harriet Tubman: The Moses of her People*. New Jersey: The Citadel Press, 1974.

Buckmaster, Henrietta. *Women Who Shaped History*. New York: Collier Books, 1966.

Day, Dorothy. *The Long Loneliness: The Autobiography of Dorothy Day*. New York: Harper and Brothers, 1952.

Day, Dorothy. *House of Hospitality*. New York: Sheed and Ward, Inc., 1939.

Day, Dorothy. *Loaves and Fishes*. New York: Harper and Row, 1963.

Foner, Phillip S. *Helen Keller: Her Socialist Years*. New York: International Publishers, 1967.

Gates, Barbara; Klaw, Susan; and Steinberg, Adria. *Changing Learning/Changing Lives: A High School Women's Studies Curriculum from The Group School*. New York: The Feminist Press, 1979.

Harrison, Barbara Grizzuti. *Unlearning the Lie: Sexism in School*. New York: Morrow Paperback Editions, 1973.

Jacobs, Sue-Ellen. *Women in Perspective: A Guide for Cross-Cultural Studies*. Chicago: University of Illinois Press, 1976.

Jones, Mary H. *The Autobiography of Mother Jones*. Chicago: Charles H. Kerr Publishing Company, 1972.

Lerner, Gerda. *The Woman in American History*. Massachusetts: Addison-Wesley, Publishers, 1971.

Lerner, Gerda. *Black Women in White America: A Documentary History*. New York: Vintage Books, 1972.

Miller, William D. *A Harsh and Dreadful Love: Dorothy Day and The Catholic Worker Movement*. New York: Liveright Publishing Company, 1973.

Rowbotham, Sheila. *Woman's Consciousness, Man's World*. New York: Penguin Books, 1973.

Rowbotham, Sheila. *Women: Resistance and Revolution*. London: Allen Lane Publishers, 1972.

Schniedewind, Nancy. *Confronting Racism and Sexism: A Practical Handbook for Educators*. New York: Common Ground Press, 1977.

Stacey, Judith; Bereaud, Susan; and Daniels, Joan, eds. *And Jill Came Tumbling After: Sexism in American Education*. New York: Dell Publishing Company, 1974.

History From the Bottom Up

Boyer, Richard O., and Morais, Herbert. *Labor's Untold Story*. Published by the United Electrical Workers, 1971.

Douglas, Frederick. *My Bondage and My Freedom*. New York: Arno Press, 1968.

Fanon, Frantz. *The Wretched of the Earth*. New York: Grove Press, 1965.

Gendzier, Irene L. *Frantz Fanon: A Critical Study*. New York: Vintage Books, 1974.

Gregory, Dick. *No More Lies: The Myth and Reality of American History*. New York: Harper and Row, 1971.

King, Martin Luther. *Stride Toward Freedom*. New York: Harper and Row, 1958.

Lynd, Alice and Lynd, Staughton, eds. *Rank and File: Personal Histories by Working-Class Organizers*. Boston: Beacon Press, 1973.

Lynd, Staughton, ed. *Nonviolence in America: A Documentary History*. Indianapolis: The Bobbs Merrill Company, Inc., 1966.

Meltzer, Milton. *Bread and Roses: The Struggle of American Labor, 1865–1915*. New York: Vintage Books, 1973.

Neuhaus, Richard J. and Berger, Peter L. *Movement and Revolution*. New York: Doubleday and Company, Inc., 1970.

Padover, Saul K., ed. *Thomas Jefferson's "Democracy."* New York: Greenwood Press, 1969.

Quarles, Benjamin, ed. *Frederick Douglas*. New Jersey: Prentice-Hall, Inc., 1968.

Terkel, Studs. *Working*. New York: Avon Books, 1975.

Terkel, Studs. *Hard Times*. New York: Pocket Books, 1978.

Malcolm X. *The Autobiography of Malcolm X*. New York: Ballantine Books, 1964.

Wasserman, Harvey. *Harvey Wasserman's History of the United States*. New York: Harper and Row, 1972.

Zinn, Howard. *Disobedience and Democracy*. New York: Vintage Books, 1968.

Zinn, Howard. *A People's History of the United States*. New York: Harper and Row, 1980.

Zinn, Howard. *The Politics of History*. Boston: Beacon Press, 1970.

Books on Teaching Reading

Ashton-Warner, Sylvia. *Teacher*. New York: Bantam Books, 1964.

Baratz, Joan C. and Shuy, Roger W. *Teaching Black Children to*

Read. Published by the Center for Applied Linguistics, Washington, D.C., 1969.

Chall, Jeanne. *Learning to Read: The Great Debate.* New York: McGraw-Hill Book Company, 1967.

Dennison, George. *The Lives of Children.* New York: Vintage Books, 1970.

Fader, Daniel. *Hooked On Books.* New York: Berkeley Publishing Corporation, 1976.

Gray, Lillian. *Teaching Children to Read.* New York: Roland Press, 1963.

Herndon, James. *How to Survive in Your Native Land.* New York: Simon and Schuster, 1971.

Koch, Kenneth. *Wishes, Lies and Dreams.* New York: Vintage Books, 1970.

Kohl, Herbert. *Reading: How To.* New York: Bantam Books, 1974.

Means, Harrison. "Nine Years of Individualized Reading," *Journal of Reading,* November, 1976.

Moffett, James and Wagner, Betty J. *Student-Centered Language Arts and Reading, K-13: A Handbook for Teachers.* Boston: Houghton-Mifflin Company, 1976.

Smith, Frank. *Reading Without Nonsense.* New York: Teachers College Press, 1978.

Spaulding, Romalda. *The Writing Road to Reading.* New York: William Morrow Publishing Company, 1969.

Williams, Frederick, ed. *Language and Poverty.* New York: Academic Press, Inc., 1970.

Notes

1. Doris Lessing is quoted from *The Golden Notebook*. See the author's special introduction in the Bantam edition (New York: Bantam Books, 1973), p. xvii.
2. Quotations from the Arizona Board of Education are extracted from the "Preamble to U.S. Course of Study," adopted by the Arizona Board on September 21, 1972. This document is no longer available to the public. According to Dr. Thomas Reno, Associate Superintendent, the document was replaced in 1976 by a revised and sanitized version. Unhappily, it is the original version which most faithfully reflects the characteristic goals and guidelines of the U.S. public schools.
3. Massachusetts educator Horace Mann is quoted from *The Republic and the School: Horace Mann on the Education Of Free Men,* edited by Lawrence A. Cremin (New York: Teachers College Press, Columbia University, 1957). A more accessible source for the same quotation is *The Great School Legend* by Colin Greer (New York: Basic Books, Inc., 1972), p. 75.
4. Sentimentalists and purblind patriots, who do not like to think ill of their former presidents, will be quick to pounce upon a shocking quotation of this kind and to insist that it is "taken out of context"and so cannot conceivably reflect "the true opinions" of its author. All the more reason, then, why teachers and writers must be extremely careful in their selection of such statements, in order to be sure that they, in fact, *do* represent the true convictions of their speakers/authors. In the case of Wilson, a small amount of research will unearth an ever-increasing volume of disturbing insight into his aristocratic and class-serving point of view. "Undoubtedly," said Wilson, in a speech delivered in Cambridge, Massachusetts in 1909, "the education which gives them [i.e., the masses of the nation] skill of hand and acquaintance

with all the means by which advancement in the practical arts are to be attained . . . is an indispensable necessity. Schools of technical training are not only desirable but indispensable, and the greater part of the education which a nation attempts must be of that kind, because that is the sort of education most universally needed—needed, I mean, by the largest number of persons. But we are not to stop there, and we are not to put our minds in confusion by placing that sort of education in competition or contrast with that which has for its object, not technical skill, but sheer enlargement of the mind. . . . And so we feel that we are entitled to be full of hope in regard to the increasing intellectual life of Princeton. I am covetous for Princeton of all the glory that there is, and the chief glory of a university is always intellectual glory. The chief glory of a university is the leadership of the nation in the things that attach to the highest ambitions that nations can set themselves, those ideals which lift nations into the atmosphere of things that are permanent and do not fade from generation to generation. I do not see how any man can fail to perceive that scholarship, that education in a country like ours, is a branch of statemanship. It is a branch of that general work of enabling a great country to use its energies to the best advantage and to lift itself from generation to generation through stages of unbroken progress. . . . No man can do anything in his generation by and of himself. He must rule his fellow-men and draw them into cooperation with himself, if he would accomplish anything. There is a touch of modern statesmanship about every piece of modern business. . . . It is as if all the powers of the world were organized and the captains of industry were making their way forward in the ranks to be generals in command of the forces of mankind. . . ." See *The Politics of Woodrow Wilson*, edited by August Heckscher (New York: Harper and Row, 1956), pp. 138, 142, 143.

5. Thomas Jefferson orginally wrote these words in a letter, dated 1787. The quotation can be found in *Democracy*, edited by Saul K. Padover (New York: Greenwood Press, 1969), p. 259.

6. William Lloyd Garrison's words are quoted from *The Politics of History* by Howard Zinn (Boston: Beacon Press, 1970), p. 147.

7. Henry David Thoreau is quoted from *Walden*. See *Walden* and *On the Duty of Civil Disobedience* (New York: Holt, Rinehart and Winston, Inc., 1948), pp. 270–71.

8. Martin Luther King, Jr.'s "Letter from Birmingham Jail" is re-

printed in *Nonviolence in America*, edited by Staughton Lynd (Indianapolis: The Bobbs Merrill Company, Inc., 1966), p. 474.

9. The quotation on obedience is taken from "Curriculum Guide in Character Education," School Document Number 11, 1962. See *Death at an Early Age* (Bantam Books: New York, 1968), p. 180.

10. The National Education Association guidebook is entitled *Discipline in the Classroom* (National Education Association, 1969), p. 39. See also *Controlling Classroom Misbehavior* (National Education Association, 1973).

11. The passage on Helen Keller quoted here is a pastiche of standard biographical works on Keller used in public schools.

12. Helen Keller is quoted from an essay written in 1913 entitled "New Vision for the Blind." See *Helen Keller: Her Socialist Years* by Philip S. Foner (New York: International Publishers, 1967), pp. 55–56.

13. The quotation on elections by Helen Keller can be found in *Helen Keller: Her Socialist Years*, p. 31.

14. Martin Luther King, Jr., is quoted here from *Movement and Revolution*, by Richard J. Neuhaus and Peter L. Berger (New York: Doubleday and Company, Inc., 1970), p. 97.

15. J. Edgar Hoover's blackmail of Dr. King is documented in *The Boston Globe*, September 3, 1975.

16. Martin Luther King, Jr. is paraphrased from *The Little Red, White and Blue Book*, edited by J. A. Rossen, (New York: Grove Press, 1969), p. 42.

17. Henry David Thoreau is quoted throughout this chapter from *Civil Disobedience*. See *Walden* and *On the Duty of Civil Disobedience*, pp. 284–85.

18. Abraham Lincoln is quoted from a speech delivered in southern Illinois in 1858. For this and other annotated material on Lincoln, see *The Politics of History*, p. 148.

19. According to the *Digest of Educational Statistics*, there were 42,900,000 students enrolled in our public education system in the 1977 academic year. This figure includes elementary and secondary students. Students in private, parochial and special schools are not incorporated in the total.

20. Since 1974, with the passage of the Family Education Rights and Privacy Act (otherwise known as The Buckley Amendment, named after its chief sponsor Senator James Buckley of New York), parents and students have had legal right of access to inspect and review "education records," defined as "those records,

files, documents and other materials which (a) contain information directly related to a student and (b) are maintained by an educational agency or by a person acting for such an agency or institution." Records are broadly defined to include "any information or data recorded in any medium, including but not limited to handwriting, print, tapes, microfilm and microfiche." There are some exceptions as to what can be examined by student or parent; but these exceptions are so few that they do not represent a substantial limitation on the right of access to all records of concern. As mentioned in the text, schools will sometimes keep a second set of records of which few parents are aware, but the 1974 legislation now insists that schools inform parents of "all types" of records maintained. For quoted material and additional information on The Buckley Amendment (including specifics regarding its limitations) see *Inequality in Education*, Volume 22, July 1977, published by The Center for Law and Education, Harvard University, 6 Appian Way, Cambridge, Massachusetts, 02138.

21. The court case affirming the right of refusal to recite the Pledge of Allegiance in school took place in West Virginia in 1943. In this landmark case, *West Virginia* vs. *Barnette*, it was determined that "the action of a State in making it compulsory for children in the public schools to salute the flag and pledge allegiance . . . violates the First and Fourteenth Amendments" (see citing 319 U.S. 624 at p. 642). For more recent cases, see *Hamilton* vs. *The Board of Regents* (293 U.S. 245), *Banks* vs. *Board of Public Instruction of Dade County, Florida* (314, Federal Supplement, 285) in 1970, *Goetz* vs. *Ansell* (477, F 2nd, 636) in 1973. For an account of one student who refused the flag pledge and won vindication in the courts, see "Girl's Flag Carrying Called 'Illegal,' 'Bizarre,' " *Boston Globe*, November 18, 1970. Another case, involving the refusal of a teacher to recite the pledge, is documented in an excellent article, "A Teacher's Right to Shun the Flag Pledge," *New York Times*, February 18, 1974.

22. For further information on certain of our oldest U.S. allies in the Latin nations, see *The Great Fear in Latin America*, by John Gerassi (New York: Macmillan Company, 1963). For more recent information see *Politics and Social Structure in Latin America*, by James Petras (New York: Monthly Review Press, 1970) and *The Politics of Latin American Development*, by Gary C. Wynia (New York: Cambridge University Press, 1978).

23. *The American Statistical Index for 1980*, published by the Congressional Information Service in Washington, D.C., refers the reader to the *Foreign Military Sales and Military Assistance Figures* for 1979, which lists the 93 nations with which the United States has military sales agreements.

24. John Milton is quoted from *The Areopagitica*. See *The Complete Prose of John Milton*, Volume 2, edited by Ernest Sirluck (Connecticut: Yale University Press, 1959), p. 561.

25. Statistics and documentation on South Africa are drawn from an article which ran in *The Boston Globe* on January 25, 1970. See "South Africa's arsenal grows, despite U.N. embargo plea," by Darius Jhalaba.

26. For a recent description of teacher centers funded and organized by the two major educational associations (the N.E.A. and the A.F.T.) see "Teacher Centers: Best Effort Yet at Upgrading Teachers," *Boston Globe*, August 3, 1980.

27. Senator George McGovern is quoted from a speech delivered on International Literacy Day, September 8, 1978. See *The Congressional Record*, Proceedings and Debates of the Ninety-fifth Congress, Second Session, Volume 124, Number 139, Washington, D.C.

28. *Lies*, by Yevgeny Yevtushenko, is included in *Yevtushenko: Selected Poems*, translated by Robin Milner-Gulland (New York: E. P. Dutton and Company, Inc., 1962), p. 52.

THE WAY AND ITS POWER

A Study of the

TAO TÊ CHING

and

Its Place in Chinese Thought

by

ARTHUR WALEY

GROVE PRESS, INC.   NEW YORK

This edition is published by arrangement with The Macmillan Company.

First Evergreen Edition 1958
Seventeenth Printing 1980
ISBN: 0-394-17207-8
Grove Press ISBN: 0-8021-4133-1
Library of Congress Catalog Card Number: 58-5092

Manufactured in the United States of America

Distributed by Random House, Inc., New York

GROVE PRESS, INC., 196 West Houston Street, New York, N.Y. 10014

Grove Press Eastern Philosophy and Literature Series
Edited by Hannelore Rosset

To
Leonard & Dorothy
Elmhirst

UNESCO COLLECTION OF REPRESENTATIVE
WORKS – CHINESE SERIES
This book has been accepted in the Chinese Translations
Series of the United Nations Educational, Scientific and
Cultural Organization (UNESCO)

CONTENTS

PREFACE

I HAVE noticed that general works[1] about the history of Man either ignore China altogether or relegate this huge section of mankind to a couple of paragraphs. One of my aims in this book is to supply the general anthropologist with at any rate an impetus towards including China in his survey. This does not however mean that the book is addressed to a small class of specialists; for all intelligent people, that is to say, all people who want to understand what is going on in the world around them, are 'general anthropologists', in the sense that they are bent on finding out how mankind came to be what it is to-day. Such an interest is in no sense an academic one. For hundreds of millennia Man was what we call 'primitive'; he has attempted to be civilized only (as regards Europe) in the last few centuries. During an overwhelmingly great proportion of his history he has sacrificed, been engrossed in omens, attempted to control the wind and rain by magic. We who do none of these things can hardly be said to represent normal man, but rather a very specialized and perhaps very unstable branch-development. In each of us, under the thinnest possible veneer of *homo industrialis*, lie endless strata of barbarity. Any attempt to deal with ourselves or others on the supposition that what shows on the surface represents more than the mere topmast of modern man, is doomed to failure.

And Man must be studied as a whole. Despite the lead

[1] e.g. A. M. Hocart's *The Progress of Man*, E. O. James's *Origins of Sacrifice*, both quite recent works.

given by unofficial historians there is still an idea that the Chinese are or at any rate were in the past so cut off from the common lot of mankind that they may be regarded almost as though they belonged to another planet, that sinology is in fact something not much less remote than astronomy and cannot, whatever independent interest or value it may have, possibly throw light on the problems of our own past. Nothing could be more false. It becomes apparent, as Chinese studies progress, that in numerous instances ancient China shows in a complete and intelligible form what in the West is known to us only through examples that are scattered, fragmentary and obscure.

It may however be objected that the particular book which I have chosen to translate is already well known to European readers. This is only true in a very qualified sense; and in order to make clear what I mean I must make a distinction which has, I think, too often been completely ignored. Supposing a man came down from Mars and seeing the symbol of the Cross asked what it signified, if he chanced to meet first of all with an archæologist he might be told that this symbol had been found in neolithic tombs, was originally a procreative charm, an astrological sign or I know not what; and all this might quite well be perfectly true. But it still would not tell the Man from Mars what he wanted to know—namely, what is the significance of the Cross to-day to those who use it as a symbol.

Now scriptures are collections of symbols. Their peculiar characteristic is a kind of magical elasticity. To successive generations of believers they mean things that would be paraphrased in utterly different words. Yet for century upon century they continue to satisfy the wants of mankind; they are 'a garment that need never be renewed'. The distinction I wish to make is between translations which set out to discover what such books meant to start with, and those which aim only at telling the reader what such a text means to those who use it to-day. For want of better terms I call the first sort of translation 'historical', the second 'scriptural'. The most perfect example of a scriptural translation is the late Richard Wilhelm's version of the *Book of Changes*. Many critics condemned it, most unfairly in my opinion, because it fails to do what in fact the author never had any intention of doing. It fails of course to tell us what the book *meant* in the 10th century B.C. On the other hand, it tells us far more lucidly and accurately than any of its predecessors what the *Book of Changes* means to the average Far Eastern reader to-day.

There are several good 'scriptural' translations of the *Tao Tê Ching*. Here again I think Wilhelm's is the best, and next to it that of Carus.[1] But there exists no 'historical' translation; that is to say, no attempt to discover what the book meant when it was first written. That is what I have here tried to supply, fully conscious of the fact that to know what a scripture meant to begin with is perhaps less important than to know what it means to-day. I have decided indeed to make this attempt only because in this case the 'Man from Mars'—the Western reader—has been fortunate enough not to address his initial questions to the archæologist. More representative informants have long ago set before him the current (that is to say, the

[1] Or rather, of his Japanese collaborator.

medieval) interpretation of the *Tao Tê Ching*. I feel that he may now be inclined to press his enquiries a little further; just as a tourist, having discovered what the swastika means in Germany to-day, might conceivably become curious about its previous history as a symbol. Fundamentally, however, my object is the same as that of previous translators. For I cannot believe that the study of the past has any object save to throw light upon the present.

I wish also to make another, quite different, kind of distinction. It has reference to two sorts of translation. It seems to me that when the main importance of a work is its beauty, the translator must be prepared to sacrifice a great deal in the way of detailed accuracy in order to preserve in the translation the quality which gives the original its importance. Such a translation I call 'literary', as opposed to 'philological'. I want to make it clear that this translation of the *Tao Tê Ching* is not 'literary'; for the simple reason that the importance of the original lies not in its literary quality but in the things it says, and it has been my one aim to reproduce what the original says with detailed accuracy.

I must apologize for the fact that the introduction is longer than the translation itself. I can only say that I see no way of making the text fully intelligible without showing how the ideas which it embodies came into existence. The introduction together with the translation and notes are intended for those who have no professional interest in Chinese studies. The appendices to the introduction and the additional and textual notes are intended chiefly for specialists. Thus the book represents a compromise—of a kind that is becoming inevitable, as facilities for purely specialist publication become more and more restricted.

After I had made my translation of the *Tao Tê Ching* and sketched out the introduction, I received Vol. IV of *Ku Shih Pien* and was delighted to find that a great contemporary scholar, Ku Chieh-kang, holds exactly the same views about the date and authorship of the work as I myself had formed.

The European scholars who have in recent years contributed most to our knowledge of ancient Chinese thought are Marcel Granet, Henri Maspero, J. J. L. Duyvendak, and Gustav Haloun. I have rather frequently expressed disagreement with M. Maspero; but this does not mean that I fail to recognize the high value of his work as a whole. Like all sinologues I owe a great debt to Bernhard Karlgren. The study of meanings is, in China at any rate, intimately associated with the study of sounds. Twenty years ago Chinese studies had reached a point at which, but for the laborious phonological researches undertaken by Karlgren, further progress, in almost every direction, was barred.

I owe a very special debt of gratitude to my friend, Dr. Lionel Giles, who read the proofs and made many suggestions and corrections. Finally, I should like to call attention to a peculiarity in my references to the *Book of Odes*. Instead of using the cumbrous and inconvenient system adopted by Legge, I number the poems 1–305, and hope that other scholars may be induced to follow suit.

INTRODUCTION

I WILL begin with a comparison. This is a passage from the *Book of History*: 'In the second year after the conquest of the Shang,[1] the king of Chou fell ill. . . . The two dukes said "let us reverently consult the tortoise on the king's behalf". But the king's other brother, the duke of Chou, said: "That is not the way to move the hearts of our ancestors, the former kings", and so saying the duke of Chou pledged his own life to ransom the king. He built three mounds on the same clearing; and for himself he made a mound to the south of these, and stood upon it, looking north. He set before him a disc of jade and in his hand he held a tablet of jade. Then he called upon the three dead kings, T'ai, Chi and Wên, and the scribe wrote his prayer upon a tablet. The duke said: "Your descendant Such-a-one[2] has met with a sharp and violent sickness. If this means that you three dead kings need some one to cherish and foster you in heaven, then take me instead of Such-a-one. For I am ready and well able to be very serviceable to ghosts and spirits; whereas your descendant the king is versed in few such arts, and would not be at all serviceable to ghosts and spirits. You, O kings, were charged by the Court of Ancestors to succour the four quarters of the land from end to end and to

[1] The Chou probably conquered the Shang early in the 10th century B.C. But the story which follows is a ritual theme (the brother who offers himself in place of the king-victim) and does not in reality belong to a particular period or instance. See, Frazer, *Golden Bough*, Pt. III, p. 160 seq. Also *Secret History of the Mongols*, Ch. XIV, 14.

[2] The king's personal name was taboo.

17

establish as best you might your sons and grandsons here on earth below. The people of the four quarters all worship and fear you. Do not frustrate the treasured mission that Heaven put upon you, and you too, O former kings, shall for ever find shelter and support.[1] I shall now ask the Great Tortoises[2] to tell me your decision. If you accept me instead of the king, I will dedicate[3] to you this disc of jade and this tablet of jade, and go home to await your command. But if you do not accept me, I shall hide away the tablet and the disc." He then consulted the three tortoises[4] and each was doubly favourable. He opened the locked-place and inspected the book of omens. This too was favourable. Then the duke of Chou said: "All is well! The king will come to no harm. I have secured a fresh mandate from the three former kings; we may make plans for an age-long futurity. Only wait; and you will see that to me they have certainly given heed." The duke of Chou went home and deposited the record of his prayer in a casket with metal clamps. By next day the king had recovered.'

The passage that I want to set in contrast to this is from *Mencius*: 'The Bull Mountain was once covered with lovely trees. But it is near the capital of a great state. People came with their axes and choppers; they cut the woods down, and the mountain has lost its beauty. Yet

[1] From the sacrifices and offerings of your descendants.

[2] Oracles were obtained from the tortoise by producing cracks in the shell by means of a red-hot stick or rod. These cracks were then interpreted as omens. Tortoise-divination is also practised in Africa. See H. A. Junod: *The Life of a S. African Tribe*, 2nd edit. 1927, II, 549.

[3] Here I follow Ku Chieh-kang, see *Ku Shih Pien* II, 69.

[4] One for each ancestor.

even so, the day air and the night air came to it, rain and dew moistened it. Here and there fresh sprouts began to grow. But soon cattle and sheep came along and broused on them, and in the end the mountain became gaunt and bare, as it is now. And seeing it thus gaunt and bare people imagine that it was woodless from the start. Now just as the natural state of the mountain was quite different from what now appears, so too in every man (little though they may be apparent) there assuredly were once feelings of decency and kindness; and if these good feelings are no longer there, it is that they have been tampered with, hewn down with axe and bill. As each day dawns they are assailed anew. What chance then has our nature, any more than that mountain, of keeping its beauty? To us too, as to the mountain, comes the air of day, the air of night. Just at dawn, indeed, we have for a moment and in a certain degree a mood in which our promptings and aversions come near to being such as are proper to men. But something is sure to happen before the morning is over, by which these better feelings are either checked or perhaps utterly destroyed. And in the end, when they have been checked again and again, the night air is no longer able to preserve them, and soon our feelings are as near as may be to those of beasts and birds; so that any one might make the same mistake about us as about the mountain, and think that there was never any good in us from the very start. Yet assuredly our present state of feeling is not what we began with. Truly,[1]

"If rightly tended, no creature but thrives;
    If left untended, no creature but pines away."

[1] See Add. Notes on Chapter I.

Confucius said:

> "Hold fast to it and you can keep it,
> Let go, and it will stray.
> For its comings and goings it has no time nor tide;
> None knows where it will bide."

Surely it was of the feelings[1] that he was speaking?'

    I have started with these two passages because they seem to me to represent, typically and forcibly, two contrasting attitudes towards life, and what I want to give some idea of in this introduction is the interplay of these two attitudes and the gradual victory[2] of the second over the first. The passage from the *Book of History* belongs to what has been called the pre-moral phase of society. All societies of which we know passed through such a stage. All the 'moral' words (virtue, righteousness, kindness, nobility), unless they are recent formations, had quite other meanings earlier in their history. 'Moral' itself of course simply meant 'customary', as did also the Greek *dikaios* (righteous). *Virtus* originally meant the inherent power in a person or thing; which is very different from what we mean by virtue. *Nobilis* meant belonging to a particular class of society. *Gentilis* did not mean 'gentle', but belonging to a certain group of families. Pre-moral is merely a negative name. It is more difficult to find a positive one, but I have got into the habit of thinking about this phase

[1] i.e. the innate good feelings.

[2] The essence of the 'moral' attitude is that it regards good as an end in itself, apart from rewards either immediate or contingent. Such a view has of course never been held in a pure and undiluted form save by small minorities. Christianity itself, with its deferred rewards, and Buddhism too, both represent a compromise.

of society as the 'auguristic-sacrificial'; for its tendency is to make thought centre largely round the twin occupations of augury and sacrifice. These however are merely means towards a further end, the maintenance of communication between Heaven and Earth. It is easy enough to see what Earth means. It means the people who dwell on earth. Now Heaven too (in China, at any rate) is a collective term and means the people who dwell in Heaven, just as the House of Lords frequently means the people who sit in that House. These 'people in Heaven' are the ancestors (*ti*) and they are ruled over by the 'supreme ancestor' (*shang ti*), first of the ancestral line. They know the whole past of the tribe and therefore can calculate its whole future; by means of augury it is possible to use their knowledge. They live in Heaven; thence comes the weather, which is 'Heaven's mood', and it is wise to share with them all such things as depend for their growth on Heaven's good mood.

Into this outlook there enters no notion of actions or feelings that are good in themselves. People of the tenth century B.C. would assuredly have been at a complete loss to understand what Mencius (in the second half of the third century B.C.) meant by his passionate and moving plea for the theory that 'man is by nature good'. Goodness, to these early people, meant obtaining lucky omens, keeping up the sacrifices (and unless the omens were favourable no sacrifice could be carried out); goodness meant conformity to the way of Heaven, that is to say, to the way of the Ancestors collectively; it meant the possession of the 'power' (*tê*) that this conformity brings. What possible meaning could it have to say that man is 'born good'?

The Way and its Power

In order to give an idea of the contrast between these two opposing phases of thought, I have chosen two characteristic passages. I want now to go back and examine each of these phases rather more closely. The world of omens and magic ritual to which the Honan oracle-bones[1] and the *Book of Changes*[2] introduce us is one with which we are already familiar in Babylonia.[3] Things that happen are divided into two classes: the things that man does on purpose and the things that 'happen of themselves'. All the latter class of things (not only in ancient but also in modern China, among the peasants, as indeed among the remoter rural populations all over the world) is ominous. 'Feelings' in different parts of the body,[4] stumbling, twitching, itching, sneezing, buzzing in the ears, trembling in the eyelids, unaccountable movements of pliant objects held in the hand—all are 'communications' from Heaven, from the Ancestors. Then there is, apart from the class of omens connected with one's own person, the whole rich category of outside omens—signs given by birds, insects, animals, thunder and lightning, the stars.[5]

[1] The best general account of these is given by W. Perceval Yetts, *Journal of the Royal Asiatic Society*, July, 1933, pp. 657-685. The inscriptions, only a small proportion of which have been interpreted, date from the 12th and 11th centuries B.C. They are the oldest Chinese writing which survives.

[2] See my article in the *Bulletin of the Museum of Far Eastern Antiquities*, Stockholm, No. 5.

[3] See Jastrow, *Religion Babyloniens und Assyriens*.

[4] *Changes* §31.

[5] The formation of the Chinese script and the evidence of early literature suggest that astrology, i.e. the linking of human fate to the motions of the stars, came comparatively late and was due to foreign influence. See Maspero, *La Chine Antique*, p. 615.

Introduction

Birds are, of course, the intermediaries between heaven and earth. But they are also the great voyagers and know what is happening to human travellers in distant parts. It is above all the wild-goose that in the *Book of Changes*, in the *Odes* and all through the subsequent course of Chinese literature, is appealed to for omens concerning the absent. Of insects the most informative is the ant (*i*) because of its 'morality' (*i*) in the primitive sense of the word—its 'orderliness' in corporate movement, and also because of its uncanny foreknowledge of weather conditions.[1] Of animals the most ominous is the swine. Indeed a large number of the Chinese characters denoting movement ('to drive out', 'to follow', 'to retreat') contain the element 'swine'. A herd of swine with white trotters crossing a stream is a portent of heavy rain.[2]

Of all elements in ritual 'none is more important than sacrifice'.[3] Constantly in early Chinese literature the maintenance of offerings to the ancestors is represented as the ultimate aim of all social institutions. A country that is unable to keep up these offerings has lost its existence. The importance of sacrifice in early China is again reflected both in the written characters and in the language. Hundreds of common words and characters in everyday use at the present time owe their origin to sacrifice and the rituals connected with it. I will give only one example. The word now written 'heart' *plus* 'blood' originally meant to draw blood from a sacrificial animal. If it bled freely, this meant that the ancestors accepted the sacrifice.

[1] If the ants come up out of their holes at Christmas there will be no further snowfall till Epiphany, say the Alpine peasants.

[2] *Odes* No. 232. [3] *Li Chi*, 25, beginning. The references are to the *Li Chi Chi Shuo* arrangement, in 49 books.

Hence, by metaphor, if one's sufferings drew a response from other people, these people were said to 'bleed' for one, in fact, to 'sympathize', which is the only meaning that the word now has. There were a host of other rituals, the nature of which is no longer clear. The Oracle Bones teem with names of rites which have not been identified.[1]

About 400 B.C.[2] or perhaps earlier a changed attitude towards sacrifice and divination begins to appear; as shown by arguments in the *Tso Chuan*,[3] put into the mouths of people who lived in very early days, but certainly reflecting a much later state of feelings: the object of sacrifice is to prove to the ancestors that their descendants are prospering. Until practical steps have been taken to make the people prosper, there should be no sacrifices. Man, it is argued comes first, the spirits second; just as 'man is near, but heaven far away'. The ritualists of the Confucian school, perhaps about 300 B.C. or earlier, go a great deal further. 'Sacrifice', says the *Li Chi*,[4] 'is not something that comes from outside. It is something that comes from inside, being born in our hearts (feelings); when the heart is uneasy, we support it with ritual.' 'Sacrifice', says Hsün Tzŭ[5] (quoting from an earlier document),

[1] I have dealt with the *hêng* ceremony, by means of which luck was 'stabilized' in my paper on the *Book of Changes*. See above, p. 22. I could now add fresh evidence on the subject.

[2] Certain passages in the *Analects* seem to regard sacrifice as only of subjective importance, e.g. III, 12.

[3] Duke Huan, 6th year; Duke Chao, 18th year.

[4] Ch. 25.

[5] *P'ien* 19, end. c.f. *Kuan Tzŭ*, 2: 'neither sacrifice nor the offering of tablets of jade and discs of jade are in themselves enough to content the spirits of the dead'.

'is a state of mind in which our thoughts turn with longing (towards Heaven, the Ancestors). It is the supreme expression of loyalty, love and respect. It is the climax of all those ritual prescriptions which we embody in patterned (*wên*) behaviour. Only a Sage can understand its real significance. It is for gentlemen and nobles quietly to carry out, for officers of state to protect it, for the common people to make it part of their common usage. The nobles know well enough that it belongs to the way of man. Only common people regard it as a service rendered to spirits of the dead.'

The attitude towards divination underwent a similar change. 'If the ruler', says *Kuan Tzŭ*,[1] 'relies on the tortoise and the divining-stalks, if he is partial to the use of shamans[2] and magicians, the result will merely be that ghosts and spirits will get into the habit of "entering into" people.' That it is not enough to receive a good omen, that one must annex it to oneself by some further ritual is a view that was certainly held in ancient China; and I imagine that parallels could be found elsewhere. Gradually, however, as we advance into the moralistic period, we find a new theory being developed: omens mean quite different things according to whether they appear to good or to bad people. 'I have heard that, though good omens are the forerunners of heavenly blessings, if one sees a good omen and then acts wickedly, the blessings will not come. So too bad omens are the forerunners of disaster. But if one sees a bad omen and acts

---

[1] *P'ien* 3.

[2] *Wu*, who performed ecstatic dances, being 'possessed' by the spirits of the dead.

virtuously, no disaster will ensue.'¹ To give these words the requisite authority they are, in accordance with an invariable Chinese practice, put into the mouth of an ancient worthy—the founder of the Shang dynasty whom we may place somewhere about the 17th century B.C. *Han Fei Tzŭ*,² in the great litany which enumerates the forty-seven causes that can bring a state to decay says: 'If a kingdom use hours and days (i.e. believes in lucky and unlucky times), if it serves ghosts and spirits, if it puts trust in divination by the tortoise or by the yarrow-stalks and loves sacrifices and intercessions it will surely decay.'

I have spoken of the shaman being 'possessed' by spirits. But there was another functionary, far more regularly connected with Chinese ritual, in whom the Ancestors, the 'royal guests' at the sacrificial banquet, habitually took their abode. This was the *shih*, the medium (literally, 'corpse') who sitting silent and composed, represented the ancestor to whom the sacrifice was made, or at funerals played the role of the dead man. Now this sort of 'medium' does not, so far as I know, form part, in other ancient civilizations, of the ritual pattern connected with sacrifice; and it is possible that this is a case of the extension of funeral ritual to the sacrificial cult of the dead. But there is no doubt about the antiquity of the custom. The medium appears not only in the ritual-books, which are records not so much of actual practice as of controversies between rival schools of ritualistic theoreticians, but also in the *Book of Odes*, one of the most unquestion-

¹ *Lü Shih Ch'un Ch'iu*, P'ien 29, beginning. There is a good translation of *Lü Shih Ch'un Ch'iu* by Richard Wilhelm. Jena. 1928.
² P'ien 15. Written in the 3rd century B.C.

ably ancient of Chinese sources. The great Chu Hsi, in
the 12th century A.D., even went so far as to say that a
medium was used in all sacrifices whether to nature-
spirits or to ancestors;[1] though he was puzzled as to
whether one was ever used in sacrificing to Heaven-and-
Earth.[2] The early Chinese, then, were accustomed to the
idea of spirits entering into human beings, and in the
moralistic period the idea began to grow up that such
spirits, if their new abode were made sufficiently attractive, might be induced to stay in it permanently, or at least
during periods other than those of sacrificial ritual. Hence
grew up the idea of 'soul', of a god or spirit more or less
permanently dwelling inside an individual. Several words
competed for this new meaning: One of them was *T'ien*,
'Heaven', 'The Abode of the Ancestors'. For example,
'Restrict your appetites and needs, abandon knowledge
and scheming, put away all crafty calculations; let your
thoughts wander in the abode of the Inexhaustible, set
your heart upon the path of that which is so-of-itself, do
this and your "heaven" shall be safe from destruction.'[3]
Or the parallel passage in *Chuang Tzŭ*:[4] 'Wander to where
the ten thousand things both begin and end, unify your
nature, foster your life-breath, concentrate your "power"[5]
till it is one with the force that created all things after
their kind—do this, and your "heaven" shall maintain its
integrity.'

[1] Quoted in *I Li I Su*, XXXIV, 14.
[2] His hesitation was well justified, for the conception of Heaven-
and-Earth as a kind of joint, twin deity is a late one. For a further
discussion of the *shih* (medium) see additional notes.
[3] *Lü Shih Ch'un Ch'iu*, P'ien 14.
[4] XIX. 2.   [5] See below, p. 31.

Another word that often comes near to meaning 'soul' is *ch'i*, the word that I have translated 'life-breath' in the passage just quoted. Originally it means a vapour that rises out of anything. As written to-day it means literally 'the vapour that rises from cooked grain'. The weather is heaven's *ch'i*; the essences (or 'spirits' as we often say) of herbs and drugs are their *ch'i*. *Ch'i* is the air. Man receives a portion of it at birth, and this is his life-breath, the source of energy, the motive-power of the senses. Another word often translated soul is *hun*, the 'cloud' that comes out of the mouth on frosty mornings. When the dualist theory became dominant in China and everything had to be classified in pairs of male and female, the *hun* became the male soul, mounting to heaven when a man died; while *p'o*, which originally meant the semen,[1] becomes the female soul, which lodges in the tomb. The word which however in the end won the day, and may be said to be, from the beginning of the Christian era onwards, the most ordinary word for soul, is *shên*. It comes from a root meaning 'to stretch'. The spirits of the dead were called 'stretchers' because they had the power to cause easy parturition, to stretch the womb. The word for thunder was written in early times with the same character as *shên*; for thunder was, in early times, as our own language attests,[2] considered to be the stretcher *par excellence*.[3]

The spirits of the dead, then, honourably called

[1] This meaning was retained by the word, in non-philosophic parlance, till modern times. See the story about hanged men in *Pên Ts'ao Kang Mu* LII (16th century).

[2] 'Thunder' is akin to Latin *tonitrus*, which, in turn, is cognate to τόνος, 'stretched string', and τείνειν, 'to stretch'.

[3] I feel now (1948) some doubt about these etymologies.

'stretchers' (*shên*), are 'nourished' by sacrifices and offerings, and at the time of the sacrifice they enter into the medium, but only as guests. The idea that a *shên* could be a permanent part of a living person's inner equipment does not occur, I think, till the 3rd century B.C.[1] Even so, we are still far from the complete conception of the soul as a kind of twin to the body. To begin with, the word in its subjective sense is used almost exclusively in connection with sages and rulers, and it is not at all clear that ordinary people were supposed to possess a *shên*.[2] 'If the monarch loses his *shên*', says *Han Fei Tzŭ*, 'the tigers[3] will soon be on his tracks.'[4]

'The Sages of old', says the *Lü Shih Ch'un Ch'iu*,[5] meaning of course legendary ancient rulers like Yao and Shun, 'did not injure their souls by petty feelings about private matters; they sat quietly and waited.'

I have still a number of other words to discuss. The reader will perhaps at this point begin to wonder whether I have lost sight of my original purpose in writing this introductory essay and have, owing to a predisposition towards philology, forgotten Chinese thought and slipped into writing a treatise on the Chinese language. I can only say that I see no other way of studying the history of thought except by first studying the history of words, and such a study would seem to me equally necessary if I were dealing with the Greeks, the Romans, the Egyptians, the

---

[1] Legge once gives *shên* a subjective sense in the *Tso Chuan* (p. 382), but this is clearly a mistranslation. There is no example in *Mencius*.

[2] In *Han Fei*, P'ien 20, an ordinary philosopher is spoken of as 'wearing out his soul'. But there are reasons for supposing that this section is late. cf. Appendix VI.

[3] i.e. his political opponents.

[4] *Han Fei*, P'ien 8.   [5] P'ien 119

Hebrews, or any other people. For example, in reading the Bible, whether for edification or literary pleasure, we do not trouble to enquire whether abstract words like 'righteousness' mean the same thing all through the Old Testament, or whether (as I should certainly expect) they mean something quite different in the more primitive parts of the Pentateuch from what they mean in the later prophets. Nor do we pause to ask what the different words rendered by 'soul', 'spirit' and so on really meant to the people who used them. But anyone studying the history of Hebrew thought would be bound to ask himself these questions, and I cannot think that it is superfluous to ask them with regard to Chinese. I will confine myself here, however, to three further words, all of which occur frequently in the *Tao Tê Ching*. The first is the word *tao* itself. It means a road, path, way; and hence, the way in which one does something; method, principle, doctrine. The Way of Heaven, for example, is ruthless; when autumn comes 'no leaf is spared because of its beauty, no flower because of its fragrance'. The Way of Man means, among other things, procreation; and eunuchs are said to be 'far from the Way of Man'. *Chu Tao* is 'the way to be a monarch', i.e. the art of ruling. Each school of philosophy had its *tao*, its doctrine of the way in which life should be ordered. Finally in a particular school of philosophy whose followers ultimately came to be called Taoists, *tao* meant 'the way the universe works'; and ultimately, something very like God, in the more abstract and philosophical sense of that term.

Now it so happens that all the meaning-extensions of this word *tao* (even including the last: 'I am the Way') also exist in European languages, so that Western scholars have had no difficulty in understanding it. The same cannot be said of another, equally important term, *tê*. It is usually translated 'virtue', and this often seems to work quite well; though where the word occurs in early, pre-moralistic texts such a translation is in reality quite false. But if we study the usage of the word carefully we find that *tê* can be bad as well as good. What is a 'bad virtue'? Clearly 'virtue' is not a satisfactory equivalent. Indeed, on examining the history of the word we find that it means something much more like the Indian *karma*, save that the fruits of *tê* are generally manifested here and now; whereas *karma* is bound up with a theory of transmigration, and its effects are usually not seen in this life, but in a subsequent incarnation. *Tê* is anything that happens to one or that one does of a kind indicating that, as a consequence, one is going to meet with good or bad luck. It means, so to speak, the stock of credit (or the deficit) that at any given moment a man has at the bank of fortune. Such a stock is of course built up partly by the correct carrying out of ritual; but primarily by securing favourable omens; for unless the omens are favourable, no rite can be carried out at all.

But the early Chinese also regarded the planting of seeds as a *tê*. The words 'to plant' (ancient Chinese, *dhyek*) and *tê* (anciently *tek*) are cognate, and in the earliest script they share a common character.[1] Thus *tê* is bound up with the idea of potentiality. Fields planted with corn represent potential riches; the appearance of a rainbow, potential disaster; the falling of 'sweet dew', potential

[1] See Takata, *Kochūhen*, under the character *tê*.

peace and prosperity. Hence *tê* means a latent power, a 'virtue' inherent in something.

Only when the moralistic position was thoroughly established, that is to say, after the doctrines of Confucianism had become a State orthodoxy,[1] did *tê*, at any rate among the upper classes, come to mean what we usually mean by virtue, that is to say, conduct beautiful and admirable in itself (as a work of art is beautiful) apart from its consequences.

The last of these 'moral' words with which I propose to deal is *i*[2] 'morality', perhaps the most important of them all. '*I*' means what is right, proper, fitting, decent; what one would expect under the circumstances; what is, as we should say, 'in order'. In 542 B.C. a noble lady was burnt to death in a palace fire owing to the fact that she would not leave the house until a chaperon could be found to escort her. Such conduct, says the historian, would have been proper in the case of a young girl; but a married woman (in this case a quite elderly one) would certainly not have been blamed for acting as was 'reasonable under the circumstances' (*i*)[3]. Or again, 'To drink only as much as is necessary to fulfil the rites and not to continue the feast till it becomes a riot—that is *i*'.[4]

But in the period centring round 300 B.C. the question[5] was asked, is not the conduct that we call *i* (moral) merely

[1] Say, from the 1st cent. A.D. onwards; but *tê* has never entirely shed its old pre-moralistic meanings, any more than our word 'virtue' had entirely discarded the sense of 'inherent power'.

[2] Giles: Nos. 5354 and 5454, which are merely two different ways of writing the same word.

[3] *Tso Chuan*, Duke Hsiang, 30th year.

[4] *Tso Chuan*, Duke Chuang, 22nd year.   [5] *Mencius*, VI. 1. 5.

the outward expression of a feeling about what is right
and wrong, and is it not this feeling, rather than the outward manifestation of it, that we ought to call morality?
Thus just as the words for soul, spirit, etc., had begun
their career as names for outside things, and ended by
being names for parts of man's interior, psychological
equipment, so the word *i*, which at first meant little more
than sensible, reasonable conduct, came in the end to mean
something very like 'conscience'. Man, indeed, was dis-
covering that he was a much more interesting creature
than he had supposed. There dwelt inconspicuously within him a strange thing called a soul, which was of the
same nature as the venerated Ancestors in Heaven, as the
spirits of the rivers, hills and groves. There was moreover, buried in his heart, a mysterious power which, if he
would but use it, enabled him to distinguish between
these two new classes into which he now divided everything—the morally-good and the morally-bad—to discriminate with a sense as unerring as that which enabled
him to tell the sweet from the bitter, the light from the
dark. Never in the most ancestor-fearing days, when
Heaven had an eye that saw all, an ear that heard all, had
it been suggested that the whole universe lay, concentrated as it were, inside the Supreme Ancestor or any one
of the Dead Kings. Yet this was the claim that Mencius
made for common man. 'The ten thousand things', he
says, meaning the whole cosmos, 'are there complete,
inside us.'[1]

[1] For the connection of Mencius with the Ch'i school of Taoism, see
below. Such passages have of course been explained away by the Confucians. Legge, though he follows the official interpretation, does so

Man on earth, then, so far from being a pale shadow of
the Ancestors, possesses within himself all the attributes
that in ancient times made the cult of the Former Kings
the supreme end of all tribal activity. · It was to himself,
as the possessor of 'heavenliness', of 'spirit', of the mysterious sense called *i* which enabled him, without con-
sulting yarrow-stalks or the tortoise, to discriminate
between right and wrong—it was to himself that each
man owed the worship and veneration that had once been
accorded to Heaven, the home of the Dead Kings. And
since the cult of the Ancestors was the main common
activity of the State at large, it followed that the transference of this cult to the individual left the State with a
sphere of action greatly limited, indeed, according to one
School,[1] reduced to nil. A perfect community, these
philosophers argued, implies perfect individuals. Let each
man perfect himself. If the State asks from him one single
act that interferes with this process of self-perfection, he
should refuse, not merely on his own account, but out
of regard for the community which corporately suffers in
as far as one of its members is 'imperfect'. 'The men of
old[2] would not have given one hair of their bodies to help
the State. Nor if every one in the State (hair by hair and

with some misgiving, remarking that the passage seems 'quite
mystical'.

[1] That of Yang Chu. See *Lieh Tzǔ* VII, which is however not an
official account, by the Yang Chu school itself, of the master's teachings, but a late hearsay account in which the original teachings of
Yang Chu are mixed up with the hedonistic doctrine which grew up
in one branch of his school. The polemic references to Yang Chu in
Mencius are mere parody.

[2] New theories were always put forward as revivals of ancient practice. See Appendix I.

34

joint by joint) had sacrificed themselves for them, would they have been willing to accept such a sacrifice. For it is only when every one in the State is whole and perfect down to the last hair and each individual attends to himself and stops thinking about benefiting the State, that the State is itself sound.'[1]

But the divine faculties of man, which make it a sacrilege to demand from him the surrender of even 'one hair from his leg', maintain a precarious existence. The *shên* (soul) is like a grandee on his travels.[2] If the inn is not well managed and tidy, he will not stay there. How, then, can the body be made a fit dwelling-place for the soul? Or if we regard the soul not as something that comes and goes but rather as a faculty fettered and impeded by the stress of daily life,[3] how can we ensure its freedom? Traditional experience concerning the behaviour of *shên*, of divinities, suggested that the first essential was abstinence and fasting. In the old sacrificial life[4] it had been regarded as useless to expect the Royal Guests (the dead kings) to descend in their spirit (*shên*) form and partake of the sacrifice, unless the sacrificer had first prepared himself by three days abstinence and fasting.[5] The term *chai* (abstinence and fasting) implied the curbing of all sensual and physical activities. The exercise, then, of any of the

[1] *Lieh Tzǔ* VII. 9. [2] *Kuan Tzǔ*, P'ien 36, beginning. [3] As in *Mencius*.
[4] I do not of course mean that sacrifice had totally disappeared, but only that it had lost its significance to the thinking classes.
[5] The original purpose of fasting was of course not self-purification (which is a relatively late, moralistic idea) but the desire to 'move the hearts' of the Ancestors. Carried to its logical conclusion it can include self-mutilation and self-disfigurement of all kinds. It was in the same spirit that suppliants to earthly potentates disfigured themselves, poured ashes on their heads, etc.

senses, whether of sight, smell, taste or hearing, the use of any sinew or limb, was regarded as a potential menace to the soul. If this menace were physical, if it were directly observable, we should all be sages. 'Suppose there were some sound which, when the ear heard it, was agreeable but which caused the ear afterwards to go deaf, we should take good care not to listen to it. Suppose there were some colour which, when the eye saw it, was agreeable but which caused blindness to follow, we should take good care not to look at it.'[1] Unhappily the wrong use of the senses is deleterious in a far subtler way; in as far then as government of any kind is needed, in a state where each person is privately perfecting his own inner nature, it will consist in the presence among the people of 'better people' who will tell them which physical satisfactions are dangerous and which profitable to the 'life within'. But these 'better people' (*hsien*) must not form a separate class supported by the labour of others, and so allowing themselves to be 'completed' at the expense of other people's 'incompleteness'. It was, I think, ideas of this kind that inspired the followers of Hsü Hsing, who dressed in coarse haircloth, wore hemp sandals instead of leather shoes and supported themselves by weaving mats; the people whom Mencius rebuked by quoting the saying: 'Some work with their minds, others with their bodies. Those who work with the mind rule; those who work with the body are ruled. Those who are ruled feed their rulers; those who rule, feed upon those they rule.' 'Which', Mencius added, 'is accepted as common sense by every one under heaven.' Sects of this kind naturally

[1] *Lü Shih Ch'un Ch'iu*, P'ien 2.

travelled about trying to find a milieu that would be sympathetic to their doctrines. Hsü Hsing and his followers had, when interviewed by Mencius,[1] already trekked some four hundred miles. If unsuccessful in this quest they settled in some remote spot outside the sphere of governmental interference. The literature of the 3rd century B.C. is full of references to recluses, people who 'lived among rocks or in holes in the ground' and 'even if they were offered salaried employments would not accept them'.[2]

'A ruler', says *Kuan Tzǔ*,[3] 'should not listen to those who believe in people having opinions of their own and in the importance of the individual. Such teachings cause men to withdraw to quiet places and hide away in caves or on mountains, there to rail at the prevailing government, sneer at those in authority, belittle the importance of rank and emoluments, and despise all who hold official posts'. As we have seen, the real reason why such persons refused to draw official salaries and insisted on living in their own way on the fruit of their own labour was that they thought society should consist of individuals each complete in himself, and it was against their consciences to be supported by 'hairs' drawn from the suffering head of the community at large. A certain Ch'ên Chung was a scrupulous recluse of this class. He belonged to an important family in the land of Ch'i (now part of Shantung). His ancestors had held high office for many generations on end, and his elder brother administered a fief from which

[1] Actually, their views were transmitted to Mencius by an intermediary.

[2] *Han Fei Tzǔ*, 45 and 49.   [3] P'ien 65.

he received a revenue of 10,000 *chung*.[1] As it was against Ch'ên Chung's principles to live on what he regarded as ill-gotten gains, he left his brother's house and set up at a remote place called Wu-ling. Here he supported himself by making hemp-sandals, his wife twisting the hemp-thread. Their livelihood was very precarious and on one occasion Ch'ên had nothing to eat for three days. 'His ears no longer heard, his eyes no longer saw.' But he knew that on a tree by the well-side there was a plum, half eaten by maggots. In desperation he groped his way to the spot, gulped the plum down, and so recovered his sight and hearing.

Once when he was staying for a while at his brother's house someone sent the family a live goose as a present. 'What use can they suppose you could make of a cackling thing like that?' Ch'ên Chung asked, frowning. A few days later his mother killed the goose and not telling him what it was gave him some for his dinner. 'I suppose you know what it is you are eating,' said his brother, coming into the room. 'That's cackle-cackle's flesh!' Ch'ên went out into the courtyard and vomited.

We might be tempted to think that Ch'ên Chung was, among his other scrupulosities, a vegetarian. But I do not think that is the point of the story. He regarded the goose, which was no doubt a gift from one of the tenants,

[1] A tenth of the revenue of a prime minister. The story of Ch'ên Chung will be found in *Mencius*, III. 2. 10. He is said also to have worked as a gardener (*Shih Chi*, 83, end). A collection of anecdotes concerning him, entitled *Wu-ling Tzŭ*, made its appearance in the 16th century, and is in all probability the work of Hsü Wei (Wên-ch'ang), 1520-1593. The surname Ch'ên was pronounced T'ien in the Ch'i state, and he is therefore sometimes called T'ien Chung.

as part of his brother's ill-gotten gains; hence his disapproval of the arrival of 'cackle-cackle' and his nausea at the thought of having partaken of such a dish.[1]

The Hedonists

The transference of attention from the dead to the living, from heaven to earth, was due not merely to the discovery that 'of all things Man is the most spirit-fraught (*ling*)', but also to a doubt whether the dead, even if they could be said in any sense to exist beyond the grave, were conscious of what happened on earth. *Mo Tzŭ*[2] devotes a chapter to the confutation of those who believe that the dead do not 'exist' and that consequently sacrifices and libations are a waste of time and food. 'It is no waste at all,' replies Mo Tzŭ, 'even admitting that there are no such things as spirits of the dead. One might call it waste indeed, if the wine and so on were merely poured into the gutter. But in point of fact, the members of the family and friends in the village all get their share, so that, at worst, sacrificing makes an excuse for bringing people together and helps us to get on to better terms with our neighbours.' This view of religion as a social bond (modern supporters of this theory are able to point to the supposed etymology of the word religion—'a binding together') is highly sophisticated. But elsewhere we find a doubt as to the consciousness of the dead side by side with

[1] A great many stories of hermits and recluses could be cited from *Chuang Tzŭ* and *Lieh Tzŭ*, but most of them are more or less in the nature of fairy-tales.

[2] P'ien 31, which probably represents the views of the Mo school c. 300 B.C. *Mo Tzŭ* has been translated into German by Alfred Forke and (part only) into English by Y. P. Mei, 1926.

the mention of very primitive practices. In 265 B.C. the wife of the former ruler of Ch'in lay dying. She was greatly attached to a stranger from the Wei state, and gave orders that he was to be sacrificed at her funeral, in order that his spirit might escort her beyond the grave. The stranger from Wei was much upset, and a friend interviewed the dying lady on his behalf, saying: 'Do you believe that the dead are conscious?' 'I do not think they are,' she said. 'If the spirit (*shên*) immanent within you indeed knows clearly that the dead are not conscious, then what possible good can it do you, great lady, that one whom you loved in life should go with you into a state where there is no consciousness? If on the other hand the dead are conscious, a fine rage the late king will be in! "Here's the queen," he will say, "who has been hovering between life and death for months past, arriving with a man from Wei! She can't have been quite as ill all the time as she led people to suppose." ' The queen said 'How true!' and desisted.[1]

The idea that morality is merely the desire to be thought well of, and that the dead do not know what we think about them, with the natural inference that it is best to get all that we can out of life, without worrying about what sort of reputation we leave behind, is attributed to the Hedonists by *Lieh Tzŭ*:[2] the whole admiration of the world is concentrated upon four paragons, Shun, the

[1] *Chan Kuo Ts'ê*, III. 52.

[2] VII. 10, end. Shun was a culture-hero, who wore himself out ploughing and potting. The Great Yü battled against the Floods. For the Duke of Chou, see above, p. 17. Legend makes Confucius the subject of a long series of insults and persecutions, due to the unpopularity of his teaching.

Introduction

Great Yü, the Duke of Chou and Confucius; yet it would be hard to imagine sorrier objects of admiration. These men led dismal and laborious lives under the impression that they were benefiting mankind and would win its eternal praises. The praise is there; but for all the difference it makes to them they might as well be clods of earth or stumps of trees. So, for that matter, might the 'bad' kings Chieh and Chou, upon whom every sort of abuse is heaped. But they at least made the most of life while it lasted, building glorious palaces, feasting far into the night, unhampered by any scruples about seemliness or morality.

The doctrine of these hedonists was called *yang-shêng*, 'nourishing the living'[1] as opposed to nourishing the dead. What most 'nourishes life' is happiness, and what leads to happiness is the freedom to satisfy desire. The ruler's duty, then (and every Chinese philosophy is formulated not as an abstract theory but as an 'art of ruling') is to give free play to every desire, whether of the body or of the mind: 'Let the ear hear what it longs to hear, the eye see what it longs to see, the nose smell what it likes to smell, the mouth speak what it wants to speak, let the body have every comfort that it craves, let the mind do as it will. Now what the ear wants to hear is music,[2] and to deprive it of this is to cramp the sense of hearing. What the eye

[1] This was, I think the earliest sense of the term. The Confucians used it in the sense of 'nurturing the living' (i.e. one's parents), as opposed to 'nurturing the dead' (i.e. sacrifice to the ancestors). *Yang-shêng* is however often taken in the subjective sense of 'nourishing one's own life', i.e. fostering one's vital energy.

[2] The Confucians discouraged all such music as was not morally uplifting; the school of Mo Tzŭ forbade music altogether.

wants to see is carnal beauty; and to deprive it is to cramp
the sense of sight. What the nose craves for is to have
near it the fragrant plants *shu* and *lan*; and if it cannot
have them, the sense of smell is cramped. What the
mouth desires is to speak of what is true and what false;
and if it may not speak, then knowledge is cramped.
What the body desires for its comfort is warmth and good
food. Thwart its attainment of these, and you cramp
what is natural and essential to man. What the mind
wants is the liberty to stray whither it will, and if it has
not this freedom, the very nature of man is cramped and
thwarted. Tyrants and oppressors cramp us in every one
of these ways. Let us depose them, and wait happily for
death to come.'[1]

Such views must have gained considerable currency, for
we find them ranged alongside of the other principal doctrines of the day (such as those of Kung-sun Lung, the
pacificist, and Mo Tzŭ) in a denunciation of doctrines
prejudicial to good government. 'A ruler of men should
on no account encourage those who preach the doctrine of
"perfecting the individual life". For should he do so,
then all his ministers will apply themselves with alacrity
to perfecting their lives, which is the same thing as nurturing their lives. And what is this "life-nurturing"? It
consists in feasting, music and love. That is the way that
the followers of this doctrine set about "nurturing life".
To encourage them is to open up the way to licence and

---

[1] *Lieh Tzŭ* VII. 5. The same sentiments are attributed to the robber
Chê by *Chuang Tzŭ* XXIX. 1, end, and by *Hsün Tzŭ* to Tzŭ Mou,
prince of Wei, who wrote a book which unfortunately has not
survived.

Introduction

depravity, to abolish the separation of the sexes, and in fact to return to the condition of wild beasts.'[1]

Quietism

There was another sect that, though its way of life was exactly the opposite of that commended by the Hedonists, met with equally severe condemnation. *Han Fei Tzŭ*[2] speaks of people who 'walk apart from the crowd, priding themselves on being different from other men. They preach the doctrine of Quietism, but their exposition of it is couched in baffling and mysterious terms. I submit to your Majesty[3] that this Quietness is of no practical value to any one and that the language in which it is couched is not founded on any real principle . . . I submit that man's duty in life is to serve his prince and nourish his parents, neither of which things can be done by Quietness. I further submit that it is man's duty, in all that he teaches, to promote loyalty and good faith and the Legal Constitution. This cannot be done in terms that are vague and mysterious. The doctrine of the Quietists is a false one, likely to lead the people astray'.

How did this doctrine arise? We have seen the gradual inward-turning of Chinese thought, its preoccupation with self and the perfection of self. We have seen how out of the ritual preparation of the sacrificer for the reception of the descending spirit grew the idea of a cleansing of the heart which should make it a fit home for the soul.

[1] *Kuan Tzŭ*, 65. *Kuan Tzŭ* like *Lieh Tzŭ* identifies the 'perfecters of the individual life' with the Hedonists. It is clear that at any rate in popular imagination the Hedonists were an offshoot of the school of Yang Chu.
[2] P'ien 51.   [3] The king of Ch'in.

Such cleansing consisted above all in a 'stilling' of outward activities, of appetites and emotions; but also in a 'returning'; for the soul was looked upon as having become as it were silted up by successive deposits of daily toil and perturbation, and the business of the 'self-perfecter' was to work his way back through these layers till 'man as he was meant to be' was reached. Through this 'stillness', this complete cessation of outside impressions, and through the withdrawal of the senses to an entirely interior point of focus, arose the species of self-hypnosis which in China is called *Tso-wang*, 'sitting with blank mind', in India *Yoga*, *dhyāna* and other names ; in Japan, Zen. A definite technique was invented[1] for producing this state of trance. The main feature of this technique was, as in India, breath-manipulation—the breathing must be soft and light as that of an infant, or, as later Quietists said, of a child in the womb. There were also strange exercises of the limbs, stretchings and postures[2] much like the *āsanas* connected with Indian *yoga*; but some Quietists regarded these as too physical and concrete a method for the attainment of a spiritual end.

The process of Quietism, then, consisted in a travelling back through the successive layers of consciousness to the point when one arrived at Pure Consciousness, where one no longer saw 'things perceived', but 'that whereby we perceive'. For never to have known 'that whereby we know' is to cast away a treasure that is ours.[3] Soon on the 'way back' one comes to the point where language, created

[1] Or borrowed. See Appendix II.   [2] *Chuang Tzŭ*, XV. 1.
[3] *Lü Shih Ch'un Ch'iu*, 23.

44

to meet the demands of ordinary, upper consciousness, no longer applies. The adept who has reached this point has learnt, as the Quietists expressed it in their own secret language, 'to get into the bird-cage without setting the birds off singing'.[1]

Here a question arises, which is indeed one which Quietists have been called upon to answer in diverse parts of the world and at many widely separated periods of history. Granted that consciousness can actually be modified by *yoga*, self-hypnotism, Zen, Quietness or whatever else one chooses to call it, what evidence is there that the new consciousness has any advantage over the old? The Quietist, whether Chinese, Indian, German or Spanish, has always made the same reply: by such practices three things are attained, truth, happiness and power.

From the theoretical point of view there is of course no reason to believe that the statements of Tao are truer than those of ordinary knowledge; no more reason, in fact, than to believe that the music we hear when our radio is adjusted to 360 is any 'truer' than the music we hear when it is adjusted to 1600. But in actual practice the visions of the Quietist do not present themselves to him merely as more or less agreeable alternatives to everyday existence. They are accompanied by a sense of finality, by a feeling that 'all the problems which all the schools of philosophers under Heaven cannot settle this way or that have been settled this way or that'.[2] Moreover, the state to which the Quietist attains is not merely pleasurable

[1] *Chuang Tzŭ*, IV. 1. Pun on *fan*=(1) bird-cage (2) return, and on *ming*=(1) sing (2) name.

[2] *Chuang Tzŭ* XVIII. 1, end. *T'ien-hsia* ('under Heaven') means the various schools of philosophy.

rather than painful. It is 'absolute joy',[1] utterly transcending any form of earthly enjoyment. And finally, it gives as the Indians say *siddhi*, as the Chinese say *tê*, a power over the outside world undreamt of by those who pit themselves against matter while still in its thralls. Nor is this aspect of Quietism confined, as is sometimes supposed, to its eastern branches. 'Sin trabajo sujetaràs las gentes y te serviràn las cosas,' says St. John of the Cross in his Aphorisms, 'si te olvidares de ellas y de ti mismo.'[2] It is this last claim of Quietism—the belief that the practicant becomes possessed not merely of a power over living things (which we should call hypnotism) but also of a power to move and transform matter—that the world has been least disposed to accept. 'Try it (*yung chih*) and find out for yourself,' has been the Quietist's usual answer to the challenge 'show us, and we will believe'.

We know that many different schools of Quietism existed in China in the fourth and third centuries before Christ. Of their literature only a small part survives.[3] Earliest in date was what I shall call the School of Ch'i. Its doctrine was called *hsin shu* 'The Art of the Mind'.[4] By 'mind' is meant not the brain or the heart, but 'a mind within the mind' that bears to the economy of man the

[1] cf. ibidem, the whole chapter.

[2] Literally 'without labour you shall subject the peoples and things shall be subject to you, if you forget both them and yourself.'

[3] Perhaps more than we think; for it is by no means certain that *Chuang Tzŭ* does not contain teachings of several different schools. Thus it seems very probable that Chapter II represents the teaching T'ien P'ien.

[4] *Hsin* means 'heart' and 'mind'. In this system it is regarded as the repository of perceptions and knowledge, and therefore 'mind' seems more appropriate.

same relation as the sun bears to the sky.[1] It is the ruler of the body, whose component parts are its ministers.[2] It must remain serene and immovable like a monarch upon his throne. It is a *shên*, a divinity, that will only take up its abode where all is garnished and swept.[3] The place that man prepares for it is called its temple (*kung*). 'Throw open the gates, put self aside, bide in silence, and the radiance of the spirit shall come in and make its home.'[4] And a little later: 'Only where all is clean will the spirit abide. All men desire to know, but they do not enquire into that whereby one knows.' And again: 'What a man desires to know is *that* (i.e. the external world). But his means of knowing is *this* (i.e. himself). How can he know *that*? Only by the perfection of *this*.'

Closely associated with the 'art of the mind' is the art of nurturing the *ch'i*,[5] the life-spirit. Fear, pettiness, meanness—all those qualities that pollute the 'temple of the mind'—are due to a shrinkage of the life-spirit. The valiant, the magnanimous, the strong of will are those whose *ch'i* pervades the whole body, down to the very toes and finger-tips.[6] A great well of energy must be stored within, 'a fountain that never dries',[7] giving

---

[1] *Kuan Tzŭ*, P'ien 12, beginning. *Kuan Tzŭ* merely uses fragments of Taoist texts as a mystic background for opportunist teaching.

[2] *Kuan Tzŭ*, P'ien 36, beginning.

[3] The fact that the *shên* is here in a transitional state, half outside divinity, half a 'soul' makes me think that this system is earlier than that of the better-known Taoists, to whom Tao was never a thing that came from outside.

[4] Ibidem, P'ien 36.

[5] See above p. 28. *Ch'i* may always be translated breath, if we add the proviso that to the Chinese 'breath' was a kind of soul.

[6] *Kuan Tzŭ*, 49 end.   [7] *Ibidem*, 37 end.

strength and firmness to every sinew and joint. 'Store it within; make of it a well-spring, flood-like,[1] even and level. Make of it a very store-pool of *ch'i*.

Never till that pool runs dry shall the Four Limbs fail;
Nor till the well is exhausted shall the traffic of the
　　Nine Apertures cease.
Thereby[2] shall you be enabled to explore Heaven and
　　Earth,
Reach the Four Oceans that bound the world;
Within, have no thoughts that perplex,
Without, suffer no evil or calamity.
Inside, the mind shall be whole;
Whole too the bodily frame.'

All this is the work of the life-breath (*ling-ch'i*) that is within the 'mind'. For it can 'come and go where it will. Be so small that nothing could go inside it; so large that nothing exists beyond it. He alone loses it who harms it by perturbation'.

What is the nature of the perturbations that cause the loss of this 'mind within the mind?' These are defined as 'grief and joy, delight and anger, desire and greed for gain. Put all these away, and your mind ("heart" would fit this particular context better) will return to its purity. For such is the mind that only peace and stillness are good for it. Do not fret, do not let yourself be perturbed and the Accord[3] will come unsought. It is close at hand,

---

[1] *Kuan Tzŭ*, 49 end. This is the famous *hao-jan chih ch'i* of *Mencius*.

[2] By an accumulation of *ch'i*. I see no reason to doubt that the passages here quoted refer, in a cryptic way, to practises of breath-manipulation such as those described in Appendix III.

[3] Harmony between the mind and the universe, which gives power over outside things.

stands indeed at our very side; yet is intangible, a thing that by reaching for cannot be got. Remote it seems as the furthest limits of the Infinite. Yet it is not far off; every day we use its power. For Tao (i.e. the Way of the Vital Spirit) fills our whole frames, yet man cannot keep track of it. It goes, yet has not departed. It comes, yet is not here. It is muted, makes no note that can be heard, yet of a sudden we find that it is there in the mind. It is dim and dark, showing no outward form, yet in a great stream it flowed into us at our birth'.[1]

The branch of Confucianism founded by Mencius was profoundly influenced by the Ch'i-country Taoism which centred round the Art of the Mind and the tending of the Vital Spirit. In this there is nothing surprising, for Mencius spent much of his life in the country of Ch'i, now part of Shantung. Indeed, the passages in which *Mencius* deals with the acquisition of the Unmoved Mind and with the use of man's 'well-spring' of natal breath are unintelligible unless we relate them to the much fuller exposition of the same theories in *Kuan Tzŭ*. Mencius, as we know, learnt the art of maintaining an 'unmoved mind' at the age of forty,[2] that is to say on his arrival in the country of Ch'i, which happened about 330 B.C. When asked about the method that he employed, he replied[3] that he had cultivated the art of using his 'flood-like breath-spirit', obviously an allusion to the system described by *Kuan Tzŭ*. Mencius however gives his own turn to this doctrine. With him the 'flood-like spirit' is

---

[1] Ibidem, 49 beginning.   [2] *Mencius* II. 1. 2.

[3] The 'I understand words' that precedes this, belongs to par. 17, which deals with quite a different topic and has crept in here by mistake.

something that is produced cumulatively by the constant exercise of moral sense (*i*). But it can only come into existence as an accessory of such exercise. Its growth cannot be aided by any special discipline or régime. It is clear that Mencius is here combatting the ideas of the *yoga*-practitioners who performed particular exercises in order to 'expel the old (i.e. the used breath-spirit) and draw in the new'. Those who try to force the growth of the spirit by means other than the possession of a tranquil conscience he compares to the foolish man of Sung who, grieved that his crops came up so slowly, tried to help them by pulling at the stalks.[1]

Taoism

In the Ch'i system of Quietism the central conception is that of the 'mind within the mind', the sanctuary (*kung*) of the spirit. *Tao* is the way that those must walk who would 'achieve without doing'. But *tao* is not only a means, a doctrine, a principle. It is the ultimate reality in which all attributes are united, 'it is heavy as a stone, light as a feather'; it is the unity underlying plurality. 'It is that by losing of which men die; by getting of which men live. Whatever is done without it, fails; whatever is done by means of it, succeeds. It has neither root nor

[1] The traditional interpretation of the psychological parts of *Mencius* (accepted by all his translators) is an attempt not to find out what Mencius actually meant but to gloss the text in such a way as to bring it into conformity with current Confucianism. Fortunately the Quietist system that Mencius grafted on to his own theory of the instinctive moral-sense is represented (not completely but in a far more explicit form) in *Kuan Tzŭ*. I hope to deal with this question in a subsequent book of essays on Chinese philosophy.

stalk, leaf nor flower. Yet upon it depends the generation and the growth of the ten thousand things, each after its kind.'[1]

The Quietists who developed this idea of Tao as the unchanging unity underlying a shifting plurality, and at the same time the impetus giving rise to every form of life and motion, were called Taoists. The ideas of other Quietists are only known to us indirectly, through writers such as 'Kuan Tzŭ' and Mencius having utilized or adopted them. With the Taoists the case is quite different. We have in two series called *Chuang Tzŭ* and *Lieh Tzŭ* a large corpus of actual Taoist works. These works clearly do not all belong to the same branch of Taoism. Some of them have been greatly affected by the metaphysical theories of the Dualists, who attributed the whole constitution of the universe to the interaction of two opposing principles, *yin* and *yang*.[2] But other parts of the Taoist corpus show no such influence, and I do not think that this dualist conception is native to Taoism. I will try in the following pages to give some idea of the conceptions that seem to me fundamental in Taoism and that are, so far as we can judge, common ground in the various Taoist schools.

The first great principle of Taoism is the relativity of all attributes. Nothing is in itself either long or short. If we call a thing long, we merely mean longer than something else that we take as a standard. What we take as our standard depends upon what we are used to, upon the general scale of size to which we belong. The fact that we endow our standard with absoluteness and objectivity, that we say 'No one could regard this as anything but

[1] *Kuan Tzŭ*, 49.   [2] See Appendix II.

long!' is merely due to lack of imagination. There are birds that fly hundreds of miles without stopping. Some-one mentioned this to the cicada and the wren,[1] who agreed that such a thing was out of the question. 'You and I know very well', they said, 'that the furthest one can ever get by the most tremendous effort is that elm there; and even this we can't be sure of doing every time. Often we find ourselves sinking back to earth, and have to give up the attempt as hopeless. All these stories about flying hundreds of miles at a stretch are pure nonsense.'

To those, then, who have rather more imagination than the cicada and the wren, all attributes whatsoever, whether they imply colour, height, beauty, ugliness, goodness, badness—any quality that can be thought of—are relative. And this applies, clearly, not only to the long and short, the high and low, but also to the 'inside' and 'outside'. The earlier Quietists regarded the soul as something that came from outside to dwell in the body. But to the Taoists, Tao was something that was at the same time within and without; for in Tao all opposites are blended, all contrasts harmonized.

Why did confidence in the absoluteness of any of the qualities that we attribute to things outside ourselves break down in China towards the end of the 4th century? Owing, I think, to rapidly increasing knowledge of what went on in the world outside China. Quite apart from the changes in material culture (use of iron, knowledge of asbestos, use of cavalry in war and adoption of non-Chinese dress in connection with it, familiarity with new forms of disposal of the dead) which these contacts

[1] *Chuang Tzŭ* I. 8.

brought, the Chinese were beginning to regard the world
they knew merely as a grain in the Great Barn.[1]

There was no end to the wonders that this great store-
house might produce. The danger was that in face of
these marvels one might, through mere bigotry and small-
mindedness, adopt the attitude of the cicada and the
wren. It was safer to believe everything, even that in the
mountains of some remote country there dwelt mysterious
beings who nourished themselves solely on air and dew,
yet by the concentration of their spirit (*shên*) acquired the
power to preserve flocks and herds from pest and cause the
crops to grow.[2] A different standard for fasting had indeed been set since the time when Ch'ên Chung[3] collapsed
after being three days without food!

The main controversy of Chinese philosophy in the 4th
century B.C. had centred round the rival claims of life and
death, of the Ancestors as against the living 'sons and
grandsons'. To the Taoist such debates were meaningless.
Looked at from Anywhere, the world is full of insecurities
and contradictions; looked at from Nowhere, it is a
changeless, uniform whole. In this identity of opposites
all antinomies, not merely high and low, long and short,
but life and death themselves merge.

'When Chuang Tzŭ's wife died, the logician Hui Tzŭ
came to the house to join in the rites of mourning. To
his astonishment he found Chuang Tzŭ sitting with an
inverted bowl on his knees, drumming upon it and singing
a song.[4] After all,' said Hui Tzŭ, 'she lived with you,

[1] *Chuang Tzŭ* XVII. 1.   [2] *Chuang Tzŭ* I. 4.
[3] See above.
[4] Both his attitude and his occupation were the reverse of what the
rites of mourning demand.

brought up your children, grew old along with you. That you should not mourn for her is bad enough; but to let your friends find you drumming and singing—that is really going too far!' 'You misjudge me,' said Chuang Tzŭ. 'When she died, I was in despair, as any man well might be. But soon, pondering on what had happened, I told myself that in death no strange new fate befalls us. In the beginning we lack not life only, but form. Not form only, but spirit. We are blent in the one great featureless, indistinguishable mass. Then a time came when the mass evolved spirit, spirit evolved form, form evolved life. And now life in its turn has evolved death. For not nature only but man's being has its seasons, its sequence of spring and autumn, summer and winter. If someone is tired and has gone to lie down, we do not pursue him with shouting and bawling. She whom I have lost has lain down to sleep for a while in the Great Inner Room. To break in upon her rest with the noise of lamentation would but show that I knew nothing of nature's Sovereign Law.'[1]

This attitude towards death, exemplified again and again in Chuang Tzŭ, is but part of a general attitude towards the universal laws of nature, which is one not merely of resignation nor even of acquiescence, but a lyrical, almost ecstatic acceptance which has inspired some of the most moving passages in Taoist literature. That we should question nature's right to make and unmake, that we should hanker after some rôle that nature did not intend us to play is not merely futile, not merely damaging to that tranquility of the 'spirit' which is the essence

[1] *Chuang Tzŭ* XVIII. 2.

Introduction

of Taoism, but involves, in view of our utter helplessness, a sort of fatuity at once comic and disgraceful. If the bronze in the founder's crucible were suddenly to jump up and say 'I don't want to be a tripod, a ploughshare or a bell. I must be the sword "Without Flaw"',[1] the bronze-caster would think it was indeed reprobate metal that had found its way into his stock.[2]

To be in harmony with, not in rebellion against the fundamental laws of the universe is the first step, then, on the way to Tao. For Tao is itself the always-so, the fixed, the unconditioned, that which 'is of itself' and for no cause 'so'. In the individual it is the Uncarved Block, the consciousness on which no impression has been 'notched', in the universe it is the Primal Unity underlying apparent multiplicity. Nearest then to Tao is the infant. Mencius, in whose system Conscience, sensitiveness to right and wrong, replaces the notion of Tao, says that the 'morally great man' is one who has kept through later years his 'infant heart'.[3] The idea is one that pervades the literature of the third century.[4] But weakness and softness in general, not only as embodied in the infant, are symbols of Tao. Such ideas as that to yield is to conquer, whereas to grasp is to lose—are indeed already inherent in the pre-

[1] Legendary heirloom of the kingdom of Wu; sharpest of mortal weapons.

[2] *Chuang Tzŭ* VI. 6.　　　　[3] *Mencius* IV. 2. 12.

[4] e.g. *Lieh Tzŭ* I. 7, *Chuang Tzŭ* XXIII. 3. What is obviously an earlier form of the Taoist hymn used by *Chuang Tzŭ* in the passage referred to occurs in *Kuan Tzŭ* twice over (P'ien 37 and 49), and each time lacks the phrases about infancy. The idea then was probably one that did not become popular till about 300 B.C. In the early centuries of the Christian era, on the other hand, it is no longer the infant but the child in the womb that is the Taoist ideal.

moralistic phase of thought. For example by retreating
from a country that one has it in one's power to lay waste,
one extorts a blessing from the soil-gods and ancestral
spirits of that country. Whereas by any act of aggression
one ranges against one a host of unseen powers. Older too
than Taoism is the idea that pride invites a fall, that the
axe falls first on the tallest tree. But it was Taoism that
first welded these ideas together into a system in which
the unassertive, the inconspicuous, the lowly, the imperfect, the incomplete become symbols of the Primal
Stuff that underlies the kaleidoscope of the apparent
universe. It is as representatives of the 'imperfect' and
the 'incomplete' that hunchbacks and cripples play so
large a part in Taoist literature. To be perfect is to invite
diminution; to climb is to invite a fall. Tao, like water,
'takes the low ground'. We have already met with the
conception of the soul as a well that never runs dry. In
Taoism water, as the emblem of the unassertive, and the
'low ground', as the home of water, become favourite
images. The question was a controversial one; for to the
early Confucians[1] the 'low ground' is the 'collecting-place
of all the impurities under heaven' and hence the symbol
of iniquity. *Kuan Tzŭ*[2] devotes a particularly eloquent
passage to water as pattern and example to the 'ten
thousand things', that is to say to everything in the universe, and to the low ground as 'dwelling-place of Tao'.
It is by absorbing the water-spirit (*shui-shên*) that vegeta-
tion lives, 'that the root gets its girth, the flower its
symmetries, the fruit its measure'. 'The valley-spirit',

[1] *Analects* XIX. 20.
[2] P'ien 39.

says another Taoist work,[1] meaning what *Kuan Tzŭ* means
by 'water-spirit', 'never dies. It is named the Mysterious
Female,[2] and the Doorway of the Mysterious Female is
the base from which Heaven and Earth sprang. It is there
within us all the while; draw upon it as you will, it never
runs dry.'

The valleys, then, are 'nearer to Tao' than the hills; and
in the whole of creation it is the negative, passive, 'female'
element alone that has access to Tao, which can only be
mirrored 'in a still pool'. Quietism consists in the culti-
vation of this 'stillness'. In its extreme forms, consciousness continues but the functions of the outward senses are
entirely suspended and the mind moves only within itself.
Between this and the normal state of consciousness there
are innumerable stages, and though definite *yoga*, with
complete suspension of the outward senses, was certainly
practised by initiate Taoists,[3] I do not think that anything
more than a very relative Quiet was known to the numerous non-Taoist schools of thought that adopted Quietism
as a mystical background to their teaching. There is no
reason for example to suppose that Mencius's[4] 'stilling of
the mind' reached an actual *samādhi*, a complete gathering
in of the consciousness into itself. But it led him to make
a distinction[5] between two kinds of knowledge, the one
the result of mental activity, the other passive and as we
should say 'intuitive'; and it is the second kind that he

1 *The Book of the Yellow Ancestor*, quoted by *Lieh Tzŭ*, I, beginning.
2 'Hills are male; valleys are female.' *K'ung Tzŭ Chia Yü* 25, end.
Huai-nan Tzŭ, Ch. IV. fol. 4.
3 See Appendix III.
4 Or whoever wrote the 'psychological' passages.
5 VII. 1. 15.

calls 'good knowledge'. Indeed, the whole of education[1] consists, Mencius says, in recapturing intuitive faculties that in the stress of life have been allowed to go astray. With him these faculties are moral; whereas the Quiet of the Taoists produces a secondary 'virtue' (*tê*) a power 'that could shift Heaven and Earth', a transcendental knowledge in which each of the 'ten thousand things' is separately mirrored 'as the hairs of the brow and head are mirrored in a clear pool'. For 'to a mind that is "still" the whole universe surrenders'.[2]

How the 'power' works is a question upon which the Taoists writers throw very little light. According to one explanation[3] it is a question of equilibrium. The perfect poise that Quietism gives to the mind can for example communicate itself to the hand, and so to whatever the hand holds. The case is cited of a philosopher who possessed this 'poise' to such a degree that he could land huge fish from a deep pool with a line consisting of a single filament of raw silk. A line snaps at the point where most strain is put upon it. But if, owing to the perfect equilibrium of the fisherman's hand, no such point exists, the slenderest thread can bear the greatest imaginable weight without breaking. The Taoists indeed saw in many arts and crafts the utilization of a power akin to if not identical with that of Tao. The wheelwright, the carpenter, the butcher, the bowman, the swimmer, achieve their skill not by accumulating facts concerning their art, nor by the energetic use either of muscles or outward senses;

[1] VI. 1. 11. [2] *Chuang Tzŭ* XIII. 1.
[3] *Lieh Tzŭ* V. 8. My interpretation of the passage differs from that of Wieger and Maspero.

but through utilizing the fundamental kinship which, underneath apparent distinctions and diversities, unites their own Primal Stuff to the Primal Stuff of the medium in which they work. Like Tao itself every 'art' is in the last resort incommunicable. Some forms of mysticism have laid stress on an oral tradition, not communicable in books; we are indeed often told that the whole Wisdom of the East is enshrined in such a tradition. Taoism went much further. Not only are books the mere discarded husk or shell of wisdom, but words themselves, expressing as they do only such things as belong to the normal state of consciousness, are irrevelant to the deeper experience of Tao, the 'wordless doctrine'. If then the Taoist speaks and still more if he writes, he does so merely to arouse interest in his doctrines, and not in any hope of communicating what another cannot be made to feel any more than you can feel the pain in my finger.

The Language Crisis

During the fourth century B.C. it began to occur to the Chinese that words move in a world of their own, a region connected only in the most casual and precarious way with the world of reality. Sometimes the mere presence of a particular word in a sentence is sufficient to label that sentence as connected solely with the region of words and not at all with the world of actualities. Such a word is 'infinite', whether applied to the infinitely small or the infinitely great. Take a stick a foot long.[1] Halve it. To-morrow halve that half, and so on day after day. Ten thousand generations hence there will still, theoretically

[1] *Chuang Tzŭ* XXXIII. 7. For the question of Hellenistic influence see Appendix II.

speaking, be something left to halve. But in reality we are obliged to stop short much sooner than this, even though we may suppose that with better eyes and a sharper knife we could still go on. In the same way it can be shown that any sentence containing the word 'infinite' belongs to the world of language, not to that of facts. Not that these two domains are totally disconnected. They share a considerable amount of common ground. Many words can be regarded as labels of particular objects, and in such cases it might seem as though there were a close correspondence between the two worlds. Unfortunately this correspondence ceases when several labels are combined; as is indeed true of actual labels in real life. For one can pile eight labels marked 'elephant' one on top of another;[1] but one cannot pile eight elephants on top of another. One can in fact (which is often very convenient) say things that sound all right, but mean nothing at all.

Now there were particular reasons, connected with the history and character not only of the Chinese language, but also of the script, which made this rift between language and actuality not merely a subject of detached philosophic enquiry, as has been the case elsewhere, not merely an easily tolerated inconvenience (as we are apt to regard it) but a burning question of the day. Chinese vocabulary was built up from a comparatively small number of original roots by a long series of meaning-extensions. The same process can of course be seen at work in all languages. But whereas this was in Chinese during its formative period the only process by which vocabulary was enriched,[2] in most other civilized languages another

[1] This image of the elephants is mine and is not used by the Chinese.

[2] No doubt isolated foreign words may have found their way into

Introduction

process was going on at the same time. For example in Japan no doubt a certain amount of meaning-extension applied to native roots has been going on since the 6th century A.D. But by far the greater number of additions to Japanese vocabulary has been made by borrowing Chinese words; and it may be said in a general way that if the Japanese wanted a new word they turned at once to Chinese, just as we to-day turn to Latin or Greek. The absence of similar borrowing and the free use of meaning-extension in ancient China had the result that the same word meant a great many different things. Thus *hsiang* meant elephant,[1] and hence ivory. Hence carved ivory tablets representing omen-objects,[2] hence anything that 'stood for' or represented something else; an image or symbol. Finally, though not, I think till well after the Christian era, the word came to mean 'like', 'as', 're-sembling', as it does in current Chinese to-day. Or to take another example, the word *ssŭ*, which now means a temple, comes from a root the basic meaning of which is 'to take in hand'. Hence (1) to hold on to in order to control. (2) to hold on to in order to support oneself. (3) a place where things are 'taken in hand', where business is handled, a courtroom. Finally, official premises assigned to foreigners for worship, and hence a Buddhist temple.[3] The words in such a series are all variations of the same root. But they were in many cases distinguished by slight

early Chinese. But no considerable influx took place till the popularization of Buddhism in the early centuries of the Christian era.

[1] The elephant did not become extinct in China till about the 5th century B.C. It is said still to exist in parts of Yünnan.

[2] A species of domino was used in divination till quite late times.

[3] Compare the word 'basilikon'. It is not certain that all the examples given are semantic developments. Possibly *hsiang* (elephant) and *hsiang* (symbol) are separate words.

differences of sound, which in process of time often developed into considerable divergencies. If Chinese had not been a written language, it would in many cases have soon been forgotten that the words in such series of meaning-extensions had any connection with one another at all. But for the fact that they are still written with the same character it would not occur to anyone, for example, that *yao* 'music' and *lo* 'to rejoice' are the same word. In point of fact they both go back to an original root 'lak'.[1]

To obviate the inconvenience caused by the fact that the same character stood for perhaps a dozen different developments of meaning, scribes took to writing what are called 'determinatives'[2] alongside of the characters. Thus when the 'hold on to' root meant 'hold in order to control' they wrote the character 'hand' at the side of it, to make sure there should be no mistake. But when it meant 'hold on to for support' and hence 'rely upon', 'have confidence in', they added the character 'heart'. Egyptian scribes, to name only one parallel, did just the same thing. But until the 3rd century B.C. this helpful practice was carried out very irregularly and inadequately. Thus in writing, different meanings of the same character were occasionally distinguished, but more often no such distinction was made; and in speech, some meaning-extensions were marked by differences of intonation or small variations in sound, but a great many were absolutely identical in pronunciation and if divorced from their context could equally well mean any of half a dozen different things.

In all languages it is the smallest and most innocent-

[1] Or 'glak', according to the current view. But I am inclined to regard the 'g' as a prefix and not part of the root.   [2] Or radicals.

looking words which have given rise to the most trouble. A large number of the tangles in which European thinkers have involved themselves have been due to the fact that the verb 'to be' means a great many different things. The fact that Chinese lacks anything exactly corresponding to the verb 'to be' might at first sight seem to put Chinese logicians at an initial advantage. But this is far from being the case. Chinese assertions take the form 'commence begin indeed', i.e. 'To commence is to begin'. And this pattern of words, attended upon by the harmless-looking particle *yeh*, 'indeed', has caused by its reticence far more trouble than any Western copulative by its assertiveness. Some of the things that this simple pattern can express are as follows: (1) Identity, as in the example given above; (2) that A is a member of a larger class, B. For example 'Boat wooden-thing indeed', i.e. 'boats are made of wood'; (3) that A has a quality B. For example 'Tail long indeed', i.e. 'its tail is long'.[1] If words have a fixed connection with realities, the Chinese argued, *yeh* ('indeed') ought always to mean the same thing. If for example it implies identity, one ought to be able to travel hundred of leagues on any 'wooden-thing'; but in point of fact one can only travel on a boat.

The absence of a plural led to similar difficulties. 'One horse is a horse' was expressed by 'One horse, horse indeed'. 'Two horses are horses' (i.e. belong to the category 'horse') was expressed by 'Two horse, horse indeed'. It appears then that in the world of language one horse is

[1] This is in reality only a special case of (2); for the category of 'long things' is a large class, embracing such tails as happen to be long. But the Chinese regarded 'qualities' in rather a different light, looking upon them as 'something added to' the thing in question.

identical with two horses; we know that in the world of fact this is not so. But not only did Chinese nouns lack number; Chinese verbs lacked tense. This creates another barrier between language and reality. If we say 'Yao sage indeed' this can only refer to the past; for Yao lived thousands of years ago. Consequently when we say 'Orphan, child minus-parent indeed' (i.e. an orphan is a child without parents), it ought to mean that an orphan is a child that never had any parents, for the same formula of words has been shown to refer, in the case of Yao, to the past, not to the present.

The people who discussed those difficulties—in Europe they have generally been called Sophists, but the Chinese called them 'discriminators' (*pien*)—did so not in order to prove, for example, that orphans never had parents, but to show how dangerous is the gulf that separates language from reality. The problem was not an abstract one; indeed, if it had been, the Chinese would not have been interested in it. For all Chinese philosophy is essentially the study of how men can best be helped to live together in harmony and good order.[1] It is only through language (*ming*), through 'orders' (*ming*, written differently but etymologically the same word) that this help can be given. Nothing is more harmful to a state than that different realities should share a common name; nothing more dangerous than that theories and doctrines which belong only to the world of language should be mistaken for truths concerning the world of fact. In the domain of language, as we have seen, the same formula expresses a

[1] 'Order (in a State) is the supreme good; disorder the supreme evil.' *Kuan Tzŭ*, 47, end.

whole series of relationships. It may mean practical identity ('To commence is to begin'); it may merely mean that
two things share certain qualities, while remaining quite
different in other respects. In language things are either
the same ('Robber man indeed') or different ('Robber
not-man indeed'). In the world of fact there are innumerable degrees of sameness and difference. A robber is the
same as a man, in that he ought not to be indiscriminately
slain; he is different from a man, in that he carries off one's
property, whereas men in general do not. Some people,
not understanding how great a gulf lies between the
world of words and the world of fact, claim that since a
robber 'is different from a man' he may be indiscriminately slaughtered.[1]

We are very scantily informed as to the history of the
'language-reforming' movement in China. My hypothesis
is that the *pien chê* ('discriminators') were the people who
discovered and to some extent analysed the discrepancy
between language and reality. No doubt there were some
among them who exploited this discovery in a merely
frivolous way, startling and bewildering their audiences
by the paradoxes that ensue if one accepts the statements
of the language-world as true of our world, or *vice versa*.
But as regards the existence of such a class of 'sophists' we
are dependent on hearsay, and it is quite certain that the

---

[1] See *Mo Tzŭ*, P'ien 44. *Hsün Tzŭ*, P'ien 22. Hu Shih's *Wên Ts'un* II.
35 seq. The school of Mo Tzŭ took up the language question in the
third century very much in the same way that some Churchmen to-day
have taken up psycho-analysis, in order to arm themselves against
modernist attack. What survives of these Mohist language-studies is a
glossary of terms used by the 'discriminators'; a commentary on that
glossary, and a memoria technica of replies to awkward questions.

average man must have regarded the whole business about 'a white horse being or not being a horse' and attributes 'not being mutually exclusive' as mere quibbling; so that in popular imagination even the most impeccably serious logicians must in any case have figured as charlatans.

Another serious difficulty was caused by the particular type of meaning-extension which is exemplified in the word *i*, 'morality'. No one was inconvenienced by the fact that *hou*, which originally meant 'a target for arrows' had come also to mean 'a chieftain, a feudal lord'; for this was merely a transition from one concrete meaning to another, and the context always made it clear which meaning was intended. With the 'moral' words, the case was different. *I* for example meant something entirely 'external' and objective, it had been applied to acts concordant with the circumstances, to behaviour such as tradition taught people to demand and expect. But now the Confucians insisted that it was something existing inside one, a sort of extra 'sense', built up and nourished by particular sorts of behaviour. The school of Mo Tzŭ also attached the greatest importance to *i*.[1] It was 'most precious of all the ten thousand things'. But whereas with them it manifested itself in loving every one equally, to the Confucians nothing was more damaging to *i* than to love anyone else as much as one loved one's parents. This claim on the part of the moralists to the possession of a special 'sense' was as irritating to the general public as is the claim of modern æsthetes to a special æsthetic sense. Both Confucians and Mohists demanded that the

1 *Mo Tzŭ*, P'ien 47, beginning.

whole administration of government should be put in the hands of the 'morally superior' (*hsien*); but when it came to deciding who these 'morally superior' were, they could not agree. In the minds of practical people a suspicion arose that *i*, like the conception 'infinite' and so many other high-sounding creations of the thinker as opposed to the man of action, belonged solely to the world of language and had no counterpart at all in actual life.

The theoretical object of the 'Ming Chia' (Language Students) was to amend language so that 'every different reality should be expressed by a different word', and this having been achieved no one should in future be allowed 'to split up existing meanings and make them into new words'.[1] Such an aim was of course, as regards ordinary parlance, quite impossible to realize. It had its effect, however, upon writing; for it was at this time (in the 4th and 3rd centuries) that the use of 'determinatives' to distinguish between different meaning-extensions of the same word began to come into much more general use.

Curiously enough the rather fruitless controversy about the improvement of language ended by escaping on to more practical ground through a loophole that admirably illustrated how urgent the need for improvement was. The word for realities as opposed to names ('language') is *hsing*, which originally meant 'shape'; hence to alter in shape, to mutilate, and so 'to punish'; for in early China punishment consisted in cutting off the nose, the ears, the feet, etc. Nowadays these two senses ('shape' and 'punishment') are distinguished in writing by the use of different determinatives. But in early China this was not

[1] *Hsün Tzǔ*, P'ien 22.

the case. Thus it came about that the controversy concerning 'words and realities' wandered off unperceived on to fresh ground, becoming in the end merely a discussion about the fitting of words (i.e. definition of crimes) to 'shapings' (i.e. their appropriate punishments).

The Realists[1]

China throughout the period that I have been discussing consisted of a number of small kingdoms, and the only state of affairs known to the Chinese by actual experience or in the records of history[2] (as opposed to mythology) was one of continual assaults and counter-assaults, raids and reprisals. Efforts to mitigate this state of continual discord and violence were not wanting. Treaties, pacts, truces, alliances followed fast upon one another. But the intentions of those who made them were not peaceable; and when, as inevitably happened, the conflict was renewed, it was further exacerbated by heated recriminations over the purely technical question as to which side had first violated the pact. At the turn of the fourth and third centuries the States of Chao and Ch'in entered into the following agreement: 'From this time henceforward in whatever Ch'in desires to do she is to be assisted by Chao; and in whatever Chao desires to do she is to be assisted by Ch'in.' Soon afterwards Ch'in attacked the kingdom of Wei, and Chao made ready to go to Wei's assistance. The king of Ch'in protested that this

[1] I use this term in its everyday not its philosophical sense. Their name in Chinese is *Fa Chia*, 'Legalists', but I feel the need of a wider term.

[2] For pre-history, see Appendix V.

68

was an infringement of the pact. But prompted by the pacifist logician Kung-sun Lung the king of Chao replied: 'According to the pact each side guarantees to help the other in whatever either desires to do. I now desire to save the State of Wei, and if you do not help me to do so, I shall charge you with infringement of the pact.'[1]

A belief however existed that China had not always been in this unhappy condition of internecine strife and disorder. Long ago the great Ancestors had exercised undisputed sway over 'everything under heaven'; and if modern rulers had not succeeded in doing more than establishing precarious hegemonies, into which the smaller and more defenceless States were absorbed, this was only because these rulers lacked the universal and all-embracing 'power' (*tê*) that can draw to itself 'everything under heaven'. Gradually the word *Ti* ('Ancestor') took on a new sense—that of Universal Ruler. The *Ti* was awaited as a kind of Messiah, and round the belief in his coming centred, in a sense, the whole of Chinese thought. For every school (Confucians, Mohists, followers of Yang Chu, Taoists) believed that it had rediscovered the *tao*, the principle by which the ancient *Ti* had ruled over the whole 'world'. To the Chinese of this period the word One (unity, singleness, etc.) had an intensely emotional connotation, reflected equally in political theory and in Taoist metaphysics. And indeed the longing, or more accurately the psychological need for a fixed standard of belief was profounder, more urgent and more insistent than the longing for governmental unity. In the long run man cannot exist without an orthodoxy, without a fixed

[1] *Lü Shih Ch'un Ch'iu*, P'ien 105.

pattern of fundamental belief. It is hard for us to-day who live in societies, like those of France or England, which despite a surface of moral anarchy, are in fact rooted upon Christian ethics, to imagine such a state of chaos as existed in China in the fourth and third centuries. The old auguristic-sacrificial outlook had, at any rate among the ruling classes, completely lost its hold, and in its place had sprung up a series of doctrines each differing from the other on questions that profoundly affected the interpretation of man's life and destiny. This is all the harder for us to realize because we are accustomed to view this period through the spectacles of a later, Confucian orthodoxy which knew little or nothing of the struggles by which it had itself been achieved. Nor even within the main schools of thought was there any semblance of an interior orthodoxy. Confucianism, for example, towards the middle of the 3rd century, was divided into eight schools each claiming to be the sole repository of the Master's teaching.[1] Every Court in China was infested by 'journeying philosophers', each in turn pressing upon a bewildered ruler the claims of Activism, of Quietism, of morality, of non-morality, of force, of non-resistance, of individualism, of State supremacy. In one thing only were they united; each claimed to possess the secret 'art of ruling' whereby the Ancestors had grown mighty in the past.

But in the minds of those who actually handled practical affairs a suspicion arose that the past could not be re-created. Obvious cultural changes such as the introduction of iron[2] and the use of cavalry, with all the changes of

---

[1] *Han Fei Tzŭ*, P'ien 50.
[2] There are references to iron in the *Yü kung* and *Tso Chuan*. But the

costume and equipment which this latter innovation involved, suggested that the Ancestors lived in a very different world. The question whether they achieved their supremacy by force, by 'morality', by *yoga*, by using only 'one word for one fact' or by correct performance of rites and ceremonies was not one which necessarily had any bearing on this very different, modern world. There arose a school of Realists, who saw no need for abstract principles such as morality and benevolence, nor for the consecration of particular emotions such as pity or love. The principles that should guide life do not need to be deducted from theories about the Five Elements, the Seasons, the Planets, the relation of Nine Times Nine to Eight Times Eight.[1] The only fundamental and relevant principles are inherent in the nature of life itself. Man needs food, clothing and shelter. To prate to him of benevolence, morality, universal love and so on, when he lacks these essential things is like 'reciting the Book of Odes to a fish out of water'. To produce food and clothing he must have fields for his rice or corn, orchards for his mulberry-trees.[2] There must be a roof over his head. To preserve these essential things for the community is the fundamental duty of the State (*kuo*) or, put in other words, of the ruler (*chu*) as symbol of the State, and all

Yü kung is now generally thought to date from the beginning of the 4th century, and there is another version of the *Tso Chuan* story, in which the word 'iron' does not occur. Iron was at first used mainly for agricultural implements, and not till the Han dynasty(?) for weapons of war.

[1] For the place of numerical conceptions in Chinese thought, see Granet's recent work, *La Pensée Chinoise*.

[2] Upon the leaves of which silkworms were fed.

other State activities are subordinate to this. Territory, then—fields, orchards and pastures—is the very life of the people, and to keep territory intact force is necessary. Other methods have been tried, but where are the States that tried them? Their national altars have been cast down, their citizens enslaved or slaughtered, their territories divided among the powerful. A philosopher from the country of Chêng asked for an audience with the king of Chao. Hoping for entertaining subtleties, the king sent for him. 'What are you going to talk to me about?' he asked. The philosopher said he proposed to talk about war. 'But I am not at all fond of war,' the king protested. The philosopher rubbed his hands, gazed at the ceiling and laughed. 'I never supposed you were,' he said, 'for of all hairy-ape games war is the vilest. . . . But suppose a strong and covetous State had concentrated its armies on your frontiers and were demanding land. Much use would it be to discourse to them upon abstract principles (*li*) or morality (*i*). In a word, so long as your Majesty does not arm, the neighbouring kingdoms can do with you as they will.' The king of Chao said: 'Tell me how to arm.'[1]

The period was one of profound disillusionment. Mencius in the second half of the 4th century had preached with exaltation and fervour the fundamental goodness of man's nature. Nowhere had the new doctrine of 'morality and kindness' been so generally accepted as in the small State of Lu, the home of Confucianism. Yet in 249 Lu was invaded and destroyed. Small wonder if Hsün Tzŭ, writing at about the time of the fall of Lu, some thirty years or more after the death of Mencius,

[1] *Chan Kuo Ts'ê*, VI. 49.

reverses his predecessor's doctrine. Man's nature, says Hsün Tzŭ, is bad. He is born greedy, jealous, lustful. Goodness is a thing that must be imposed upon him from without, as wood is rendered serviceable by straightening its 'obliquities' in the press. This is the view of a Confucian. The Realists went much further. Honest people may exist. One might even find twenty or thirty of them in a State. But of what use is a score when one is looking for hundreds?[1] The Confucians and Mohists had insisted that the task of government must be entrusted to *hsien* 'morally superior' people. Unfortunately the attributes of moral superiority are so easy to counterfeit that from the moment when it is known that *hsien* are to be promoted, the country teems with pseudo-benevolence and pseudo-morality.[2] The Realists were also very distrustful of what one may call short-term emotions. Pity for individuals too often entails cruelty towards the community at large. They were fond of using the simile of hair-washing.[3] He who washes his head inevitably loses a certain number of hairs. But if for that reason one refrained from ever washing the head, there would soon be no hairs left at all. 'A polity that does not involve hardship, national achievements (*kung*) that do not entail suffering have never yet existed under heaven.' Life in its essence is stern and hard:

> No lake so still but that it has its wave;
> No circle so perfect but that it has its blur.
> I would change things for you if I could;
> As I can't, you must take them as they are.[4]

[1] *Han Fei Tzŭ*, 49.   [2] *Han Fei Tzŭ*, 7.
[3] *Ibid.*, 46; repeated in 47.   [4] *Ibid.*, 47.

So ran an old rhyming proverb. We must take the facts of life and human nature as we find them. 'Ordinary people (*min*) are lazy; it is natural to them to shirk hard work and to delight in idleness.'[1] If in times of scarcity we give grain doles to the poor we are merely taxing those whose providence and industry have enabled them to save, in order to supply the wants of those whose own idleness and improvidence has reduced them to penury.[2] The result of such mistaken benevolence can only be general idleness, followed by general indigence and misery. The common people are incapable of looking ahead. They do not wish to be enslaved by foreigners, they do not wish to have their homes burned, but they would not if left to themselves take any long-sighted measure to prevent these disasters. 'They want security, but hate the means that produce security.' The State therefore is all the time demanding from the people things that are hard and irksome. Sophists, Confucians, Mohists, Hedonists, half a dozen other sects and persuasions, are only too ready to take advantage of this fact, and delude the people into thinking that there is a way of safety which is not 'hard'. But the Realist knows that all these doctrines are founded on illusions, on the idea that in this world of blurs and smears a perfect circle can yet be drawn. There can be no compromise with these doctrines. 'Ice and embers cannot lie in the same bowl.' 'If the horses are pulling different ways the coach will not advance.' There must be no private doctrines (*ssŭ hsüeh*); no religion indeed save that of the Realists which alone is founded on facts, not on abstractions or what is almost as

---

[1] *Han Fei Tzŭ*, 54.   [2] *Ibid.*, 50.

bad, on the experience of exceptional people. The philosopher Lao Tan said that 'he who is content with what he has got can never be despoiled, he who knows when to stop can never be destroyed'. On the basis of this some politicians pretend that the whole object of government is to give the people as much of everything as they can desire; whereupon they will instantly become orderly and contented. This might be true if the common people were all philosophers. The only maxim true of the world as it exists is that the more people have, the more they want.[1] The Confucians are compared by Han Fei Tzŭ[2] to the quack magicians who pretend that by their prayers and incantations they can make their customers live 'a thousand autumns, ten thousand years'; yet for all their gabblings and antics no one has ever yet been known to obtain the slightest benefit of any kind by patronizing them. So the Confucians pretend that by studying the records of remote antiquity and the achievements of long-dead kings they have discovered a secret that will enable the modern ruler to confound his enemies. 'But the enlightened ruler pays attention only to facts and ideas that are of practical use at the moment. He does not concern himself with benevolence and morality; or listen to the empty discourses of learned people.' In the remote past the population was small and there was plenty and to spare for everybody. It was easy enough then and in no wise meritorious to exercise the virtues of 'sharing' and 'yielding' that the Confucians attributed to the ancient sages. To-day everything is changed. We live in troublous times and it is no more possible to rule a great modern

[1] *Han Fei Tzŭ*, 46.   [2] *Ibid.*, 50.

kingdom as though it were a village in which everyone was related to everyone else, than it is possible for a wheelbarrow to keep pace with a chariot. The wise ruler has no use for 'wheelbarrow' government.[1] Needless to say, the whole of the sacrificial-auguristic side of public life must be ruthlessly discarded. 'That a State should keep times and days, serve ghosts and spirits, trust in divination by the tortoise or by the yarrow-stalks, be fond of prayers and sacrifices, is a portent of doom.'[2] This is part of the forty-seven portents of political decay, each clause ending with the word *wang* ('doom', 'destruction') that clangs like a warning bell across these powerful and impressive pages.

The school that came perhaps into most active conflict with the Realists was that of Mo Tzŭ, whose doctrine of universal love demanded that one should 'feel towards all people under heaven exactly as one feels towards one's own people, regard other States exactly as one regards one's own State'. It becomes necessary at this point to digress a little, and see what had hitherto been the Chinese attitude to war. While the old belief in the Ancestors and Heaven (the abode of the Ancestors) was in full sway, war like every other activity was hedged round by innumerable precautions and restrictions. It was safe to attack only when one had reason to believe that the enemy had forfeited the support of their Former Kings; for 'against Heaven none can war'. This view gave rise in the moralistic period to the familiar distinction between righteous and unrighteous wars, the aggressors acting in the former

[1] *Han Fei Tzŭ*, 47.
[2] *Han Fei Tzŭ*, 15.

as agents of Heaven, and bringing a well merited chastise-
ment to those who had sinned against Heaven. This was
particularly the case with wars resulting in the establishment of a new dynasty. Each dynastic line ends with a
wicked monarch whose sins 'cry to Heaven'. At the same
time weapons, used on behalf of whatever cause, are
'unlucky implements'.[1] The metal of which they are
made has been wrested from the earth, and earth is loth
to lose her treasures. War causes the crops to fail and the
streams to dry. It was indeed hard for the governing
classes to uproot from the minds of the people this conception of war as essentially baleful and ill-omened. Yet
not to train the people for war is to abandon them to the
mercy of their enemies. The idea that weapons are
'baleful' is combatted in the *Ta Tai Li Chi*.[2] Peace and war
are permanent features in man's environment, Confucius
is represented as saying, just as rage and delight are permanent elements in his emotional constitution. This,
however, was only the view of certain Confucian schools.
During the 4th century, when the Yang Chu doctrine
that the perfect State consists of whole and 'intact' individuals was at the height of its vogue, Confucianism too
was influenced by the individualist doctrine. It was man's
first duty to keep himself intact. So far this Confucian
school was in agreement with Yang Chu. But whereas the
followers of Yang Chu perfected the individual in order
that there might be a perfect aggregation of individuals,
the Confucian perfected himself in order that his duty
towards his parents might be carried out by a perfect

[1] Quoted as a proverbial saying by *Han Fei Tzǔ*, 2, beginning.
[2] P'ien 75, 'on the use of arms'.

individual. It is for this reason that it is his duty not to risk any diminution of his physical or mental efficiency. He may neither 'climb up on to high places nor look down into deep places'.[1] He remembers at every instant that his body is a sacred trust, committed to him by his parents. No hair, no tissue of his whole frame must ever be wilfully imperilled.[2] It is doubtful however whether this doctrine obtained much currency till the Han period. The real enemies of violence were the Mohists, and the great upholder of pacifism was the Mohist Kung-sun Lung, also famous as a logician. He succeeded in partially converting to his theories King Hui of Chao, who came to the throne in 298 B.C. 'I have now been aiming at the suppression of arms for ten years,' the king said to Kung-sun Lung one day, 'but with very little success. Don't you think the truth may be that arms cannot be suppressed?' 'The doctrine of the suppression of arms', said Kung-sun Lung, 'is the outcome of universal love, felt equally towards everyone under heaven. If such love exists only in words but not in actuality this policy can certainly never be carried out.' Kung-sun Lung goes on to point out that the king's state of mind was one which could not possibly lead to the realization of the aims which he professed. He was manifestly still obsessed by the old hatred of the western kingdom of Ch'in. When two towns voluntarily placed themselves under Ch'in rule, King Hui (the philosopher reminded him) went into mourning; but on hearing that the Ch'ins had lost a castle he celebrated the occasion by a banquet.[3] But the truth is, as a Realist

[1] *Li Chi*, I. [2] *Book of Filial Piety*, beginning.
[3] *Lü Shih Ch'un Ch'iu*, 101.

writer[1] points out, that 'the most the benevolent man can do is to be benevolent to others; he cannot cause others to be benevolent to him. The most the moral man can do is to exercise his love upon other people; he cannot make other people love one another'. The necessity for self-defence was generally admitted, and the Mo Tzŭ school gave special attention to the arts of fortification, freely admitting that to love every one equally does not necessarily entail being loved by everyone equally. But a purely defensive policy has, as Kuan Tzŭ points out, great disadvantages. In actual practice the status of soldiering, in countries that adopt such a policy, is a low one, pay is inadequate, interest in the military arts is at a low ebb. Sooner or later the integrity of the 'defensive' State is threatened from abroad, and the only result of this 'defensive' policy is that the aggressors operate with a trained army, we with a hastily summoned levy; they are led by skilled generals, we by mere incompetents;[2] with the inevitable result. Accordingly even the State that does not contemplate aggression must foster an aggressive state of mind in the people. Even more dangerous to the State than the upholders of the purely defensive policy are those whom 'the world honours with the name of *kuei-shêng* ("esteemers of the individual life")', but who are in reality 'mere runaways, afraid for their skins'.[3] The tendency of peasant populations to shoulder their ploughs and hearth-stones and flee before an invader was one which sorely troubled early Chinese rulers. The nomadic period was indeed not so far away, and stories really belonging to

---

[1] *Shang Tzŭ*, 18. [2] *Kuan Tzŭ*, 65, beginning.
[3] *Han Fei Tzŭ*, 46, beginning.

such a period could be quoted in defence of non-resistance. Had not old father Tan, a Chou Ancestor, when his territory was threatened by another tribe, successively offered them skins, silk, horses, dogs, pearls, jade, in the hopes of bribing them off; and at last finding it was land and land alone that his enemies desired, had he not quietly surrendered his territory and trekked with his tribesmen all the way from Pin to the foot of Mount Ch'i?[1] To attach the people to their homes and prevent them from trekking off, from 'evading difficulties', as such emigrations were called, at the first hint of trouble, was no easy matter.

But to return to the doctrine of the Realists. The first essential, as we have seen, was that the State should maintain its frontiers intact. The second was that the people should have food and clothing. Soldiering must be the profession that holds the highest status in the whole corporate life; and next to it must come agriculture. Admittedly the life of the peasant is much less agreeable than that of the scholar, the roaming politician, the manufacturer of luxuries and toys. For this very reason the State must do everything in its power to stem the inevitable drift from agriculture, on which the existence of the country depends, into unessential occupations. Above all, the rising influence of the merchant must be checked,[2] for the whole power of the State lies in its power to punish or reward, and the existence of a class which 'rewards itself', and consequently has no incentive to seek public reward,

[1] The story is told in *Mencius, Chuang Tzŭ, Huai-nan Tzŭ* and elsewhere. It is still popular, being cited, for example, in a recent propaganda pamphlet of the Manchukuo government.

[2] *Han Fei Tzŭ*, 49, end.

is a menace to society. The number, then, of those who enrich themselves whether by commerce or by any form of unessential craft, is to be limited to the barest minimum, and their social position is to be lowest in the State.

A vast system of punishments and rewards is indeed to take the place of any appeal to public feeling, decency or morality. For such virtues function even at best in a sporadic and irregular way and in the majority of men maintain an existence shadowy indeed when contrasted with the two active and prominent motives of mankind— 'love of profit and love of fame'. A few exceptional people can draw a perfect circle without using a compass, estimate the weight of grain without using scales; but if the making of wheels and the selling of grain depended on the use of such people, the markets would languish and waggoning soon be at a standstill. 'Morality' as apart from 'legality' is merely an unnecessary factor, disintegrating because of its uncertain and irregular operation, inconsistent with the great Realist principle of unity, in that it introduces and sanctions a sort of private, secondary Law.

Codification is, I suppose, always connected with spread of empire. In a small, homogeneous community law is merely 'what is customary'. But if other communities with other customs are conquered and absorbed it becomes necessary to decide which alien customs can be tolerated and which are inimical to the new, larger society. For it is not in practice ever possible completely to eradicate all usages save those of the conquering tribe. It is easy to see that the 'codification' movement in China was part of a general tendency towards unification of manners in the widest sense. It is reflected in the activity of the 'ritualist' school of Confucianism which, faced with a multiplicity of conflicting usages and traditions, attempted to construct, at any rate for the *chün-tzŭ*, the upper classes, a uniform code of conduct which should embrace not only every branch of public activity, but also personal relationships and domestic life. The earliest penal code preserved is that attributed to King Mu of the Chou dynasty.[1] The object of this very confused document seems to be the justification of fines as a substitute for corporal mutilation. Such a change may be regarded on the one hand as a cultural advance, similar to the substitution of clay figures for human sacrificial victims. It certainly also represents a victory for the propertied classes, who alone were able to take advantage of the innovation and so preserve their ears and noses intact. At the same time it opened up for the State an important new source of revenue. The code of King Mu deals with punishments only. But in all later documents we find a mating of punishments and rewards, due I think to the growing influence of the Yin-yang (Dualist) School,[2] deterrents and encouragements forming as it were the 'light' and 'shade' of government. In the doctrine of the Realists this appeal to hope and fear is the only *ch'ang-tao*, the only fixed principle. Its application depends solely on the circumstances of the moment, on the nature of the tasks that the State needs to perform, on the condition of the subjects who are to perform these tasks. The type of rather crude propaganda that was used

[1] 'Book of History': *Lü Ching.* Mu probably reigned in the 9th century B.C. The document in question, however, is not history, but propaganda in justification of a social change, welded on to a legend about the wickedness and ultimate destruction of a first race of men.

[2] See below, p. 110.

to justify this doctrine is well instanced by the following story, in which Confucius is made to figure as a Legalist: The men of Lu had set fire to some bushlands to the north of their capital in order to clear the ground and make it fit for agriculture. A strong north wind sprang up, the fire spread and the capital was threatened. The duke of Lu was so much perturbed that he collected the inhabitants of the city and led them in person to the scene of the fire. But the people were soon busy chasing the game that the fire had startled, and the duke presently found himself entirely deserted. In this predicament he sent for Confucius. The sage said: 'To chase animals is pleasant; to put out a fire is hard work. So long as the chasing of animals involves no penalty and the putting out of the fire brings no reward, the fire will continue to blaze.' With the duke's permission Confucius accordingly made it known that anyone who failed to help in putting out the fire would rank as a deserter on the battlefield and be dealt with accordingly; while those who were caught running after animals would be treated as though they had violated holy ground.

The fire was completely extinguished while the order was still being circulated.[1]

The Mystic Basis of Realism

It is not surprising that all surviving expositions,[2] despite their repudiation of abstract principles and ideals, do in fact seek a foundation in Taoist mysticism. The Realist system professed to be founded solely on human

[1] *Han Fei Tzŭ*, 30, second set of 'traditions'.
[2] Except *Shang Tzŭ*; see below, p. 85.

facts, and the facts which it chose for its basis are vital ones. But they are far indeed from constituting the whole truth about man and the functions of human society. The beliefs embodied in the old auguristic-sacrificial life and afterwards transmuted by the moralists into ethical conceptions were not, as the Realists claimed, mere illusion. Just as much as the opportunist doctrine of the realists, those older beliefs were founded on facts, on fundamental actualities of human existence. True, these facts concerning as they did the subtler parts of man's equipment, were more easily overlooked than those related to the broad necessities of his physical existence; but this did not make them any the less vital. It was the failure to enquire even in the most superficial way into the nature and function of the things they sought to discard that caused the Realists to build an edifice which, despite its coherence and solidity, never became and could never hope to become a dwelling-place for the human spirit. Long sections, in works such as *Han Fei Tzǔ* and *Kuan Tzǔ*, put forward the Realist position in a complete and uncompromising form. But as I have said, these works in very frequent passages make an attempt to reconcile this position with Taoism, which in the third century had become the dominant religion of China, at any rate in the sense that it coloured the works of all other schools.[1] The Taoist maxim 'Cling to the Unity' was divested of its metaphysical sense and turned into a political maxim—the absolute unification of everything in the State. Many of the incidental tenets of Taoism could, as it happened, be

[1] cf. the strong Taoist influence on the *Chung Yung, Hsi Tz'ǔ, Mencius, Lü Shih Ch'un Ch'iu, Han Fei Tzǔ, Kuan Tzǔ*, etc.

accepted as they stood. Taoists and Realists concurred in their contempt for *hsien* (people of superior morality), for book-learning, for morality and benevolence, for commerce and 'unnecessary' contrivances; both schools decried ceremony and advocated return to simple ways of life.

There was one State in China where simple ways (including human sacrifice) had never been abandoned. This was the north-western kingdom of Ch'in. Confucianism and, we may suppose, moralistic ideas in general, had hardly penetrated there.[1] Legend attributed to the Lord Shang, a 4th century statesman in Ch'in, an important part in the creation of Realist doctrine, though it is by no means certain that such ideas existed in China at all until the 3rd century. We possess a book called *Shang Tzŭ*, dating from the end of the 3rd century, which purports to give an account of Lord Shang's teaching. This short work[2] entirely eliminates all mysticism and idealism. It is not, like previous works of the kind, a receipt for maintaining frontiers intact, with the vaguely suggested possibility of uniting several states into some sort of hegemony. It is an exaltation of war; a handbook for the rearing of a race of conquerors. 'At home and in the streets, at their eating and at their drinking, all the songs that the people sing shall be of war.'[3] 'The father shall send his son, the elder brother his younger brother, the wife her husband,

[1] *Hsün Tzŭ*, P'ien 16.

[2] Admirably edited and translated by J. J. L. Duyvendak (Probsthain's Oriental Series, Vol. XVII. 1928), under the title *The Book of Lord Shang*. I here give only a very cursory account of *Shang Tzŭ* and refer the reader to Duyvendak's introduction.

[3] *Shang Tzŭ*, 17.

each saying when she speeds him: "Conquer, or let me never see you again!" '

The Ch'in conquered; and in 221 B.C. the king of Ch'in, which till a generation or two ago had been a small, outlying, insignificant principality, became First Emperor of all China. It seemed as though at any rate the efficiency of Realism had been triumphantly demonstrated. But some ten years later the new dynasty was already tottering, and in 206 it disappeared. Those who founded it believed that a State based upon 'facts' and not upon sentimental 'illusions' such as compassion and morality, would necessarily be eternal. This belief, however, soon turned out to be itself another example of illusion.

The 'Tao Tê Ching'

About 240 B.C. an anonymous[1] Quietist produced a small book, in only two *p'ien*, known from the early centuries of the Christian era onwards as the *Tao Tê Ching*. It was an extremely polemical work, directed in the main against the Realists, but at the same time siding with them in their condemnation of Confucianism and of the doctrines of Yang Chu. A superficial reader, dipping into the early parts of the book, might easily have supposed that he had before him another of those treatises, so fashionable at the time, in which the ruthless doctrines of the Realists were diluted with a specious basis of Taoist mysticism. He would have found that the art of ruling consisted in 'emptying the people's minds and filling their bellies, weakening their wills[2] and strengthening their

[1] For the circumstances which led posterity to connect the work with the name of Lao Tzŭ, see below, p. 106.
[2] cf. *Shang Tzŭ*, P'ien 20.

86

bones', in 'treating the hundred families like straw dogs', that is to say, not allowing any private feelings of pity towards individuals, any short-range sentimentalities to stand in the way of the general will of the State. He would have found this anonymous author using with apparent approval such Realist slogans as *wu-ssŭ*, 'nothing private', that is to say, the State can tolerate no aims, no opinions, no activities that are not its own. He would have found the usual Realist condemnation of book-learning (i.e. the study of the past, which may lead to dangerous criticisms of the present), of government by *hsien* (morally superior persons), of that private and individual law which we call conscience and which the Confucians of Mencius's school called *i*. Such a reader, if we may suppose him not to have had much of an eye for subtleties or ironies, might have read on happily through more than a quarter of the work, believing himself in perfectly safe and conventional hands, till he came to the statement that 'kingdoms cannot be made strong by force of arms; for such a policy recoils on the heads of those who use it'. At this point it becomes clear that the author is not a safe or sound person at all; and such a view of him is amply confirmed by subsequent passages in which he undermines the very corner-stone of Realist domestic policy by declaring that capital punishment, mutilations, imprisonment and the like do not in point of fact act as deterrents from crime.

The Realists called themselves *fa chia*, 'Legalists', and their doctrine was based on the idea that the decadence of the State is due to its tolerating private standards of good and evil, and failing clearly to 'label', to give names (*ming*) to the things that are good and evil from the public point of view. This leads to a discrepancy between 'names' and 'facts' (i.e. realities as conceived of by the State), creates in the network of Law innumerable loopholes, of which interests hostile to the public good will not scruple to avail themselves.

The author of the *Tao Tê Ching* combats, in the first place, the idea that there is such a thing as 'public good'. Society is a complicated structure, consisting of myriads of individuals, 'some blowing hot, some blowing cold, some loading, some setting down'. The ambition of the State to 'join the tallies', to absorb all these conflicting interests in one central purpose, is futile. The most it can do is to benefit some individuals at the expense of others. Equally delusive is its claim to save society by attaching an unalterable name to every fact. For the Quietist knows that the vast majority of facts—all those, indeed, that he becomes aware of when the ordinary sense-channels are closed—have no names, are in their very essence Nameless. Yet it is the knowledge of these nameless facts, the existence of which is undreamt of by the Realist, that gives *tê*, the only power that can 'benefit without harming', that can dissolve the myriad contradictions and discordances of phenomenal existence. The mysticism of the *Tao Tê Ching* is, then, essentially that of earlier Taoist works, save that owing to the rise of the Realist school, the question of 'names' is not merely a metaphysical one, but has become topical and controversial.

Another controversy of the times, which finds prominence in the *Tao Tê Ching*, centred round the word *yü*, 'desire'. Yü does not merely mean sexual desire (though it includes this), but all the desires of all the senses, the desire of the eye for human beauty,[1] of the ear for music, of the mouth for pleasant tastes, and so on. Doctors held that the unrestricted gratification of desires was dangerous to health;[2] moralists, that it diminished the powers of conscience,[3] which was conceived of, as has been shown above, as a sort of *shên* or divinity, precariously housed in the human frame. That abstinence touches the hearts of heavenly spirits, that the presence or help of such spirits can only be obtained by fasting and self-denial, was a principle universally admitted in the sacrificial-auguristic stage of Chinese society. The Taoists believed that by 'desirelessness' (*wu yü*) the ruler could become possessed of a *tê* ('power') which would turn his subjects away from their unruly desires.[4] Precisely the same view is reflected, I think, in the passage of the *Analects*[5] where in response to a question about how to deal with robbers Confucius says: 'If only you yourself were desireless they would not steal even if you paid them to.' The commentators have been at pains to deprive the passage of its Taoist flavour.

Mo Tzŭ believed in universal love, the natural corollary of which was the abolition of war. We have seen Mo Tzŭ's follower Kung-sun Lung finding that, though people were willing to subscribe to these principles in theory, their real state of mind was entirely inconsistent with a policy of peace and goodwill. The obstacle, so Sung Tzŭ[6] discovered in the second half of the 4th century

---

[1] *Sê.*   [2] cf. *Tso Chuan*, Chao Kung, year 1 (Legge, p. 573).
[3] *Mencius*, VII. 2. 35.   [4] *Chuang Tzŭ*, XII. 1.   [5] XII. 18.
[6] See *Mencius*, VI. 2. 4, *Chuang Tzŭ*, I. 3 and XXXIII. 3, *Hsün Tzŭ*, P'ien 18 and *Han Fei Tzŭ*, P'ien 50. Sung's personal name is written in three different ways; but all point to an approximate Archaic

B.C., was the prevalent belief that the 'desires' which cause conflict and mutual distrust are deeply-rooted and numerous. On the contrary, man's desires are 'shallow and few'; to prove which Sung Tzŭ deployed, as *Hsün Tzŭ* tells us, a great wealth of argument and imagery. But the most convincing proof that 'desire' can be practically eliminated lay in the life led both by Sung himself and by his numerous disciples: 'Constantly rebuffed but never discouraged, they went round from State to State helping people to settle their differences, arguing against wanton attack and pleading for the suppression of arms, that the age in which they lived might be saved from its state of continual war.[1] To this end they interviewed princes and lectured the common people, nowhere meeting with any great success, but obstinately persisting in their task, till kings and commoners alike grew weary of listening to them. Yet undeterred they continued to force themselves on people's attention. Troublesome though they were, it must be confessed that what they did on behalf of others was unlimited; while what they asked for themselves was little indeed. They said all they needed was to have half a peck of rice in store. Often enough the master himself got little to eat and the disciples even less. But never for a moment did they forget what they had vowed to do for all people under heaven, and hungry though they were, never

Chinese *gieng* or *giweng*. The lack of uniformity is due to the fact that he 'travelled about everywhere under heaven'; consequently the name is preserved in various dialectal forms.

[1] We know from *Mencius* that Sung based his argument against war on expediency (*li*), that is to say, on the plea that war does not 'pay'. Mencius attributes Sung's failure to this fact, and urges him to base his appeal on moral grounds.

rested either by night or day. . . . They thought indeed that anyone who is not helping all people under heaven had far better be dead.'[1]

But Hsün Tzŭ in his chapter on the necessity of improving language,[2] shows that those who claim to be 'without desire' or to have 'few desires' are not expressing themselves accurately. In reality they have just as many desires as other people; but they have decided not to satisfy these desires. There does indeed exist a state in which desire is absent. But this state is death. We must not assume then either that we can abolish desires or that there would be any advantage in doing so. On the contrary, we must help people to choose wisely among their desires, selecting for gratification those which 'pay', those which do not stand in the way of too many other gratifications. It is simply, says Hsün Tzŭ, a matter of doing a sum, of 'counting the cost', of balancing profit and loss just as is done every day in the market-place.

The *Tao Tê Ching* uses the two expressions *wu-yü* 'desirelessness' and *kua-yü* 'reduction of desires' interchangeably. Absence or at any rate a relative absence of desire is accepted by the author of this book, as indeed by all Taoists, as an essential for the practice of Quietism.

The Shêng

The Taoists however did not, I think, ever envisage a whole community or society consisting of ascetics. The way of life discussed in their books is believed by them to be an old one. It was followed by the *shêng*, the sage Ancestors who ruled mute and motionless over the em-

[1] *Chuang Tzŭ*, XXXIII. 3.   [2] *Hsün Tzŭ*, XXII. Paragraph 9.

pires of the past. True, the subjects of these Sages were insensibly led in a Quietist direction; but it is never suggested that they themselves actually practised Quietism or became possessed of its mysterious 'power'. The *Tao Tê Ching* is not in intention (though anyone may treat it as such, if he so chooses) a way of life for ordinary people.[1] It is a description of how the Sage (*shêng*) through the practice of Tao acquires the power of ruling without being known to rule. In Chinese, as we have seen, tense is not usually expressed. Every sentence in the *Tao Tê Ching* refers as much to the past as to the present. 'The Sage does this or that' means that the Sages of the past did so and that anyone who wishes to possess their miraculous power must do so again. Throughout the book it is assumed (as everyone except the Realists assumed) that an ideal state of society once existed. All reform simply means a return to the remote past. A very remote past indeed; for as far back as history went—that is to say, to the 8th century B.C.—no trace could be discovered of anything save just such violence and disorder as still prevailed in the 3rd century. But behind the historic period stretched legendary epochs which, though removed from the present by whole millennia seemed, and to a great extent still seem to the Chinese much nearer than the historic past. For mythology was in a fluid state, and these legendary eras could, from generation to generation, be remoulded to suit current longings and aspirations. Thus though nothing new could be recommended that was not according to the way of the Ancestors, the

[1] In *Chuang Tzŭ*, however, Taoism is in certain passages treated as a way of life for individual adepts.

Introduction

Ancestors themselves could be reformed. Ku Chieh-kang[1] has shown the humanizing process through which the legend of the San Miao, a race of rebellious 'first men', has passed. In the first stage of the legend the Supreme Ancestor annihilates them. In the second, they are banished to a remote corner of the earth. In the final stage, they are peacefully converted by a display of *tê*, of magico-moral 'power'. And it is by *tê*, not by war, that the Sage of the *Tao Tê Ching* 'wins the adherence of all under heaven'. Such a method is indeed the only one consistent with Quietism.[2] What strikes us at first sight as inconsistent with Quietism is the idea of founding an empire at all. By the middle of the third century, however, it had been generally recognized that the peace for which everyone longed could only come through the unification of China under one strong State. It was believed that such a unification had existed in the past, and all political thought of the period centered upon schemes for the restoration of this hypothetical Empire. But often it seems as though cultural rather than political conquest were envisaged. 'A nation,' Mussolini has said,[3] 'becomes imperial when directly or indirectly it rules other nations; it need not necessarily have conquered a single yard of territory.' The actual territory of the Ancestors Yao and Shun is often said, by those who believed most fervently in the existence of the early Empire, not to have extended more than a few miles. But the whole of China was subject to their 'power'. It is as well to bear this in mind when reading the political chapters of the *Tao Tê Ching*.

[1] *Ku Shih Pien*. Introduction, p. 53.
[2] As is indeed stated in the *Tao Tê Ching*, Ch. 30.
[3] *Enciclopedia Italiana*, Vol. 14.

The Way and its Power

An important difference between this book and other Taoist works is its attitude towards war. We have seen that pacificism arose out of the 'universal love' of Mo Tzŭ, and was preached at the close of the 4th century B.C. by the logician Kung-sun Lung and the altruist Sung Tzŭ. In the whole of the great Taoist corpus which is constituted by the forty one p'ien of Chuang Tzŭ and Lieh Tzŭ there is no specific condemnation of war. It is assumed as self-evident that violence of any kind is contrary to the principles of Tao, which 'acts' only through its own specific tê or 'power'. The Tao Tê Ching however devotes three chapters (30, 31 and 69) to the condemnation of war, and though chapter 31 has unfortunately reached us in a corrupt state, it is quite clear what the views of the author are. In condemning war he is addressing not the Quietist, whose principles in any case forbade violent action, but the average 'worldly person'. He cannot like Mencius appeal to morality, for two reasons: in the first place, the existence of morality (as opposed to legality) was no longer generally admitted; and secondly, the Quietist system itself rejected such conceptions as morality and altruism. He might like Sung Tzŭ have attempted to meet the common man on his own ground, by proving that apart from all moral or religious considerations, war is to be condemned, like any other bad bargain, for the simple reason that it costs more than it is worth. This is one of the arguments used by the Mo Tzŭ school.[1] A small castle may often cost as much as 10,000 lives. Multiply 'victories' indefinitely and you will have a vast territory, but no soldiers left to defend it. The same sort of argument,

[1] Mo Tzŭ, P'ien 18.

Introduction

based on 'profit and loss', was apparently used by Sung
Tzŭ. Such appeals to the mercantile spirit meet with a
response only from those who are already opposed to war.
Among primitive peoples the object of war is to renew the
waning vigour of the tribe,[1] and wherever the warring
instinct survives it is grounded not in a belief that war
pays in the material sense, but in the belief that (as a
modern Fascist writer has said) 'it sets once more the
stamp of nobility upon a people'. Mo Tzŭ, however,
makes an alternative appeal to the belief of the
masses. 'Whoever slays men', he says,[2] 'is destroying those
upon whom Spirits depend for their sustenance, and is
thus at the same time annihilating Former Kings.' The
warrior, then, as has already been pointed out, is at grips
not only with his own kind, but with unseen Powers
whose existence, no less than that of their descendants, is
at stake. It may be that the Ancestors in Heaven are dis-
gusted with their descendants and are ready to come over
to our side; indeed 'Heaven's hatreds are unaccountable'.
But in general war is 'unlucky', that is to say, it is bound
to give offence somewhere in the Halls of Heaven, and
the result will be pest, famine, earthquakes, storms,
eclipses. It is on this line of argument, directly based on
Mo Tzŭ, that the Tao Tê Ching condemns offensive war,
while admitting (like Mo Tzŭ and unlike the 'life-
esteemers' of the Yang Chu school) the right of the community to defend itself against attack.

In chapter 31, which deals with war, a commentary[3] has

[1] By absorbing, through various rites ranging from cannibalism to
drinking out of the enemy's skull, etc., the vigour and valour of
another tribe.   [2] Ibid., P'ien 19.   [3] Possibly that of Wang Pi
(3rd century A.D.), see below, pp. 129 and 182.

become incorporated in the text. Numerous efforts have been made to restore the chapter to its original state. Not one of these yields anything that at all resembles the usual style of the *Tao Tê Ching*, with its paradoxical twisting-round of other people's maxims, its epigrammatic and pungent quality. I am inclined to think that the author has here inserted with very little adaptation a passage from some lost pacifist work of the Mo Tzŭ school.

The Literary Methods of the Book

All argument consists in proceeding from the known to the unknown, in persuading people that the new thing you want them to think is not essentially different from or at any rate is not inconsistent with the old things they think already. This is the method of science, just as much as it is the method of rhetoric and poetry. But, as between science and forms of appeal such as poetry, there is a great difference in the nature of the link that joins the new to the old. Science shows that the new follows from the old according to the same principles that built up the old. 'If you don't accept what I now ask you to believe,' the scientist says, 'you have no right to go on believing what you believe already.' The link used by science is a logical one. Poetry and rhetoric are also concerned with bridging the gap between the new and the old; but they do not need to build a formal bridge. What they fling across the intervening space is a mere filament such as no sober foot would dare to tread. But it is not with the sober that poetry and eloquence have to deal. Their *tê*, their essential power, consists in so intoxicating us that, endowed with the recklessness of drunken men, we dance across the chasm, hardly aware how we reached the other side.

The appeal of the *Tao Tê Ching* is entirely of this second kind. 'What others have taught', says the author, 'I too will teach.' We are not, he promises, to be tempted across any chasm. Our feet are firmly planted on the safe, familiar shore. Yet long before we have closed the book we find to our astonishment that the chasm is behind us. Magically, without bridge or ferry, we have been transported to the other shore.

Proverbs of the people and of the patricians (*chün-tzŭ*), maxims of the strategist and realist, of the individualist (Yang Chu school); above all, sayings of the older Taoists which though they had very little apparent influence on conduct were at that period accepted as 'spiritual' truths, much as the Sermon on the Mount is accepted to-day—all these conflicting elements the author of the *Tao Tê Ching* reproduces or adapts, subtly weaving them together into a pattern perfectly harmonious and consistent, yet capable of embracing and absorbing the most refractory elements. The method here carried to an extreme point was not in itself new or exceptional. A great part of ancient thought, whether Christian, Buddhist or Mohammedan takes the form of giving fresh contents and hence new meanings to accepted maxims. Often these maxims were embodied in texts the letter of which was immune from criticism. But such texts were for a variety of reasons[1] fragmentary and ambiguous. They left ample

[1] Absence of 'determinatives' made early Chinese writing a very imperfect form of notation. Absence of vowels had the same effect in Semitic texts. Religious texts tend in general to be in obsolete or foreign languages.

room for manipulation, could be interpreted literally or figuratively, could in fact within certain limits be made to mean whatever the interpreter desired. Never has such manipulation been handled more ingeniously than by the Confucian school in China, particularly from the 1st century B.C. onwards when Confucianism had become a national orthodoxy. But in the 3rd century no such orthodoxy existed and the *Tao Tê Ching*, not being addressed exclusively to Confucians, to Mohists, to Taoists or to any one of the Twelve Schools, but comprehensively to the public at large, applies the method of 'reinterpretation' not only to the maxims of each philosophic school in turn, but also to the traditional code of thought and conduct embodied in proverbs whether plebeian or patrician.

The whole of 3rd century thought is shaken and shuffled like a kaleidoscope. Black is no longer black, nor white, white. One by one each cherished stand-by, each pivot of thought collapses, sheds its trappings and accessories, returns with no apparent intervention on the author's part to the 'state of the Uncarved Block'. The literary method of the book is indeed a triumphant exhibition of *tê*, of the 'power' that masters all complicated, all difficult and re-calcitrant things by reducing them to their alternative state of unity and simplicity.

In using a method which is essentially that of poetry[1] the author was returning, I think, to the practice of the 4th century Quietists, portions of whose apocalyptic utterances are preserved for us in *Chuang Tzŭ*, *Lieh Tzŭ*,

[1] I am not here merely referring to the fact that most of the book is in rhyme: cf. Bernhard Karlgren, *The Poetical Parts in Lao Tsi*, Göteborg, 1932.

Kuan Tzǔ and *Hsün Tzǔ*.[1] These early Taoist hymns were however clearly intended chiefly for the initiate. Then followed a period of Taoist expansion and propaganda, giving rise to the method of teaching by fable and anecdote which is typical of the 3rd century. This resource the *Tao Tê Ching* discards entirely. Its aim indeed is not to produce conviction upon any one point or understanding of any particular doctrine, but to create in the reader a general attitude favourable to Quietism. For the art of Tao is in its essence not merely incommunicable (as indeed are all arts) but secret, as is every technique in the pre-scientific world. Nevertheless, as a sort of Masonic sign to initiate readers that the author himself is an initiate, a certain number of passages do allude in a veiled way to the physical technique of Taoism, to breath-control and sexual régime. In such passages—there are not more than four or five of them—there is a double meaning, an esoteric and an exoteric. But the esoteric meaning is not intended to convey information. It is merely as it were a greeting to fellow Taoists into whose hands the book might chance to fall.

The Author

The reader may at this point well ask why I have all this time said nothing about the author of the book. The reason is a simple yet cogent one. There is nothing to say. We do not know and it is unlikely that we shall ever know who wrote the *Tao Tê Ching*. But for two thousand years the name of Lao Tan or 'Master Lao' (Lao Tzǔ) was connected with this book. To understand how this happened

[1] P'ien 21.

one needs to know something about the history of authorship in China, and as the subject is a rather complicated one, I shall discuss it in a separate essay.[1]

Meanwhile, before closing this introduction, I should like to meet two possible lines of criticism. It may be said that in my account of early Chinese thought I have wandered from author to author, picking out a scrap here or there, and taking no notice of the surrounding context. My answer is that several of my main sources (*Kuan Tzŭ*, *Han Fei Tzŭ*) are in themselves essentially a patchwork, in that they constantly quote early Quietist rhymes and maxims, and then proceed to reinterpret them in a Realist way. It is quite legitimate to divorce the text from the sermon.

It will certainly be said that my account of the Realists is coloured by recent events in Europe—that I have 'touched up' the picture, so as to give it the added interest of topicality. I can only ask anyone who thinks this to read J. Duyvendak's translation of *Shang Tzŭ*, a work which came out some five years ago and reads like a prophecy of recent events in Germany.

[1] Appendix I.

APPENDIX I

Authorship in Early China, and the Relation of the Lao Tan Legend to the 'Tao Tê Ching'

THE EARLIEST use of connected writing (as opposed to isolated magic pictures, developing into magic patterns) was as an aid to memory. That is to say, its purpose was to help people not to forget what they knew already; whereas in more advanced communities the chief use of writing is to tell people things that they have not heard before. Writing in early China, for example, was used to record the taking of omens, in order to assist in the correct interpretation of future omens. It was used to record infrequent rites, such as those of coronation[1] which might occur only once in a generation and were consequently apt to be imperfectly remembered. It was used to record the *libretti* of the great sacrificial dances that attended the worship of dynastic founders,[2] to record the main events (campaigns, reprisals, visits from other tribes, together with portents and omens other than those obtained by divination) of tribal life. All such writing as this was necessarily anonymous. No notion of 'authorship' attended it. It was merely the work of scribes, mechanically setting down things that were in danger of being forgotten.

Then came a time when men were interested in words and thoughts, as well as in actions. There arose a new kind of person, such as Confucius himself, who said

[1] See *Book of History*, Ku Ming.
[2] Such as the Great War Dance celebrating the defeat of the Shang by the Chou. Considerable parts of its *libretto* survive in the *Book of History* and elsewhere.

things that their followers were anxious not to forget. Tzŭ-ch'ang, we know, once wrote down a memorable saying of the Master's upon the lappet of his sash. There is no reason to doubt that the pupils of the early philosophers frequently recorded remarks in this way. Later on such jottings were collected and, along with oral traditions, framed into works such as the *Analects* and *Mencius*. But still there was no notion of 'authorship' in the modern sense of the word. Nor was there any idea that a book must have a title, a fixed name. Take for example the work that Europeans call the *Book of History*. The 'History' part of the title is our invention, and not a very happy one. For no book could be less historical. The early sources generally call it simply *Shu*, 'the writings', or they quote it by the names of individual sections in the work, or else they say 'in the writings of the Chou', 'in the writings of the Hsia', etc.; since then it has had a variety of other names. Nor is this tendency to describe books by any name that seemed to suit their contents confined to early times; there are books that, written long after the Christian era, only arrived at their present titles in the Sung dynasty or later.

Thus people in early China were used to regarding books as records of tradition. Their purpose was to save ancient and venerable things from oblivion. Consequently it was perfectly natural that when real authorship began writers should give their books the appearance of being records of ancient things, rather than present their ideas as new and personal discoveries. This was as natural and as inevitable as that the first railway carriages should imitate stage coaches. These early products of authorship were not, strictly speaking, what Western bibliographers call pseudepigraphs. No pretence was made that the books in question were written by the Ancients (though this was often believed in after ages by people who could only think in terms of modern authorship). It was merely pretended that what was now set down had once been taught by such or such an Ancient. Had this method not been adopted the people could not have been induced to read the books,[1] any more than travellers could have been persuaded to enter a railway carriage if it had not looked something like a stage coach.

Thus in the huge collection of writings known as *Kuan Tzŭ* a great many opinions are put into the mouth of a certain Kuan Chung who is supposed to have been Minister in Ch'i in the 7th century B.C. We should be wholly mistaken, however, if we supposed (as a famous modern scholar has done) that these opinions were such as the 3rd century writers who compiled the book had good reason to accept as Kuan Chung's. It would never have occurred to them to ask, for example, whether iron was really used in Kuan Chung's time. But when they had advice to give about the control of the iron industry (already flourishing in the 3rd century, but almost certainly non-existent in the 7th) they naturally and without a thought put this advice into Kuan Chung's mouth. In the same way the author of *Shang Tzŭ*, who lived in the 3rd century, in order to give weight to his extreme Realist views puts them into the mouth of, or at any rate often appeals to the authority of Shang Yang, a 4th century Minister. Again, a Taoist wrote the *Book of the Yellow*

[1] As is explained by *Chuang Tzŭ*, 27. 1.

Ancestor, now known to us only in quotation. The Yellow
Ancestor lived, as we have seen, somewhere about the 4th
millennium B.C., being relegated to this remote period
because there was no room for him in any other. There
was no suggestion that the book was actually written by
this fabulous divinity, but only that it embodied his
teachings, which had afterwards been handed down orally
from generation to generation. And finally the *Tao Tê
Ching*, owing to its constant use of sayings which everyone
connected with the name of Lao Tan (Lao Tzŭ, the Master Lao), naturally came to be regarded as embodying the
teaching of this legendary Quietist. Whether it was definitely put into the world as a record of the teachings of Lao
Tan or whether this ascription was merely one that grew
up in the minds of readers we cannot know.

Thus in regard to a whole series of Chinese books a
rather complicated state of affairs exists, which was completely misunderstood in China until quite recent times,
and appears still to be very imperfectly understood by
European scholars. In each case we get (1) an ancient
Worthy, (2) centuries later, a book 'sheltering itself' (as
the Chinese say) under his name. It occurred very early to
the Chinese that some of these books were not in point of
fact by the ancient worthies in question. But already the
conventions of primitive authorship, the ritual of self-
effacement that custom imposed upon it, were completely
forgotten, and to the medieval Chinese there appeared to
be only two alternatives: either the book really was by the
Worthy, or else it was by a forger, and therefore must not
be read. For forgery is wicked, and nothing useful can be
learnt from the books of wicked men. Now such is the

spell that the *Tao Tê Ching* has always had over the minds
of all save the most narrow and rigid sectaries of Confucianism that so long as no middle way presented itself
China has been obliged, despite every evidence to the contrary, to accept the book as a work of a legendary Worthy,
Lao Tan; for the only alternative was to admit that it was
a forgery, in which case it could not be read. I am speaking, of course, of the ordinary public. In the Taoist
Church the book had long ago become a sacred scripture,
the authenticity of which it was profanity to question.

In 'fathering' their works upon the Ancients or in issuing them anonymously in such a form that the public
would accept them as inspired by the Ancients, early
Chinese writers were in point of fact doing nothing disreputable, but merely conforming to the accepted ritual
of authorship. Such a view is only just beginning to be
accepted in China, and there is still a great deal of confusion between proving (1) that a work is not by its
'sheltering' Worthy, (2) proving that it is not by an
anonymous writer of the period when the 'sheltering'
ritual still prevailed. Nor is this confusion confined to
Chinese works. Thus in trying to prove that *Kuan Tzŭ* is
a forgery of the 4th century A.D. a French scholar mentions
that in one place *Kuan Tzŭ* adopts the chronology of the
State of Lu, 'absurd for a Minister of Ch'i' in the 7th
century B.C. If this were true, it would merely prove that
Kuan Tzŭ is not a work by its 'sheltering' Worthy, Kuan
Chung. It would have no bearing whatever on whether
Kuan Tzŭ is an anonymous work of the 3rd century B.C.
or a forgery of the 4th century A.D.

Historicity is a quantitative matter. Queen Victoria

is indubitably an historical character and not a mere legend. Yet among the things that we believe about her, some at least are likely to be false. The Cid is mainly legendary; yet embedded in this legend are certain grains of fact. The Worthies upon whom the Chinese of the 3rd century B.C. fathered their books represent varying degrees of historicity. There is not much doubt that a Ch'i Minister called Kuan Chung existed at the date alleged; but we know very little about him. Shang Yang is perfectly historical. The Yellow Ancestor is, I suppose, as mythical as it is possible to be. Lao Tan, the ancient Worthy under whose ægis the *Tao Tê Ching* has sheltered, is hard to classify, being a composite figure, made up of very heterogeneous elements. I do not intend here to analyse his legend, inextricably interwoven as it is with that of another sage called Lao Lai-tzŭ, to a lesser extent with that of Grandfather P'êng, the Chinese Methusaleh, and finally with the facts concerning a perfectly historical personage, also called Lao Tan, who was Treasurer of the Chou State about 374 B.C. When in the 1st century B.C. Ssŭ-ma Ch'ien attempted[1] to write a life of Lao Tan (whom he naturally regarded as the author of the *Tao Tê Ching*) he found himself confronted, as he confesses, with a mass of conflicting legend, which he was entirely unable to disentangle. The information he gives can be analysed as follows:

1. Birthplace, derived from the Lao Lai Tzŭ legend.

2. Nomenclature (surname, *tzŭ* etc., all complete as

[1] *Shih Chi*, 63.

though he were a T'ang dynasty official), an interpolation, as early quotations show.

3. Rank (Treasurer of Chou), derived from identification of Lao Tan with the 4th century Chou official of the same name. This is, of course, inconsistent with the meeting with Confucius, who lived a century earlier.

4. Story about Lao Tan's meeting with Confucius. An anti-Confucian Taoist legend similar to those in *Chuang Tzǔ* and elsewhere, no more relevant to historical facts than are the Taoist stories of Confucius's discomfiture at the hands of the Brigand Chê.

5. Story of Lao Tan's departure through the Pass. (cf. *Lieh Tzǔ* III. 2.) At the request of the Pass keeper Yin Hsi (also a famous Taoist Worthy) he writes a book in two *p'ien* 'embodying his ideas about *Tao* and *Tê*, and running to somewhat more than 5,000 words'.

6. Question as to whether Lao Tan and Lao Lai Tzǔ are not really the same person (Ssǔ-ma Ch'ien knew that Lao Lai Tzǔ figures instead of Lao Tan in stories about Confucius very similar to the one he has just told.)

7. Records that some people said Lao Tan lived to be 160; while others put the figure at over 200.

8. Quotes an historical reference to the Lao Tan who was Treasurer in 374 B.C., and remarks that though some say he is identical with Lao Tan the philosopher, others say no.

9. Quotes a genealogy by which the Li family in the 2nd century B.C. tried to establish its descent from Lao Tan whom they clearly identify with the historical Treasurer of the 4th century B.C.

10. Reflections on the mutual and quite unnecessary hostility of Taoists and Confucians.

In short, Ssŭ-ma Ch'ien's 'biography' of Lao Tzŭ consists simply of a confession that for the writing of such a biography no materials existed at all.

APPENDIX II.

Foreign Influence

IT HAS often been suggested that the Quietism of early China (4th and 3rd centuries B.C.) was to some extent moulded by Indian influence. It has been suggested that other trends of Chinese thought belonging to the same period[1] were also due to foreign influence. Thus it has been said that the theory of the Five Elements (Wu Hsing) may be connected with the Greek στοιχεῖα. Admittedly the Greek system enumerates the elements differently. But *hsing* means 'to walk', 'to go', and the Greek word for elements means literally 'steps'. It has also been said that the Dualist theory, which divides everything in the universe into the two categories *yin* and *yang*, is derived from Zoroastrianism. Finally, it has been claimed that the conundrums of the language-discriminators or 'sophists' were merely confused echoes of Greek thought.

Here we are only directly concerned with the question of a possible Indian influence on Taoism. The probability of such an influence becomes, however, much stronger if it can be shown that other branches of Chinese thought were being affected by outside influences at the same period. Let us examine these three allegations one by one.

1.—*The Five Elements*

Though *hsing* means 'to walk', 'to go', 'to set in motion',

[1] In common with most scholars in China and Japan I see no reason

109

'to operate', 'operation', 'conduct' (a man's 'walk' being taken as symbolic of behaviour in general, c.f. our 'walk warily', meaning 'behave with caution'), it never means 'a step'. What was the original sense of *hsing* in this connection? I fancy *Wu hsing* meant the Five Operations, i.e. the operations of the five constituent parts of nature, wood, fire, earth, metal and water. In that case the idea 'element' is not expressed, but understood, and it is irrelevant to compare *hsing* with στοιχεῖον.

2.—*Yin and Yang*

These terms mean literally 'dark side' and 'sunny side' of a hill. Hence, the shady side of anything, as opposed to the side that is in the sun. Suddenly, in a work[1] which is partially of the 4th century B.C. we find these terms used in a philosophical sense. *Yin* and *yang* are categories, corresponding to male and female, weak and strong, dark and light. At the same time they are (though this view has been recently combated) quite definitely forces; for *yin* is the vital-energy (*ch'i*, the life-breath of Earth, just as *yang* is the life-breath of Heaven). The work in question is currently printed in 24 paragraphs; only in three of these are the terms *yin* and *yang* used at all. The division into paragraphs is of course relatively modern, and I only

to place the Five Element theory earlier than the 4th century. The question is too complicated to discuss here.

[1] The *Hsi Tz'ŭ*, Appendix III to the *Book of Changes* in Legge's edition. There is one mention of *yin-yang* in the *Chou Kuan* chapter of the *Book of History*. This chapter is one of those which are generally regarded as the work of a third century A.D. forger.

mention it to show how very small a part these terms play in the Dualist theory. There is however little doubt that they assumed a much more important rôle in the speculations of Tsou Yen,[1] who flourished in Ch'i at the end of the 4th and beginning of the 3rd century B.C.; and they figure considerably in some of the Taoist treatises that form the collections *Chuang Tzŭ* and *Lieh Tzŭ*. It is however an exaggeration to say that 'the theory of *yin* and *yang* spread rapidly. From the end of the 5th century it was generally adopted by all philosophers'.[2] In the *Analects*, which were in process of formation at any rate down till about 350 B.C., there is no mention of *yin* and *yang*. In the works of the Mo Tzŭ school there is only one stray reference. In important Confucian works such as *Mencius*, the *Chung Yung*, the *Ta Hsüeh*, these terms do not occur at all. Out of the 76 surviving *p'ien* of *Kuan Tzŭ* only some half dozen mention *yin* and *yang*. Even in the second half of the 3rd century the Dualist theory was not widely accepted. It had little influence on Hsün Tzŭ or Han Fei Tzŭ. It is utilized in the calendrical parts of the *Lü Shih Ch'un Ch'iu*, but hardly at all in the other parts of this very catholic encyclopædia. Now my purpose in emphasizing the relative unimportance of the Dualist theory during the 4th and 3rd centuries is to explain why it is that the terms *yin* and *yang* figure so sparingly in my account of early Chinese thought, whereas some works on early China, particularly those dealing with archæology,

[1] His works (running to over 100,000 words, according to the *Shih Chi* of Ssŭ-ma Ch'ien) no longer survive; some account of them however is given by the *Shih Chi* in an appendix to the biography of Mencius.

[2] Maspero, *La Chine Antique*, p. 485.

attempt to explain every phenomenon in the light of the *yin-yang* Dualism. I will now return from this short digression, and ask what evidence there is that the Dualist conception was imported from the Iranian world.

In Zoroastrianism Darkness is essentially evil; the principle of Light, essentially good. The fundamental conception of *yin* and *yang* is quite different. They are two interdependent and complementary facets of existence, and the aim of *yin-yang* philosophers was not the triumph of Light, but the attainment in human life of perfect balance between the two principles. I will not here speculate as to how this conception arose in China.[1] In order to do so we should have to examine the whole history of yarrow-stalk divination, the fancies that wove themselves round the properties of the numbers that played important parts in this system of divination, which is essentially a development of primitive omen-taking by 'odds' and 'evens'. Suffice it to say that while it is quite easy to see how the *yin-yang* theory may have grown up out of native divination, it is very difficult indeed to imagine that even the most confused and distorted account of Persian religion could have given rise to the *yin-yang* system as we know it in China.

3.—Greek Influence on the Sophists

Chuang Tzŭ (XXXIII. 7) enumerates themes which were dealt with by the Chinese 'sophists'. Among these three have been supposed to show an affinity with topics discussed by the Greeks.

[1] It is noteworthy that an apparently arbitrary classification of all objects into two or more categories is found among primitives, for example in Australia.

Foreign Influence

a. 'The Tortoise is longer than the snake.' This seems at first sight to be merely a stupid pun on two senses of the *ch'ang*, which means 'long' in time as well as 'long' in space. But to the 'word-discriminators' such inadequacies of language were no joke at all. See above, p. 65. Cumulatively they made effective government impossible. In the present case it is shown that whereas in the world of fact length in time does not necessarily involve length in space, in the world of language no such distinction is made. There is no reason to think that we here have a confused echo of 'Achilles and the Tortoise'.

b. Something about an arrow which, as it stands, makes no sense. It is true that by supplying words which are not there, we can easily make the topic appear to have something to do with the arrow of Zeno; but such a proceeding is quite unscientific. What the proposition probably expressed (judging by similar Chinese propositions) is that all movement is relative. In relation to the earth, the arrow-tip moves; in relation to the shaft of the arrow, it stays still.

c. The proposition about halving a stick, which I have already dealt with above (p. 59). It is another way of stating the problem of Achilles and the tortoise; but at the same time it belongs entirely to Chinese thought, being merely part of a general demonstration that the world of language is quite a different place from the world of reality. In the latter, infinites do not exist.

In the three cases examined above (the Five Elements,

Yin and Yang, Logic) an outside influence is then not an impossibility; but its existence is far indeed from having been proved. We cannot, therefore, say that the formative period of Chinese Quietism (the 4th century) was one when outside influences on thought were general. On the other hand Quietism developed and expanded during a period when such influences were demonstrably beginning to be of great importance. All scholars are, I think, now agreed that the literature of the 3rd century is full of geographic and mythological elements derived from India.[1] I see no reason to doubt that the 'holy mountain-men' (*shêng-hsien*) described by *Lieh Tzŭ* are Indian *rishi*; and when we read in *Chuang Tzŭ* of certain Taoists who practised movements very similar to the *āsanas* of Hindu *yoga*, it is at least a possibility that some knowledge of the *yoga*-technique which these *rishi* used had also drifted into China. It has been said that merchants, who were undoubtedly the main carriers of information about the outside world, are not likely to have been interested in philosophy. This is a notion derived from a false analogy between East and West. It is quite true that Marco Polo 'songeait surtout à son négoce'. But the same can hardly be said of Indian or Chinese merchants. Buddhist legend, for example, teams with merchants reputedly capable of discussing metaphysical questions; and in China Lü Puwei, compiler of the philosophical encyclopædia *Lü Shih Ch'un Ch'iu*, was himself a merchant. Legend even makes a merchant of Kuan Chung; which at any rate shows that

[1] See Maspero, *loc. cit.* 608-609, and Lionel Giles, Two Parallel Anecdotes in Greek and Chinese Sources (i.e. *Lieh Tzŭ*), offprint from the *Bulletin of the School of Oriental Studies*.

philosophy and trade were not currently supposed to be incompatible. I see no reason, then, to doubt that the Chinese technique of self-hypnosis may have been supplemented in the 3rd century, particularly towards its close, by hints from abroad. But we are not at present in a position to prove that this was so.

APPENDIX III.

Taoist Yoga

THAT THE Chinese Quietists practised some form of self-
hypnosis no one familiar both with the yoga literature of
India (whether Hindu or Buddhist) and with Taoism
would, I think, be likely to dispute. Take these three
passages from *Chuang Tzŭ*:[1] 'The philosopher Ch'i sat
propped upon a stool, his head thrown back, puffing out
his breath very gently. He looked strangely dazed and
inert, as though only part of him were there at all. "What
was happening to you?" asked his disciple Yen Ch'êng,
who had been standing at his side. "You seem able to
make your body for the time being like a log of wood,
your mind like dead embers. What I have just seen lean-
ing against this stool appeared to have no connection with
the person who was sitting there before." "You have put
it very well," said Ch'i; "when you saw me just now my
'I' had lost its 'me'." '

In the second passage the Quietist ruler is said to sit like
a *shih*. This is generally translated 'corpse'; but I think it
is much more likely to mean the medium (*shih*) who sits
motionless and silent at the sacrifice waiting for the spirit
of the Ancestor to descend upon him. In the third passage we are told that on one occasion when Confucius
visited Lao Tan he found him 'so inert as hardly to
resemble a human being'. 'Confucius waited for a while,
but presently feeling that the moment had come for

[1] II. 1, XI. 1, and XXI. 4.

announcing himself addressed Lao Tan saying: "Did my eyes deceive me or can it really have been so? Just now you appeared to me to be a mere lifeless block, stark as a log of wood. It was as though you had no consciousness of any outside thing and were somewhere all by yourself." Lao Tan said: "True. I was wandering in the Beginning of Things." '

That these passages describe some form of self-induced trance is beyond dispute; and that this trance was closely akin to the *dhyāna* of the Buddhist is shown by the fact that the Chinese term for practising *dhyāna* (*tso-ch'an*,[1] literally 'sitting *dhyāna*') is modelled on the term by which the old Taoists describe the practice referred to in the above extracts. The Taoist term in question is *tso-wang*, 'sitting with blank mind' and is defined[2] as: Slackening limbs and frame, blotting out the senses of hearing and sight, getting clear of outward forms, dismissing knowledge and being absorbed into That which Pervades Everything.

The technique of self-hypnosis is often connected with some form of breath-control. In early Buddhism a state of trance was induced by concentrating the whole of conscious attention upon the incoming and outgoing breaths. There were other methods; but this was by far the commonest.[3] It is not certain whether this method was used in China before the advent of Buddhism. But breath-control was certainly part of Taoist discipline, of the

---

[1] Ancient Chinese approximately *dian*.   [2] *Chuang Tzŭ*, VI. 10.
[3] See for example the *Rāhulovāda* of the Majjhima Nikāya, the *Brahmacariya* of the Samyutta Nikāya, the *Path of Purity* (Pali Text Society Translations, No. 17) Pt. II, p. 305 seq. And in Chinese, the *Ta-an-pan Shou-i Ching*. Nanjio 681, Takakusu XV. 163.

régime by which the initiate became a *chên-jên* or Purified One. We have seen above[1] that in one place *Chuang Tzŭ* condemns physical exercises analogous to the yoga *āsanas*; but elsewhere (*Chuang Tzŭ* VI. 2) it is said that the breathing of the Sage is not like that of ordinary men: 'He breathes with every part of him right down to the heels.' 'He keeps the Great Treasure (i.e. the initial life-breath) intact and uses only the new breath. He sees to it that his "clarified breath" is daily renewed, his evil breath entirely eliminated.'[2] The breathing of the Sage, we read in many passages, must be like that of an infant. Later Taoist writers[3] go a step further, saying that it must be like that of a child in the womb. This 'womb-breathing' is the 'essence of breath-control', he who has mastered it can 'cure every disease, expose himself with immunity to epidemics, charm snakes and tigers, stop wounds from bleeding, stay under the water or walk upon it, stop hunger and thirst, and increase his own life-span'. The beginner draws in a breath through his nose, holds it while he counts mentally up to 120, and then breathes out through his mouth. Neither in being inhaled nor exhaled must the breath be allowed to make any sound. And more must always be breathed in than is breathed out. A goose-feather should be put (?) above the nostrils, and when such proficiency has been reached that the breath is expelled without causing the feather to tremble, the first stage of the art may be said to have been mastered. The counting should then be gradually increased up to a thousand, at which point the practicant will find himself

---

[1] p. 44.   [2] *Lü Shih Ch'un Ch'iu*, 13.
[3] *Pao P'u Tzŭ*, 4th century A.D. Nei P'ien VIII.

growing daily younger instead of older. . . . 'My great-uncle whenever he was very drunk or the weather was uncomfortably hot, used to jump into a pond and remain at the bottom for as much as a whole day. What enabled him to do this was solely his mastery over the art of breath-closing and womb-breathing.'

It is clear that the above passage deals with the abnormal physiological states which are the aim of the fakir rather than of the *yogi*. The reason for this is not far to seek. The *yoga* element in Chinese religious life had during the past century gradually been absorbed in Buddhism. The earliest Chinese works on Buddhist *yoga* date from the 2nd century A.D.[1] Their terminology is partly derived from that of Taoist *yoga*. Thus *dhyāna* is translated by the word *kuan*, which occurs so often in Taoist texts. *Kuan* means originally to 'watch' for omens,[2] and in the dictionaries it is defined as 'looking at unusual things', as opposed to ordinary seeing or looking. Hence, in accordance with the general 'inward-turning' of Chinese thought and vocabulary, it comes to mean 'what one sees when one is in an abnormal state'; and in Taoist literature it is often practically equivalent to our own mystic word 'Vision'. The root from which *dhyāna* comes has however nothing to do with 'seeing' but means simply 'pondering, meditating'; and it was only because *kuan* already possessed a technical sense closely akin to that of *dhyāna* that

---

[1] Nanjio, 681, attributed to An Shih-kao (fl. 148-170 A.D.), is one of the 30 An Shih-kao works accepted by Tao-an (314-385 A.D.). It has a preface by K'ang Sêng-hui (died 280 A.D.). It is not a translation of an Indian work, but a paraphrase, with commentary. I see no reason to doubt that it belongs to the 2nd century.

[2] See the *Book of Changes*, section 20.

it was chosen as an equivalent, in preference to some such word as *nien*, or *ssŭ*, which are the natural equivalents.

Chinese Quietism, however, though it found a temporary lodging place in the general Buddhist fold, was never entirely at home there. Gradually[1] it detached itself and formed a sect that owed its metaphysic to Mahayana Buddhism and not to Taoism, but which nevertheless eventually became the 'conductor' for exactly the same psychological forces that had in early days expressed themselves in Taoism. This new sect, called Ch'an in China and Zen in Japan, was like Taoism a 'wordless doctrine'. Like Taoism it discarded outward ceremonies, and like Taoism it startled the novice, loosened his sense of 'is' and 'isn't', by conundrums and paradoxes. Thus Zen which has played so great a part in the spiritual life of China and Japan, which is probably destined to exert before long a considerable influence on the West, is psychologically if not doctrinally the heir of 4th and 3rd century Chinese Quietism.

[1] Possibly from the 6th, certainly from the 7th century A.D. onward. It is now recognized that the sect was an internal movement in Chinese Buddhism and owed nothing to India. The whole story of Bodhidharma is a late legend, designed to give status and authority to the movement. See Pelliot, *T'oung Pao*, Vol. XXII, p. 253; and Hu Shih, *Wen Ts'un*, Series 3, p. 395 seq.

APPENDIX IV.

Date; Text and Commentaries

THERE ARE two current methods of dating Chinese texts, both of which have their dangers and disadvantages. The first we may call the bibliographical. This consists in searching literature for references to the text we are examining. We may find them in special book-catalogues or in general literature. Or again, we may find quotations from the text in question in books of known date, and thus get a clue as to its period. This method has been extensively used in China since the 18th century. In itself it is a scientific method; but only so long as it is used in a scientific way. In China it has frequently been used in a very unscientific way; and Europeans, hailing the method as congenial to Western ideas of research, have unfortunately borrowed not only the method, but also a most unscientific use of it. Examples of this have been collected by Professor Karlgren in an article on the authenticity of early Chinese texts.[1] I will deal here only with some further aspects of the question that particularly concern the present introduction and translation.

What is a quotation? M. Maspero[2] says that the *Analects* 'quote' a passage of the *Tao Tê Ching* ('Requite ill-feeling with *tê*'). I should say that both works make use of a stock saying. M. Maspero says[3] that *Lieh Tzŭ* is 'quoted' by the *Lü Shih Ch'un Ch'iu* and must therefore be previous. I

[1] *Bulletin of the Museum of Far Eastern Antiquities,* No. 1.
[2] *La Chine Antique,* p. 546.   [3] Op. cit. p. 491.

should say that there existed a common oral fund of stories about Quietist sages, and that if one author tells two such stories it certainly does not prove that he derived them from a second author who tells the same stories. Again, it is said[1] that the *Analects* of Confucius must be anterior to the *Ta Hsüeh* ('Great Learning') and *Chung Yung* ('Doctrine of the Mean'), 'which quote passages from it'. But if three Reminiscences of the 'Nineties all told the same story about Oscar Wilde, we should not arbitrarily decide that any one of them was 'quoting' the other. We should regard it as probable that all three were drawing on a common stock of Oscar Wilde tradition. Only if one book said 'As Pennell tells us in his Reminiscences', or something of that kind, should we regard the Wilde saying as a literary quotation. But when we examine the four passages in which the *Analects* are 'quoted' in these two books, we find no mention of the source. It is not said 'in the *Analects* it is written' or the like, but at most 'the Master said'.[2] What possible reason have we to suppose that all three books are not drawing on a common stock of tradition, just as in the modern parallel mentioned above? The same is true of the 'quotations' from the *Analects* that Maspero finds in *Chuang Tzŭ*,[3] *Lieh Tzŭ* and *Mencius*. I venture in these instances to express disagreement with M. Maspero, to whose work I owe so much, merely in order to show that the 'bibliographical' method needs to

[1] Op. cit. p. 546.

[2] Moreover, there is only verbal identity in one passage.

[3] *Analects*, XVIII. 5. cf. *Chuang Tzŭ*, IV. 8; the story of the Madman of Ch'u. This is a typical Taoist story, told in a much more complete form by *Chuang Tzŭ*. I hope to deal with this question elsewhere.

be handled scientifically, which in this case means imaginatively; in other words, it must be linked with an effort to reconstruct in our minds the conditions under which early Chinese books were produced.

Apart from quotations, we may find references in general literature (the question of catalogues has been dealt with by Professor Karlgren) to a text we are trying to date. In reference to the *Book of History* and its recovery after the supposed eclipse of learning during the short-lived Ch'in dynasty, the *Ju-lin Chuan*, the 121st chapter in Ssŭ-ma Ch'ien's History, has been often quoted. A *chuan*, as the character with which it is written shows, is a tradition 'passed from person to person'. No doubt in later days it comes to mean merely a written record. But I think it preserved its sense of 'oral tradition' well into the Han dynasty. The *chuan* inserted in *Han Fei Tzŭ* are certainly of this sort; and the *chuan* attached in the Han dynasty to the *History, Odes,* etc., were supposed to represent teaching orally handed down in the Confucian schools. If we compare Ssŭ-ma Ch'ien's annalistic sections[1] with the *chuan,* we feel at once that we are in a different world. To my mind it is the difference between written and oral tradition. The accounts of the kingdoms are chiefly founded on written annals; the biographies and most of the other *chuan* are hearsay, in which facts have become transformed, systematized, romanticized in the process of passing from mouth to mouth. True, many of these *chuan* deal with recent events. But it is not one's experience in

[1] Taking them as a whole; but where adequate annalist material was wanting he has been obliged to pad out even these sections with legendary matter. cf. Yao Ming-ta in *Ku Shih Pien* Vol. II (p. 118 seq.).

actual life that facts require centuries, or even years, to accomplish the process of turning into fiction, particularly where an atmosphere of excitement prevails. A great deal of excitement attended the recovery of literature in the 2nd century B.C., and I see no reason to accept Ssŭ-ma Ch'ien's description of the finding of the *Book of History*, any more than I should accept offhand a story about the finding of lost books of Livy. Indeed I see no reason to suppose that in his *chuan*, consisting essentially of things 'told by one person to another' and not based on contemporary written annals, Ssŭ-ma Ch'ien was any more critical than the average modern newspaper. It has not been noticed that next door to the story about the recovery of the *History* is one about the transmission of the *Book of Changes*, which is frankly legendary, at any rate in its earlier part. Ssŭ-ma Ch'ien describes the transmission of Confucius's teaching about the *Changes* through nine generations of master and pupil down to a certain Yang Ho, who flourished about 134 B.C. There is not the slightest evidence, however, that the *Book of Changes* was adopted by Confucianism until late in the 3rd century B.C.; and it does not figure on a par with the *Odes*, *History*, etc., as an accepted element of Confucian curriculum till the Han dynasty.[1]

I mention this only to show that the *Ju-lin Chuan* is a mixture of fiction and fact, as is inevitably the case with all works that depend on oral tradition rather than on

[1] As is well known, the passage (*Analects* VII. 16) in which Confucius himself is made to appear as a student of the *Changes* has probably been tampered with. We know that in the Lu version of the *Analects* the passage ran differently and contained no reference to the *Book of Changes*.

annals in which events were recorded one by one, as they occurred.

The alternative method of dating texts is one that we may call 'internal' or 'evolutionary'. Without going beyond the text itself it attempts to fix the point of evolution revealed on the one hand by grammar, vocabulary and pronunciation (as evidenced by rhymes); and on the other by ideas, legends and general range of allusion. The historical study of Chinese grammar was begun by Karlgren in 1920. He showed, for example, that certain laws obeyed almost without exception in the *Analects* have begun to break down in *Mencius*.[1] The historical study of vocabulary is still in its infancy. It is worth pressing much further. Here again Karlgren has been a pioneer. He has shown for example that in early works the word for boat is *chou*, and that the modern word *ch'uan* does not make its appearance till *Chuang Tzŭ*. I have pushed the enquiry a little further and can show that the new word also occurs in *Mo Tzŭ* (P'ien 45), in the *Lü Shih Ch'un Ch'iu* (P'ien 119), in *Han Fei Tzŭ* (P'ien 28), in *Kuan Tzŭ* (P'ien 13), in the *Chan Kuo Ts'ê* (V. 19); it does not however seem to occur in *Hsün Tzŭ*. Broadly speaking, we may say that this word began to come in during the 3rd century and by Han times had definitely replaced *chou* as the general word for a boat. There are no doubt many other words that could be subjected to the same sort of historical analysis. I have collected and hope to publish a few other examples. It will be seen that it ought to be possible ultimately to build up on this principle a very

[1] The same question was treated from a rather different angle by Hu Shih (*Wên Ts'un*, Vol. II).

useful series of word-tests. Karlgren again has dealt with the subject of rhyme, showing for example in his *The Poetical Parts in Lao-tsi* (1932) that the rhyme-system of the *Tao Tê Ching* is typical of the period at which I place the work.

But there exists a species of 'internal' test more important than the purely philological ones just described. I have given an example of it above (p. 93) in connection with the story of the wicked San Mao. As an example of the evolution of beliefs one might take the case of the *hsien* ('mountain-men'), the Immortals of later Taoism. In *Lieh Tzŭ* they are mysterious people who live in a far-off land. There is no suggestion that anyone in China can 'become' a *hsien*. It is not till well into the Han dynasty that to 'turn into a *hsien*' becomes the aim of Taoist asceticism. An example of evolution in legends is supplied by the story of the 'Tyrant' Chou, last ruler of the Yin dynasty. Let us examine the references to him in three works, representing the successive stages in the development of the story. In the *Book of History* (canonical portions only, showing the progress of the legend down to about 500 B.C.) the king drinks excessively, is under the influence of women, sets aside old-established dignitaries and puts scamps in their place, fails to sacrifice to the ancestral-spirits in Heaven, in the conviction that the Divine Right, once given, cannot be forfeited. In the *Lü Shih Ch'un Ch'iu* (showing development in the next 250 years) King Chou not merely drinks excessively but constructs a 'lake of wine'. He is not merely under the influence of women, but commits atrocities in his dealings with them; for example, rips open the belly of a pregnant woman to see what is happening inside. He does not merely set aside the trusted officers of state, but slays them, and flouts Heaven by a whole series of other atrocities, such as putting all his own feudal barons under arrest, and making minced meat of envoys sent from neighbouring lands. The crescendo continues during the Han dynasties, and finally when we reach the *Ti Wang Shih Chi*[1] of Huang-fu Mi (4th century A.D.) the tyrant Chou, though he still cooks envoys, tortures prisoners and feeds his tame tigers on human flesh, has risen to a sort of Satanic grandeur: 'There came a great wind and rain. Oxen and horses were blown off their feet, trees and houses were cast down, a fire from Heaven burnt his palace, for two whole days it blazed, till it was utterly destroyed. But still, though the spirits of the dead wailed and the hills lamented, King Chou was not afraid.'

The above examples are sufficient, I think, to show what an important part the study of the history of thought and the history of legends and myths might play in the dating of early works. Indeed this method, when combined with linguistic tests, is in my view the surest standard; and where literary tradition, as established by bibliographical researches, conflicts with the results of this internal method, I personally am prepared to jetison literary tradition.

Applying these same methods to the *Tao Tê 'Ching* we find that in grammar it is typical of 3rd century B.C. philosophers.[2] In vocabulary there are elements (such as

[1] Now known only in quotation. I am indebted to Ku Chieh-kang for the above account of the expansion of this legend.

[2] Applying Karlgren's nine tests. The only exception is *ssŭ* in the sense of 'thereupon' (Ch. 3). But it occurs in certain fixed combinations of which this (*ssŭ . . . i*) is one.

chiao in Ch. 1 and *chia*, 'fine' in Ch. 31) that point to the latter part of the 3rd century. The rhymes I have already referred to. But it is above all the point of evolution reached by the ideas alluded to in the book that makes its date certain beyond any doubt. It is a controversial work, and the opponents with which it deals did not exist till the 3rd century. There is, moreover (without actual quotation), a continual use of phrases, metaphors and topics derived from *Hsün Tzŭ*, *Han Fei Tzŭ* and the *Lü Shih Ch'un Ch'iu*, or at any rate from sources that these works also used. Failure to realize this fact has made it frequently impossible to extract any meaning from the text, even a purely 'scriptural' one; whereas for anyone who has these contemporary writers in mind very few passages present any difficulty at all. A particularly good example is Chapter 60, the wording of which seems to me to postulate the presence in the author's mind of a whole series of other texts. We have in such cases something vaguely analogous to, but far from identical with, the allusiveness of later Chinese literature. The latter is ornamental; that of the *Tao Tê Ching* is combative and ironical. I have not thought it worth while to tabulate all these correspondences; but many of them will be found in the footnotes and commentary.

Text

The earliest surviving edition of the *Tao Tê Ching* is that of Wang Pi (226-249), an extremely short-lived scholar most of whose life was devoted to the 'scripturalization' of the *Book of Changes*. His text was evidently a very sound one. It has been tampered with here and there; but his commentary was not brought into line with such changes, so that (except in the case of phrases upon which he happened not to comment) we can restore the original reading. We are helped too by the phonetic glosses of Lu Tê-ming (564-635 A.D.).[1] Some time about the 4th century A.D. an unknown Taoist produced what purported to be an independent text, together with what he pretended was a lost Han commentary. It can however easily be shown that this edition is simply the Wang Pi text furnished with a few variants mostly either trivial or erroneous, and a commentary designed to bring the *Tao Tê Ching* into line with contemporary Taoism, which was a very different thing indeed from the Taoism of six hundred years before.

All the commentaries, from Wang Pi's onwards down to the 18th century, are 'scriptural'; that is to say that each commentator reinterprets the text according to his own particular tenets, without any intention or desire to discover what it meant originally. From my point of view they are therefore useless. The 18th century opens up a new era. The study of textual variants begins, and also the historical study of grammar. The latter is of vital importance;[2] the former, as I shall try to show, has not in the case of this particular work, achieved results com-

[1] Wang Pi's commentary is rather corrupt and so is Lu Tê-ming's work. But both are adequately serviceable for the purpose in view. The interpretations of passages from the *Tao Tê Ching* to be found in *Han Fei Tzŭ* and *Huai-nan Tzŭ* can also be regarded as partial commentaries.

[2] Cf. Wang Sung-nien's little treatise on the conjunction *yen* in *Tu Shu Tsa Chih*, Yü P'ien, fol. 16.

mensurable with the vast amount of labour expended upon it.

Variant readings, in such a case, are only of value if they go back to a source which is surer and better than the text we already possess. The variants collected by scholars from Pi Yüan in the 18th century down to Ma Hsü-lun in our own day are of two classes. The first is drawn from quotations of the *Tao Tê Ching* in early works. These quotations are always short, and judging from every known analogy we may presume that they were made from memory. In our own books Shakespeare, Keats, the Bible are constantly misquoted. Why should we repose a vast faith in the accuracy of early Chinese quotations? If there were a case where the original was hopelessly corrupt and an early writer quoted a version that not merely looked convincing but gave us some inkling of how the corruption arose, then we should be justified in bringing the text into line with the quotation. But no such case· exists. In the few places where the text is obviously corrupt the variants are, in my opinion, simply more or less intelligent suggestions,[1] such as we could perfectly well make for ourselves. There is not the slightest evidence that any single variant based on an early quotation really goes back to an independent and better text. In one case a quotation—that of the 6th century commentary on the *Shih Shuo Hsin Yü*—supplies a smooth and easy version of a sentence which in the text as we have it (Ch. 13) is hard to

---

[1] The variants in *Han Fei Tzŭ* and *Huai-nan Tzŭ* are hardly of this class. Both books are interpreting the text in a manner so totally divorced from its original meaning that they end, so it seems to me, by becoming somewhat reckless even concerning the wording of the text itself. Both, too, were probably quoting from memory.

construe. Here again, it is unlikely in the extreme that the commentator rushed to a copy of the *Tao Tê Ching* in order to quote a single sentence. He quoted from memory, and his memory unconsciously smoothed out and simplified the difficult clause. It is far wiser to make the best we can of the text as it stands, rather than use this probably quite unintentional emendation.

So much for quotations. There remains the question of early texts. Several times during the T'ang dynasty the *Tao Tê Ching* was engraved on stone, and some of these slabs still survive. All of them follow the spurious 4th century text, embellishing it with a great variety of small emendations and simplifications. Where these merely concern unessential particles they become little more than a matter of 'typography' and need not detain us. Their efforts to 'make better sense' of the original are almost always connected with the fact that the whole context meant something quite different to them from what was intended by the author. This also holds good of the T'ang MSS. recovered from Tun-huang,[1] which include at least one partial Wang Pi version. Their emendations are either negligible or are due simply to misunderstanding. As to Sung, Yüan and Ming texts—it seems to me pure waste of time to tabulate all their small differences.

Checked by Lu Tê-ming's glosses and the Wang Pi commentary, our text is at least as satisfactory as that of other early Chinese works. Occasionally modern writing conventions require us to alter a determinative; in one or two instances we have to take a reading from the 'spurious' text; for it and the Wang Pi text have to some slight

[1] Now in the British Museum and Bibliothèque Nationale.

extent become mutually contaminated. Of actual emendations really affecting the sense I have made only one, consisting in the omission of a single negative; and in this case it is easy to see how the corruption arose.

APPENDIX V

The Formation of Chinese Pre-history

THE GRADUAL rise of the idea of empire, of a great State 'without rival under Heaven' was accompanied by the theory that the Ancestors had ruled over such an Empire. In actual fact, however, the Chinese knew practically nothing about their own past previous to the 8th century B.C. Tradition indeed said that from the 11th to the 9th century the Chou had exercised a sort of glorified hegemony far more complete than those actually witnessed in the historic period. We have no reason to reject this tradition altogether; but what the extent of this hegemony was, whether it was mainly cultural or also political, we do not know and certainly cannot discover except through archæological finds.[1] As for the Yin, the ancient Chinese knew nothing about them except the names of their kings. To-day, owing to the discovery of the Honan oracle bones (11th century B.C.), we know something about the life and preoccupations of the Yin people; but nothing that can be called history.

European writers, not understanding the process by which Chinese prehistorical chronology was built up, have till recently been apt to assume that, even if such figures as the Yellow Ancestor (Huang Ti) whom this chronology

[1] A certain amount of information can be gleaned from archæological evidence already existing; for example, from inscriptions on bronzes. But the pitfalls in such a line of research are obviously numerous. The best collection of inscriptions is Kuo Mo-jo's *Liang Chou Chin Wên Tzŭ Ta Hsi*, Tōkyō, 1932.

133

places in the 3rd millennium B.C.) are legendary, the stories told about them do actually reflect the state of culture in China during the third millennium or at any rate during a very early period. Legend, for example, says that the Yellow Ancestor cast nine bronze tripods; therefore even if the Ancestor is mythical (so this argument runs) we may at least conclude that the use of metal was known thousands of years before history. Such an argument would not be used if it were understood that the Yellow Ancestor was put into this remote period by the chronologists merely in just the same way as someone arriving late at a crowded concert is put at the back of the room. Each Chinese tribe had at the outset its own ancestral cult and ancestral mythology. The establishment of successive hegemonies brought about a constant merging of ancestral cults. So long as Ancestors (such as Yao, Shun, the Great Yü) were conceived of merely as Former Kings of a particular tribe, they could exist in popular imagination side by side, floating in a vague past. But when the idea of Empire arose, and it was asserted as a justification of an Imperialist policy that the Chou, for example, once ruled over everything under Heaven, having conquered the Yin who also ruled the world, it was no longer possible to place a mighty and venerated Ancestor such as Yao at the same period as the Yin or Chou 'Empires', and thus make him a subject of Yin or Chou. To bring him down to the historical period was obviously impossible, and the only alternative was to give him the vacant space previous to the dominance of the Yin. Yao and Shun do not appear in the earliest literature and still figure very dimly in the *Analects*. The Yellow Ancestor was an even later comer, and had consequently to be accommodated 'behind' Yao, in an even more remote corner of prehistory. Thus the chronology was built up backwards, and has no relation whatever with an actual time-sequence.

APPENDIX VI

Sources of Doubtful Date

Kuan Tzŭ

B. KARLGREN has shown (*Bulletin of the Museum of Far Eastern Antiquities*, No. 1) that none of the 'bibliographical' arguments which would relegate *Kuan Tzŭ* to the 3rd or 4th century A.D. are valid. Internal evidence for the 3rd century B.C. as the date for this work as a whole is overwhelming. See Lo Kên-tsê, *Ku Shih Pien*, IV. 615. Certain parts are older; see Haloun, *Asia Major*, IX. 3 (1933).

Lieh Tzŭ

European opinion (Karlgren, Maspero) tends (quite rightly) to put *Lieh Tzŭ* in the 3rd century B.C.; but it seems as though Ma Hsü-lun's 'Doubts about the Authenticity of *Lieh Tzŭ*' (written some 14 years ago) still holds the field in China. None of the arguments used by Ma Hsü-lun and his supporters are of a kind that I can regard as in any way valid, and internal evidence points to the 3rd century B.C. for a large part of the contents.

Han Fei Tzŭ

It is agreed that the chapters in this collection fall into three classes: (1) those which are certainly by Han Fei himself, (2) those which show strong affinity in style and content with the Han Fei chapters, (3) the rest.

Two chapters form a sort of commentary on parts of the *Tao Tê Ching*, interpreting it (in a very forced way) according to a syncretist philosophy in which Taoism and Realism both play a part. It has never been suggested that these chapters belong to class (1) or (2). If anyone succeeded in proving that they were by Han Fei himself, we should know that they were earlier than 235, the date of his death. Various other problems would arise, so hypothetical that they need not here be dealt with.

Chan Kuo Tsʻê

Is the débris of a work composed in the early years of the Han dynasty? For the question of its authorship, see *Ku Shih Pien*, IV. 229.

Kʻung Tzŭ Chia Yü

In order to establish this book as part of the Confucian curriculum, Wang Su (3rd century A.D.) provided it with forged credentials. The idea, however, that the work we possess is not part of that which circulated in Han times, is quite unfounded. Wang Su may have tampered with certain passages. But this cannot often be the case; for there are only ten paragraphs in the whole book which have not (as regards content, though not as regards phrasing) exact parallels in early literature. A list of most of these parallels is given by Gustav Haloun in *Asia Major* VIII. fascicule 3, where the inadequacy of the usual arguments against the authenticity of the *Chia Yü* is shown. The Chinese were faced with the alternative of regarding the *Chia Yü* as a late forgery or of accepting its *logia* as genuine utterances of Confucius. For us this dilemma does not exist. The *Chia Yü* represents the Confucian legend as it developed during the 3rd century B.C.

137

TAO TÊ CHING

TAO TÊ CHING

CHAPTER I

The Way that can be told of is not an Unvarying Way;
The names that can be named are not unvarying names.
It was from the Nameless that Heaven and Earth sprang;
The named is but the mother that rears the ten thousand
    creatures, each after its kind.
Truly,[1] 'Only he that rids himself forever of desire can see
    the Secret Essences';
He that has never rid himself of desire can see only the
    Outcomes.[1]
These two things issued from the same mould, but never-
    theless are different in name.
This 'same mould' we can but call the Mystery,
Or rather the 'Darker than any Mystery',
The Doorway whence issued all Secret Essences.

Paraphrase

The Realists demand a *ch'ang-tao*, an 'unvarying way' of
government, in which every act inimical and every act
beneficial to the State is codified and 'mated' to its
appropriate punishment or reward. The Taoist replies
that though there does exist a *ch'ang-tao*,[2] 'an unvarying

---

[1] See additional notes.   [2] *Han Fei Tzu*, 51.

Way', it cannot be grasped by the ordinary senses nor described in words. In dispassionate vision the Taoist sees a world consisting of the things for which language has no names. Provisionally we may call them *miao*, 'secret essences'. The Realist, his vision distorted by desire, sees only the 'ultimate results', the Outcomes of those essences, never the essences themselves. The whole doctrine of Realism was founded on the conviction that just as things which issue from the same mould are mechanically identical, 'cannot help being as they are',[1] so by complete codification, a series of moulds (*fa*), can be constructed, which will mechanically decide what 'name' (and consequently what reward or punishment) should be assigned to any given deed. But the two modalities of the Universe, the world as the Taoist sees it in vision and the world of everyday life, contradict the basic assumption of the Realist. For they issue from the same mould ('proceed from a sameness'), and nevertheless are different as regards name. Strictly speaking, the world as seen in vision has no name. We can call it, as above, the Sameness; or the Mystery. These names are however merely stop-gaps. For what we are trying to express is darker than any mystery.

---

1 *Kuan Tzŭ*, 36, just after middle.

CHAPTER II

IT IS because every one under Heaven recognizes beauty as beauty, that the idea of ugliness exists.

And equally if every one recognized virtue as virtue, this would merely create fresh conceptions of wickedness.

For truly 'Being and Not-being grow out of one another;

Difficult and easy complete one another.

Long and short test[1] one another;

High and low determine one another.

Pitch and mode give harmony to one another.

Front and back give sequence to one another .

Therefore[2] the Sage relies on actionless activity,   *wu wei*

Carries on wordless teaching,

But the myriad creatures are worked upon by him; he does not disown them.

He rears them, but does not lay claim to them,

Controls them, but does not lean upon them,

Achieves his aim, but does not call attention[3] to what he does;

And for the very reason that he does not call attention to what he does

He is not ejected from fruition of what he has done.

Paraphrase

The Realists say that virtue (i.e. what the State desires)

[1] See textual notes.

[2] Because 'action' can only make one thing high at the expense of making something else low, etc.

[3] Lit.: 'does not place (i.e. classify) himself as a victor'. cf. *Mencius*, II. 1. 2. 19.

must, by complete codification, be made as easily recognizable as beauty. When people see Hsi Shih (the legendary paragon of beauty) they at once know that she is the most beautiful of women; but when they see good men (i.e. those who are strong-limbed but docile, see *Shang Tzŭ*) they mistake them for boors. This can only be avoided if the State clearly labels the good as good.

But, says the Taoist, by admitting the conception of 'goodness' you are simultaneously creating a conception 'badness'. Nothing can be good except in relation to something that is bad, just as nothing can be 'in front' except in relation to something that is 'behind'. Therefore the Sage avoids all positive action, working only through the 'power' of Tao, which alone 'cuts without wounding', transcending all antinomies.

The type of the Sage who in true Taoist manner 'disappeared' after his victory is Fan Li[1] (5th century B.C.) who, although offered half the kingdom if he would return in triumph with the victorious armies of Yüeh, 'stepped into a light boat and was heard of no more'.

---

[1] *Kuo Yü*, 21. The passage is closely akin to the *Tao Tê Ching* both in language and thought.

CHAPTER III

IF WE stop looking for 'persons of superior morality' (*hsien*) to put in power, there will be no more jealousies among the people. If we cease to set store by products that are hard to get, there will be no more thieves. If the people never see such things as excite desire, their hearts will remain placid and undisturbed. Therefore the Sage rules

By emptying their hearts
And filling their bellies,
Weakening their intelligence[1]
And toughening their sinews
Ever striving to make the people knowledgeless and
    desireless.

Indeed he sees to it that if there be any who have knowledge, they dare not interfere. Yet through his actionless activity all things are duly regulated.

Commentary

This chapter is a bait for Realists. The author shows that like them he is against the raising of *hsien*, is against knowledge, trade, luxury, etc. But he slips in *wu-yü*, desireless (see Introduction, p. 89) and *wu-wei*, 'non-activity', i.e. rule through *tê* ('virtue', 'power') acquired in trance.

---

[1] Particularly in the sense of 'having ideas of one's own'.

CHAPTER IV

The Way is like an empty vessel
That yet may be drawn from
Without ever needing to be filled.
It is bottomless; the very progenitor of all things in the world.
In it all sharpness is blunted,
All tangles untied,
All glare tempered,
All dust[1] smoothed.
It is like a deep pool that never dries.
Was it too the child of something else? We cannot tell.
But as a substanceless image[2] it existed before the Ancestor.[3]

[1] Dust is the Taoist symbol for the noise and fuss of everyday life.

[2] A *hsiang*, an image such as the mental images that float before us when we think. See Introduction, p. 61.

[3] The Ancestor in question is almost certainly the Yellow Ancestor who separated Earth from Heaven and so destroyed the Primal Unity, for which he is frequently censured in *Chuang Tzŭ*.

CHAPTER V

Heaven and Earth are ruthless;
To them the Ten Thousand Things are but as straw dogs.
The Sage too is ruthless;
To him the people are but as straw dogs.
Yet[1] Heaven and Earth and all that lies between
Is like a bellows
In that it is empty, but gives a supply that never fails.
Work it, and more comes out.
Whereas the force of words[2] is soon spent.
Far better is it to keep what is in the heart.[3]

Commentary

Jên, which I have here translated 'ruth' and elsewhere 'gentle', 'kind', etc., is cognate to *jên* 'man'. I believe that *jên* did not originally mean mankind in general, but the members of one's own tribe or group, for whom one has feelings of 'nearness'. (The *Shuo Wên* defines *jên* as *ch'in*, 'akin', 'near'.)

Compare the origin of 'kind' from 'kin' and 'gentle' from *gens*, Latin for a clan. Hence (because members of one's own ethnic group are better than members of other groups) 'good' in the most general sense. In the *Book of*

---

[1] Though ruthless (as the Realists never tired of maintaining), nature is perpetually bounteous.

[2] Laws and proclamations.

[3] For *chung* as 'what is within the heart', see *Tso Chuan*, Yin Kung 3rd year and *Kuan Tzŭ*, 37, beginning. The comparison of Heaven and Earth to a bellows is also found in *Kuan Tzŭ* (P'ien 11, beginning).

Odes, jên only occurs coupled with *mei*—'handsome and good', i.e. true member of the tribe both in appearance and character. In early Confucianism *jên* acquires a mystic sense, 'The Highest Good', and comes near to playing the part that the term Tao plays in Quietist terminology.

It is to be noted that in the earliest literature (e.g. *Odes* Nos. 249, 256, 257; *Book of History,* Hung Fan) *jên*, 'men of rank', 'men of the tribe' are contrasted with *min*, 'subjects', 'the common people'.

CHAPTER VI

The (Valley Spirit) never dies. *feminine spirit*
It is named the Mysterious Female.
And the Doorway of the Mysterious Female
Is the base from which Heaven and Earth sprang.
It is there within us all the while;
Draw upon it as you will, it never runs dry.[1]

[1] For these six lines see Introduction, p. 57. *Lieh Tzŭ* quotes them as coming from the *Book of the Yellow Ancestor*; but it does not follow that the *Tao Tê Ching* is actually quoting them from this source. They may belong to the general stock of early Taoist rhymed teaching. For *ch'in* compare below, p. 206, line 9, and *Huai-nan Tzu* I, fol. 2.

149

CHAPTER VII

Heaven is eternal, the Earth everlasting.
How come they to be so? It is because they do not foster
    their own lives;
That is why they live so long.
Therefore the Sage
Puts himself in the background; but is always to the fore.
Remains outside; but is always there.
Is it not just because he does not strive for any personal end
That all his personal ends are fulfilled?

humility

CHAPTER VIII

favorite image of Tao

THE HIGHEST good is like that of water.[1] The goodness of water is that it benefits the ten thousand creatures; yet itself does not scramble, but is content with the places that all men disdain. It is this that makes water so near to the Way.

And if men think the ground the best place for building a
    house upon,
If among thoughts they value those that are profound,
If in friendship they value gentleness,
In words, truth; in government, good order;
In deeds, effectiveness; in actions, timeliness——
In each case it is because they prefer what does not lead
    to strife,[2]
And therefore does not go amiss.

[1] For water as a Taoist symbol see Introduction, p. 56.
[2] Even ordinary people realize the importance of the Taoist principle of 'water-like' behaviour, i.e. not striving to get on top or to the fore.

CHAPTER IX

Stretch a bow[1] to the very full,
And you will wish you had stopped in time;
Temper a sword-edge to its very sharpest,
And you will find it soon grows dull.
When bronze and jade fill your hall
It can no longer be guarded.
Wealth and place breed insolence
That brings ruin in its train.
When your work is done, then withdraw!
Such is Heaven's[2] Way.

asceticism

---

[1] The expression used can also apply to filling a vessel to the brim;
but 'stretching a bow' makes a better parallel to 'sharpening a sword'.
[2] As opposed to the Way of man.

152

CHAPTER X *Taoist Yoga*

Can you keep the unquiet[1] physical-soul from straying,
   hold fast to the Unity, and never quit it?
Can you, when concentrating your breath, make it soft
   like that of a little child?
Can you wipe and cleanse your vision of the Mystery till
   all is without blur?
Can you love the people and rule the land, yet remain
   unknown?
Can you in opening and shutting the heavenly gates play
   always the female part?[2]
Can your mind penetrate every corner of the land, but you
   yourself never interfere?
Rear them, then, feed them,
Rear them, but do not lay claim to them.
Control them, but never lean upon them;
Be chief among them, but do not manage them.
This is called the Mysterious Power.

Commentary

For other versions of the old Taoist hymn which the
author here adapts to his own use, see *Chuang Tzŭ*,
XXIII. 3, and *Kuan Tzŭ* 37 (near beginning). For the
physical-soul or *p'o* see Introduction, p. 28. But as we
have seen *p'o* literally means semen, and there is here an
allusion to a technique of sexual hygiene parallel to

1 See textual notes.
2 Read *wei*, not *wu*. This is the original Wang Pi reading, as the
commentary shows.

153

breathing technique. For the necessity of soft breathing, see Appendix III. The female (i.e. passive) opening and shutting of the heavenly gates also refers to the opening and shutting of mouth and nostrils. This however was a mildly esoteric meaning; the completely uninitiated would take it in the sense: 'Handle the weightiest affairs of state', as indeed does Wang Pi, the earliest commentator.

Huai-nan Tzǔ (Ch. XII) is quite aware that the opening passage of this chapter deals with the technique of Taoist *yoga*, for in illustration of it he quotes the story (*Chuang Tzǔ*, VI. end) of Yen Hui and his practice of *tso-wang*, 'sitting with blank mind'. See Appendix III.

The phrase *pao-i* or *chih-i* ('holding to the Unity') has a curious history, very typical of the way in which the various schools, while retaining the same time-hallowed watchwords, adapted them to their own needs. In *Mencius* (VII. 1. 26) it means having a 'one-sided' view, and is the opposite of *chih-chung*, 'holding to the middle' between two extremes. In Quietist language it has a metaphysical sense, meaning to 'hold fast to' the One as opposed to the Many, to utilize the primal, 'undivided' state that underlies the normal consciousness. Finally, to the Realists the phrase meant to maintain the ruler's or the State's absolute, undivided sway. Writers such as Kuan Tzǔ, who base their Realism on a mystic foundation, pass bewilderingly from the Quietist to the political application of the phrase, often seeming to attach both meanings to it simultaneously.

CHAPTER XI

We put thirty spokes together and call it a wheel;
But it is on the space where there is nothing that the
usefulness of the wheel depends.
We turn clay to make a vessel;
But it is on the space where there is nothing that the
usefulness of the vessel depends.
We pierce doors and windows to make a house;
And it is on these spaces where there is nothing that the
usefulness of the house depends.
Therefore just as we take advantage of what is, we should
recognize the usefulness of what is not.

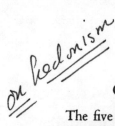

CHAPTER XII

The five colours confuse the eye,
The five sounds dull the ear,
The five tastes spoil the palate.
Excess of hunting and chasing
Makes minds go mad.
Products that are hard to get
Impede their owner's movements.
Therefore the Sage
Considers the belly not the eye.[1]
Truly, 'he rejects that but takes this'.[2]

Commentary

This is an answer to the Hedonists; see Introduction, p. 39. Any attempt to exploit to the full the use of the senses leads to a dulling of those senses. There is a proverb 'Poverty does not impede movement' (cf. *Yen T'ieh Lun*, XVI); whereas riches do, because they tempt bandits to attack. This is sometimes interpreted in a moral sense: 'Poverty is no impediment to (virtuous) courses.' I do not think that the moral sense of *hsing* is intended here.

---

[1] The belly in this instance means 'what is inside him', his own inner powers.

[2] For this use of 'that' and 'this' (i.e. the world outside and the powers within oneself) cf. *Kuan Tzŭ*, 36, middle.

CHAPTER XIII

'FAVOUR AND disgrace goad as it were to madness;[1] high rank hurts keenly as our bodies hurt.' What does it mean to say that favour and disgrace goad as it were to madness? It means[2] that when a ruler's subjects[3] get it[4] they turn distraught, when they lose it they turn distraught. That is what is meant by saying favour and disgrace goad as it were to madness. What does it mean to say that high rank hurts keenly as our bodies hurt? The only reason that we suffer hurt is that we have bodies; if we had no bodies, how could we suffer? Therefore we may accept the saying: 'He who in dealing with the empire regards his high rank as though it were his body is the best person to be entrusted with rule; he who in dealing with the empire loves his subjects as one should love one's body is the best person to whom one can commit the empire.

Commentary

In this chapter the author takes a number of Individualist (Yang Chu school) sayings and adapts them to his own use. Every individual must devote himself to the perfection of his own life, regardless of outside opinion. 'High rank is greatly detrimental to your (*jo*) body', i.e. to your self-perfection. Such, I think, is the original meaning of this sentence. But our author is at constant war with this 'self first' school, and by taking *jo* not as 'your' but in its alternative sense 'like', 'as', he extracts the meaning:

[1] See additional notes. [2] See textual notes. [3] *Hsia*. [4] i.e. favour.

'High rank hurts even as the body hurts'. For the body, the self, which in Yang Chu's doctrine must be put before everything else, is in fact (our author points out) the source of all pain. But so long as we regard the body in this light we can accept the Individualist saying:[1] 'Only he who in dealing with the empire makes the perfection of his own body (i.e. self, life) the primary consideration, may be entrusted with rule. Only he who cares for his own body is fit to govern an empire'—reinterpreting it however as meaning that he must regard his own high position just as he regards his body, that is to say, as the potential source of pain; and he must regard his subjects in the same light.

In *kuei i shên, ai i shên* the *i* has a limiting force. Compare *Analects*, I, 5. 'He must employ the people only at the proper times', and not when they have work to do in the fields. For the Buddhist interpretation of this passage, see additional notes.

[1] Cf. in the summary of Individualism in *Lü Shih Ch'un Ch'iu*, P'ien 7: 'He alone may be entrusted with empire who does not let empire interfere with his own life-culture'. *Chuang Tzŭ* (XI. 1. and XXVIII. 1) adapts similar sayings.

CHAPTER XIV *mystery of the universe*

Because the eye gazes but can catch no glimpse of it,[1]
It is called elusive.
Because the ear listens but cannot hear it,[1]
It is called the rarefied.
Because the hand feels for it but cannot find it,
It is called the infinitesimal.
These three, because they cannot be further scrutinized,
Blend into one.
Its rising brings no light;
Its sinking, no darkness.
Endless the series of things without name
On the way back to where there is nothing.
They are called shapeless shapes;
Forms without form;
Are called vague semblances.
Go towards them, and you can see no front;
Go after them, and you see no rear.
Yet by seizing on the Way that was
You can ride[2] the things that are now.
For to know what once there was,[3] in the Beginning,
This is called the essence[4] of the Way.

---

1 This is the traditional description of ghosts and spirits (cf. *Doctrine of the Mean*, paragraph 16) adopted as a description of the Way.
2 i.e. dominate.
3 Macrocosmically, in the Universe. Microcosmically, in oneself.
4 Literally, main-thread.

CHAPTER XV

Of old those that were the best officers of Court
Had inner natures subtle, abstruse, mysterious, penetrating,
Too deep to be understood.
And because such men could not be understood
I can but tell of them as they appeared to the world:
Circumspect they seemed, like one who in winter crosses
    a stream,
Watchful, as one who must meet danger on every side.
Ceremonious, as one who pays a visit;
Yet yielding, as ice when it begins to melt.
Blank, as a piece of uncarved wood;
Yet receptive as a hollow in the hills.
Murky, as a troubled stream——
Which of you can assume such murkiness, to become in
    the end still and clear?
Which of you can make yourself inert,[1] to become in the
    end full of life and stir?
Those who possess this Tao do not try to fill themselves to
    the brim,
And because they do not try to fill themselves to the brim
They are like a garment that endures all wear and need
    never be renewed (?).

Commentary

Jung (appearance, attitude, 'how they appeared to the
world') is a technical term with a long history. In fulfill-
ing religious rites it is not sufficient merely to say the

[1] Text doubtful. It is better to omit *chiu*.

160

right words or perform the right actions. Each rite requires also an appropriate 'attitude', one of reverence, eagerness, reluctance, joy, gloominess, etc. These 'attitudes' are always defined in Chinese by quasi-onomatopœic words, rather of the 'cock-a-hoop' type; they are often reduplicatives, and are always followed by an exclamatory or adverbial particle. Among the Confucians the study of correct attitudes was a matter of prime importance. The *Analects* (especially Book X) constantly defines these attitudes, and mnemonic jingles were current, in which a whole string of *jung* were connected into a sort of didactic poetry. The literature of the 3rd century B.C. teems with *jung*, modelled on those of the ritualists, but often defining a correct attitude towards life in general, rather than one appropriate to a particular ceremony. Thus in *Chuang Tzŭ*[1] we find a *jung* of the ancient *chên-jên* (Taoist adept, 'perfected, purified man'), and another[2] of the possessor of 'power', *tê*. The *Lü Shih Ch'un Ch'iu*[3] gives a *jung* of the perfect State officer, rather on Taoist lines. *Hsün Tzŭ* has general *jung*, like that of the 'perfect gentleman'[4] and the Sage;[5] but also a more ritualistic definition of the attitudes to be adopted by fathers and elder brothers, sons and younger brothers, and finally by pupils in relation to their masters.

The 'which of you can assume murkiness . . . to be clear' is a *fan-yen*, a paradox, reversal of common speech. Thus 'the more you clean it the dirtier it becomes' is a common saying, applied to the way in which slander 'sticks'.[6] But the Taoist must apply the paradoxical rule: 'The more you dirty it, the cleaner it becomes.'

[1] VI. 2.   [2] XII. 12.   [3] P'ien 79   [4] P'ien 3.   [5] P'ien 8.
[6] *Hsün Tzŭ*, P'ien 4 and P'ien 27.

CHAPTER XVI

Push far enough towards the Void,
Hold fast enough to Quietness,
And of the ten thousand things none but can be worked on by
    you.
I have beheld them, whither they go back.
See, all things howsoever they flourish
Return to the root from which they grew.
This return to the root is called Quietness;
Quietness is called submission to Fate;
What has submitted to Fate has become part of the always-so.
To know the always-so is to be Illumined;
Not to know it, means to go blindly to disaster.
He who knows the always-so has room in him for everything;
He who has room in him for everything is without prejudice.
To be without prejudice is to be kingly;
To be kingly is to be of heaven;
To be of heaven is to be in Tao.
Tao is forever and he that possesses it,
Though his body ceases, is not destroyed.

immortality ?

Commentary

To have room in one for everything (*jung*) is cognate
both in writing and etymology with 'to be without prejudice' (*kung*). But *kung* happens also to mean a royal Duke,
the person next in rank to the king. There is here a play
on these two senses of *kung*. That the resemblance of two
words may be due to a series of phonological accidents is a

162

conception that is quite recent in the history of thought. All early thinkers, including the Greeks,[1] attributed a profound significance to such resemblances. *Kung*, then, is a sort of king. And kings are, as has been thought all over the world, delegates of Heaven. Heaven in our author's thought is synonymous with Tao. Tao is the absolute, the enduring, the ever-so.

Such a passage, depending on rhyme, plays on words and resemblance of characters, is of course bound to appear pointless in translation.

[1] With the exception of certain rare passages, such as Plato's *Timaeus* (38 b) where rather irrelevantly, in a sort of parenthesis, and in a work which teems with plays on words, it is noted that the verb to be has two uses (1) as a connecting word, (2) meàning 'to exist'; more generally, Hermogenes says in the *Cratylus* (384 D and E) he 'cannot believe' that names are otherwise than conventional.

CHAPTER XVII

Of the highest[1] the people merely know that such a one
    exists;

The next they draw near to and praise.

The next they shrink from, intimidated; but revile.

Truly, 'It is by not believing people that you turn them
    into liars'.[2]

But from the Sage it is so hard at any price to get a
    single word[3]

That when his task is accomplished, his work done,

Throughout the country every one says 'It happened of
    its own accord'.

---

[1] i.e. most Taoist.

[2] The same saying is quoted in Ch. 23. Cf. Ch. 49: 'The truthful
man I believe; but the liar I also believe, and so he (the liar) gets
truthfulness.' Similarly it is 'lack' in the ruler which creates in the
people every other fault and crime.

[3] Literally: 'How, reluctant, he raises the price of his words!'

CHAPTER XVIII

It was when the Great Way declined
That human kindness and morality arose;
It was when intelligence and knowledge appeared
That the Great Artifice began.
It was when the six near ones[1] were no longer at peace
That there was talk of 'dutiful sons';[2]
Nor till fatherland was dark with strife
Did we hear of 'loyal slaves'.[3]

[1] Father, son, elder brother, younger brother, husband and wife.
[2] Read *tzŭ* 'son' not *tz'ŭ* 'compassionate', as in the *Yung Lo Ta Tien* text.
[3] As Ministers called themselves.

CHAPTER XIX

Banish wisdom, discard knowledge,
And the people will be benefited a hundredfold.
Banish human kindness, discard morality,
And the people will be dutiful and compassionate.
Banish skill, discard profit[1],
And thieves and robbers will disappear.
If when these three things are done[2] they find life too
    plain and unadorned,
Then let them have accessories;
Give them Simplicity to look at, the Uncarved Block to
    hold,
Give them selflessness and fewness of desires.

raw silk

ung to universe

Commentary

For *jên* (human kindness) see above, p. 147. For *i*
(morality) see Introduction, p. 66. The virtues which the
author here discards were also discarded by the Realists,
who maintained that loyalty, for example, may exist in
exceptional people, but is absent in most; whereas the
love of gain exists in everyone. Consequently, government should be based solely on a complete system of
punishments and rewards. The Taoist ruler, on the other
hand, creates in his subjects the qualities and tendencies
that he desires solely by the exercise of the *tê* that Tao
confers.

[1] i.e do away with skilful artisans and enterprising traders, who
supply things likely to attract thieves.

[2] I suspect that a negative has fallen out in front of 'these three', and
that the original ran: 'If without these three . . . they find life, etc.'

'Simplicity' (*su*) means literally 'raw silk'. It is the symbol of the 'attributeless' nature of Tao. The Uncarved Block is the symbol of the primal undifferentiated unity underlying the apparent complexity of the universe. *Ssŭ* (the 'self' element in the word translated selflessness) is the opposite of *kung*, 'public'. It means absence of personal ambition. For *kua-yü* 'fewness of desires', see Introduction, p. 89.

CHAPTER XX

Banish learning,[1] and there will be no more grieving.
Between *wei* and *o*
What after all is the difference?
Can it be compared to the difference between good and bad?[2]
The saying 'what others avoid I too must avoid'
How false and superficial it is!
All men, indeed, are wreathed in smiles,
As though feasting after the Great Sacrifice,
As though going up to the Spring Carnival.[3]
I alone am inert, like a child that has not yet given sign;[4]
Like an infant that has not yet smiled.
I droop and drift, as though I belonged nowhere.
All men have enough and to spare;
I alone seem to have lost everything.
Mine is indeed the mind of a very idiot,
So dull am I.
The world is full of people that shine;
I alone am dark.

[1] 'Learning' means in particular learning the '3300 rules of etiquette'. *Wei* and *o* were the formal and informal words for 'yes', each appropriate to certain occasions. For 'learning' in the sense of knowing which words are taboo at which Courts, see *Kuo Yü*, 15, fol. 3.

[2] Good and bad in the Taoist sense, i.e. like and unlike the Way. This leads up to the description of the great gulf that separates the Taoist from other men. This description is in the form of a generalized *jung* (see Ch. 15, above) and cannot be taken as in any sense a self-portrait of the author. The sense of the first six lines is very doubtful.

[3] See additional notes. I read *têng ch'un t'ai*.

[4] A child 'gives sign' by stretching its hand towards some object. This is an important omen concerning its future.

They look lively and self-assured;
I alone, depressed.
I seem unsettled[1] as the ocean;
Blown adrift, never brought to a stop.
All men can be put to some use;
I alone am intractable and boorish.
But wherein I most am different from men
Is that I prize no sustenance that comes not from the
  Mother's[2] breast.

Commentary

The saying 'What others avoid I too must avoid' refers
to keeping the same taboos, ritual avoidances, etc., as
people with whom one finds oneself in contact. Thus
Confucius (*Analects*, VII, 9), if he found himself eating
side by side with someone who was in mourning imposed
upon himself the same abstentions as were required of the
mourner. Conversely of course, it is ill-omened to weep
when others are rejoicing. But the Taoist, who is the anti-
thesis of other men, cannot obey these rules.

[1] For this sense of *tan*, see *Lü Shih Ch'un Ch'iu*, P'ien III, line 7.
[2] i.e. the Way's. The image may equally well be that of a child in
the womb, 'feeding on the mother'.

CHAPTER XXI

Such the scope of the All-pervading Power
That it alone can act through the Way.
For the Way is a thing impalpable, incommensurable.
Incommensurable, impalpable.
Yet latent in it are forms;[1]
Impalpable, incommensurable
Yet within it are entities.
Shadowy it is and dim;
Yet within it there is a force,
A force that though rarefied
Is none the less efficacious.
From the time of old till now
Its charge[2] has not departed
But cheers onward the many warriors.
How do I know that the many warriors are so?
Through this.[3]

[1] Thought-images, ideas.
[2] See additional notes.
[3] Through inward knowledge, intuition.

CHAPTER XXII

'To remain whole, be twisted!'
To become straight, let yourself be bent.
To become full, be hollow.
Be tattered, that you may be renewed.
Those that have little, may get more,
Those that have much, are but perplexed.
Therefore the Sage
Clasps the Primal Unity,
Testing by it everything under heaven.
He does not show himself; therefore he is seen everywhere.
He does not define himself, therefore he is distinct.
He does not boast of what he will do, therefore he
    succeeds.
He is not proud of his work, and therefore it endures.
He does not contend,
And for that very reason no one under heaven can contend
    with him.
So then we see that the ancient saying 'To remain whole,
be twisted!' was no idle word; for true wholeness can only
be achieved by return.[1]

[1] To the Way.

CHAPTER XXIII

To BE always talking is against nature. For the same reason a hurricane never lasts a whole morning, nor a rainstorm all day. Who is it that makes the wind and rain? It is Heaven-and-Earth.[1] And if even Heaven-and-Earth cannot blow or pour for long, how much less in his utterance should man? Truly, if one uses the Way[2] as one's instrument, the results will be like the Way; if one uses the 'power' as one's instrument, the results will be like the power. If one uses what is the reverse of the 'power', the results will be the reverse of the 'power'. For to those who have conformed themselves to the Way, the Way readily lends its power. To those who have conformed themselves to the power, the power readily lends more power. While to those who conform themselves to inefficacy, inefficacy readily lends its ineffectiveness. 'It is by not believing in people that you turn them into liars.'[3]

Commentary

Wind and rain are taken as the utterances of nature, parallel to speech in man. 'Talking' here refers to government by laws and proclamations. Tê, the power of Tao, also means 'getting' as opposed to 'loss', success as opposed to disaster. The author puns on these two senses, which were often expressed by the same character. For the silence of heaven, see *Analects*, XVII. 19; and for that of heaven and earth, see *Hsün Tzǔ*, P'ien 3, middle.

[1] Nature, as we should say.

[2] The text is here somewhat confused; but the general meaning is clear.   [3] See above, Ch. 17. If one uses disbelief as one's instrument of government, the result will be a nation of liars.

CHAPTER XXIV

'He who stands on tip-toe, does not stand firm;
He who takes the longest strides, does not walk the fastest.'
He who does his own looking sees little,
He who defines himself is not therefore distinct.
He who boasts of what he will do succeeds in nothing;
He who is proud of his work, achieves nothing that
    endures.
Of these, from the standpoint of the Way, it is said:
'Pass round superfluous dishes to those that have already
    had enough,
And no creature but will reject them in disgust.'
That is why he that possesses Tao does not·linger.[1]

[1] Over the scene of his successes, thus calling attention to them.
Cf. Ch. 2.

CHAPTER XXV

There was something formless yet complete,
That existed before heaven and earth;
Without sound, without substance,
Dependent on nothing, unchanging,
All pervading, unfailing.
One may think of it as the mother of all things under
     heaven.
Its true name[1] we do not know;
'Way' is the by-name that we give it.
Were I forced to say to what class of things it belongs I
     should call it Great (*ta*).
Now *ta*[2] also means passing on,
And passing on means going Far Away,
And going far away means returning.[3]

Thus just as Tao[4] has 'this greatness' and as earth has it
and as heaven has it, so may the ruler also have it. Thus
'within the realm[2] there are four portions of greatness',
and one belongs to the king. The ways of men are con-
ditioned by those of earth. The ways of earth, by those
of heaven. The ways of heaven by those of Tao, and the
ways of Tao by the Self-so.[5]

---

[1] i.e. we do not know to what class of things it belongs.

[2] See textual notes.

[3] Returning to 'what was there at the Beginning'.

[4] Henceforward I shall use the Chinese word Tao instead of the
Way; to do so avoids many inconveniences.

[5] The 'unconditioned'; the 'what-is-so-of-itself'.

Tao Tê Ching

Commentary

The intention of this 'chain-argument' (a rhetorical form very commonly used by early Chinese writers) is to show that a line of connection may be traced between the ruler and Tao. This connection exists macrocosmically, in the line ruler, earth, heaven, Tao; but also microcosmically, in that by passing on and on through successive stages of his own consciousness back to the initial Unity he can arrive at the Way which controls the multiform apparent universe. The ecstasy called Far Away Wandering[1] is also known as the Far Away Passing On.[2]

The Realists insisted that there must be only one 'Greatness' in the realm—that of the State. I suspect that the clause 'There are four portions of greatness . . .' is adapted from a saying of the logicians. See Textual Notes.

---

[1] The subject of one of the *Ch'u Elegies*. These travels, these 'wanderings alone with Tao in the Great Wilderness' (*Chuang Tzǔ* XX. 2.) are not external journeys, but explorations of oneself, back to the 'Beginning of Things'.

[2] For example, in the *Li Sao*.

CHAPTER XXVI

As the heavy must be the foundation of the light,
So quietness is lord and master of activity.
Truly, 'A man of consequence[1] though he travels all day
Will not let himself be separated from his baggage-wagon,[2]
However magnificent the view, he sits quiet and dispassionate'.
How much less, then, must be the lord of ten thousand
    chariots
Allow himself to be lighter[3] than these he rules!
If he is light, the foundation is lost;
If he is active, the lord and master[4] is lost.

[1] Reading *Chün-tzŭ*, which has considerable ancient support; cf.
Ma Hsü-lun's *Lao Tzŭ Fu Ku*.
[2] Literally, 'his covered heavy', 'heavy' being the Chinese name for
carts as opposed to light travelling carriages. There is a play on the
two senses of 'heavy'. This is a patrician proverb, a maxim of the
chün-tzŭ, 'gentlemen'.
[3] i.e. more easily moved.
[4] i.e. Quietness, the magical passivity that is also called *wu-wei*.
There is a secondary meaning: 'His lordship is lost.'

CHAPTER XXVII

perfection 6 Tao

Perfect activity leaves no track behind it;
Perfect speech is like a jade-worker whose tool leaves no mark.
The perfect reckoner needs no counting-slips;[1]
The perfect door has neither bolt nor bar,
Yet cannot be opened.
The perfect knot needs neither rope nor twine,
Yet cannot be untied.
Therefore the Sage
Is all the time in the most perfect way helping men,
He certainly does not turn his back on men;
Is all the time in the most perfect way helping creatures,
He certainly does not turn his back on creatures.
This is called resorting to the Light.[2]
Truly, 'the perfect man is the teacher of the imperfect;
But the imperfect is the stock-in-trade[3] of the perfect man'.
He who does not respect his teacher,
He who does not take care of his stock-in-trade,
Much learning though he may possess, is far astray.
This[4] is the essential secret.

---

[1] Slips of bamboo thrown into little bowls; forerunner of the abacus.
[2] 'Light' has been defined above as self-knowledge. 'This' means the way in which the Sage saves the world, though apparently shunning it. For 'resorting to' see additional notes.
[3] Cf. *Chuang Tzŭ*, I. 4.
[4] The power to influence mankind through Tao. The commonest charge brought against Taoists was that of being merely interested in self-perfection without regard for the welfare of the community as a whole. The present chapter is devoted to rebutting that charge.

NB

CHAPTER XXVIII

'He who knows the male, yet cleaves to what is female
Becomes like a ravine, receiving all things under heaven,'[1]
And being such a ravine
He knows all the time a power that he never calls upon in vain.
This is returning to the state of infancy.[2]
He who knows the white, yet cleaves to the black
Becomes the standard by which all things are tested;
And being such a standard
He has all the time a power that never errs,
He returns to the Limitless.
He who knows glory, yet cleaves to ignominy
Becomes like a valley that receives into it all things under
    heaven,
And being such a valley
He has all the time a power that suffices;
He returns to the state of the Uncarved Block.
Now when a block is sawed up it is made into implements;[3]
But when the Sage uses it, it becomes Chief of all Ministers.
Truly, 'The greatest carver[4] does the least cutting'.

---

[1] Adapted from a Lao Tan saying. See *Chuang Tzŭ*, XXXIII. 5.
[2] Cf. Introduction, p. 55.
[3] Play on the double sense of this word which also means 'a subordinate', 'an instrument of government'.
[4] Play on *chih* 'to cut', 'to carve', and *chih* 'to rule'. The secondary
meaning is that the greatest ruler does the least chopping about.

CHAPTER XXIX

Those that would gain what is under heaven[1] by tampering with it—I have seen that they do not succeed. For that which is under heaven is like a holy vessel, dangerous to tamper with.

Those that tamper with it, harm it.

Those that grab at it, lose it.

For among the creatures of the world some go in front, some follow;

Some blow hot when others would be blowing cold.

Some are feeling vigorous just when others are worn out.

Some are loading[2] just when others would be tilting out.

Therefore the Sage 'discards the absolute, the all-inclusive,[3] the extreme'.

---

[1] i.e. empire.

[2] Read *tsai*.

[3] *Shê* means (1) 'spread out' (2) dissipated. It is the first meaning which is appropriate here. The author is, however, certainly adapting a maxim that was aimed against dissipation, luxury etc. cf. *Han Fei Tzŭ*, P'ien 8, beginning.

social content of Taoism

CHAPTER XXX

He who by Tao purposes to help a ruler of men
Will oppose all conquest by force of arms;
For such things are wont to rebound.[1]
Where armies are, thorns and brambles grow.
The raising of a great host
Is followed by a year of dearth.[2]
Therefore a good general effects his purpose and then
    stops; he does not take further advantage of his victory.
Fulfils his purpose and does not glory in what he has done;
Fulfils his purpose and does not boast of what he has done;
Fulfils his purpose, but takes no pride in what he has done;
Fulfils his purpose, but only as a step that could not be
    avoided.[3]
Fulfils his purpose, but without violence;
For what has a time of vigour also has a time of decay.
This[4] is against Tao,

violence

And what is against Tao will soon perish.

---

[1] Lit. 'To be reversed'. He who overcomes by violence will himself
be overcome by violence.

[2] This does not only refer to direct destruction, but also to the curse
that war brings upon herds and crops by its intrinsic 'balefulness'.

[3] For the construction compare *Chuang Tzŭ* XXIII. 6: 'To move
only when movement cannot be avoided, that is the true power.' This
principle of *pu tê i* 'action as a last resort' was preached by the 4th
century Quietist Shên Tao, and pervades *Chuang Tzŭ*.

[4] Violence.

CHAPTER XXXI

FINE[1] WEAPONS are none the less ill-omened things. That is why, among people of good birth,[2] in peace the left-hand side[3] is the place of honour, but in war this is reversed and the right-hand side is the place of honour. The Quietist,[4] even when he conquers, does not regard weapons as lovely things. For to think them lovely means to delight in them, and to delight in them means to delight in the slaughter of men. And he who delights in the slaughter of men will never get what he looks for out of those that dwell under heaven. A host that has slain men is received with grief and mourning; he that has conquered in battle is[5] received with rites of mourning.

Commentary

In this chapter, as has been generally recognized, a considerable amount of commentary has become inextricably confused with the text. Now upon this chapter Wang Pi[6] makes no comments. The natural inference, as

[1] *Chia* also means 'auspicious', e.g. *chia jih*, 'a lucky day'. I see no reason to tamper with the text.

[2] Of good birth, and consequently of good manners.

[3] See additional notes.

[4] For this expression cf. *Han Fei Tzŭ*, P'ien 51, near end, and *Chuang Tzŭ*, X, end.

[5] Whether such a custom actually existed we do not know; but we learn from *Huai-nan Tzŭ* (15, end) that the general, having received his marching orders, cuts his nails (as was done by mourners before a funeral), dresses in mourning garb, and leaves the city by a 'gate of ill-omen' constructed for the purpose.

[6] 226-249 A.D. The earliest commentator on the *Tao Tê Ching* whose work survives.

the Japanese scholar Tojo Hiroshi has pointed out,[1] is that the text as we have it is an amalgamation of the original with the lost Wang Pi commentary. Several attempts[2] have been made to separate this intrusive commentary from the text. My reconstruction comes fairly close to that of Ma Hsü-lun (1924).[3]

[1] In his *Roshi Ochu Hyoshi*, 1814.

[2] e.g. by T'ao Fang-chi, Li Tz'ŭ-ming and Ma Hsü-lun.

[3] It should however be noted, in connection with the above line of argument, that there is also no Wang Pi commentary on Ch. 66.

CHAPTER XXXII

Tao is eternal, but has no fame (name);[1]
The Uncarved Block,[2] though seemingly of small account,
Is greater than anything that is under heaven.[3]
If kings and barons would but possess themselves of it,
The ten thousand creatures would flock to do them homage;
Heaven-and-earth would conspire
To send Sweet Dew,[4]
Without law or compulsion, men would dwell in harmony.
Once the block is carved,[5] there will be names,[6]
And so soon as there are names
Know that it is time to stop.
Only by knowing when it is time to stop can danger be avoided.
To Tao[7] all under heaven will come
As streams and torrents flow into a great river or sea.

1 See textual notes.
2 See Ch. 28.
3 Literally 'under Heaven no one dares regard it as an inferior'.
4 'Sweet Dew tastes like barley-sugar or honey; it falls only when a kingdom is at complete peace.' *Lun Hêng*, XIX. 2. See also *Kuan Tzŭ*, P'ien 20, fol. 16, and *Lü Shih Ch'un Ch'iu*, 115, end.
5 Secondary meaning 'Once there is government'.
6 Categories, distinctions. Things depending on contrast with something else; as opposed to Tao, which 'is so of itself'.
7 i.e. to the possessor of Tao. The last two lines resume the thought of lines 4 and 5.

CHAPTER XXXIII

To understand others is to have knowledge;
To understand oneself is to be illumined.
To conquer others needs strength;
To conquer oneself is harder still.
To be content with what one has is to be rich.
He that works through[1] violence may get his way;
But only what stays[2] in its place
Can endure.
When one dies one is not lost;[3] there is no other longevity.

Commentary

Shou longevity means, strictly speaking, potential longevity, 'staying-power', what we should call having a good constitution, and is a quality that may be possessed by the young as well as the old. One branch of the 'life-nurturing' school sought it by means of diet, hygiene, drugs, etc. For the Taoist view of death see Introduction, p. 54.

[1] The word *hsing* implies movement as well as action.
[2] As, for example, mountains.
[3] One's left arm may become a cock; one's right arm a bow; one's buttocks wheels (*Chuang Tzŭ* VI. 6). In any case, no part of one will be lost.

CHAPTER XXXIV

Great Tao is like a boat that drifts;
It can go this way; it can go that.
The ten thousand creatures owe their existence to it and it does
    not disown them;
Yet having produced them, it does not take possession of them.[1]
Tao, though it covers the ten thousand things like a garment,
Makes no claim to be master over them,
And asks for nothing from them.
Therefore it may be called the Lowly:
The ten thousand creatures obey it,
Though they know not that they have a master;
Therefore it is called the Great.
So too the Sage just because he never at any time makes a show
of greatness in fact achieves greatness.

---

1 Cf. Chapter 2, where similar words are used of the Sage, who is
identified with Tao. For the reading, see textual notes.

CHAPTER XXXV

He who holding the Great Form goes about his work in
 the empire
Can go about his work, yet do no harm.
All is peace, quietness and security.
Sound of music, smell of good dishes
Will make the passing stranger pause.
How different the words that Tao gives forth!
So thin, so flavourless!
If one looks for Tao, there is nothing solid to see;
If one listens for it, there is nothing loud enough to hear.
Yet if one uses it, it is inexhaustible.

Commentary

 The Great Form is the form that is formless, i.e. Tao.
Strictly speaking the word means a mental image as
opposed to concrete reality.

 See introduction p. 61, *hsiang*.

CHAPTER XXXVI

What is in the end to be shrunk
Must first be stretched.
Whatever is to be weakened
Must begin by being made strong.
What is to be overthrown
Must begin by being set up.
He who would be a taker
Must begin as a giver.
This is called 'dimming' one's light.[1]
It is thus that the soft overcomes the hard
And the weak, the strong.
'It is best to leave the fish down in his pool;
Best to leave the State's sharpest weapons where none can
    see them.'

Commentary

The Sage must 'stoop to conquer', must make himself
small in order to be great, must be cast down before he
can be exalted. He must remain like the fish at the bottom of the pool. The last two lines are a maxim of common statecraft, here applied in a metaphorical way: the
'sharp weapons' symbolize the Taoist sage who is a kind
of secret armament on whom the safety of the state depends. The fish symbolizes armour because both have
'scales'. Compare the *I Chou Shu* 52, where it is said that
on the tenth day of spring the fish come up above the ice.
If they fail to do so, this is a sign that armour is being secret-
ed in the houses of private people with a view to rebellion.

1 *Wei* means (1) 'obscure because so small', (2) 'obscure because so
dark'. It is etymologically connected with *mei* 'dark'.

CHAPTER XXXVII

Tao never does;
Yet through it all things are done.
If the barons and kings would but possess themselves of it,
The ten thousand creatures would at once be transformed.
And if having been transformed they should desire to act,
We must restrain them by the blankness[1] of the Unnamed.
The blankness of the Unnamed
Brings dispassion;
To be dispassionate is to be still.
And so,[2] of itself, the whole empire will be at rest.

[1] Literally, 'the uncarven-wood-quality'.
[2] If the Sage is 'still'.

CHAPTER XXXVIII

The man of highest 'power' does not reveal himself as a
   possessor of 'power';
Therefore he keeps his 'power'.
The man of inferior 'power' cannot rid it of the appear-
   ance of 'power';
Therefore he is in truth without 'power'.
The man of highest 'power' neither acts[1] nor is there any
   who so regards him;[2]
The man of inferior 'power' both acts and is so regarded.[3]
The man of highest humanity, though he acts, is not so
   regarded;
Whereas a man of even the highest morality both acts and
   is so regarded.
While even he who is best versed in ritual not merely
   acts, but if people fail to respond
Then he will pull up his sleeves and advance upon them.
That is why it is said:[4] 'After Tao was lost, then came the
   "power";
After the "power" was lost, then came human kindness.
After human kindness was lost, then came morality,
After morality was lost, then came ritual.
Now ritual is the mere husk[5] of loyalty and promise-
   keeping

   1 Does not act separately and particularly, but only applies the
'power' in a general way.
   2 Regards him as a possessor of power. Compare *Kuan Tzŭ*, P'ien 5,
paragraph 2.   3 i.e. is regarded as a possessor of *tê*.
   4 The same saying is quoted by *Chuang Tzŭ*, XXII. 1.
   5 Or 'attenuated form'; but it balances *hua* ('flower', as opposed to
fruit) and it is better to indicate the vegetable metaphor.

And is indeed the first step towards brawling.'
Foreknowledge[1] may be the 'flower of doctrine',
But it is the beginning of folly.
Therefore the full-grown man[2] takes his stand upon the
    solid substance and not upon the mere husk,
Upon the fruit and not upon the flower.
Truly, 'he rejects that and takes this'.

(The repeated use of nouns as verbs, not possible in English to the same extent as in Chinese, makes anything but a clumsy paraphrase of the first ten lines of the chapter impossible.)

---

[1] See additional notes.   [2] Full-grown in Tao.

CHAPTER XXXIX

As for the things that from of old have understood the Whole—
The sky through such understanding remains limpid,
Earth remains steady,
The spirits keep their holiness,[1]
The abyss is replenished,
The ten thousand creatures bear their kind,
Barons and princes direct[2] their people.
It is the Whole that causes it.
Were it not so limpid, the sky would soon get torn,
Were it not for its steadiness, the earth would soon tip over,
Were it not for their holiness, the spirits would soon wither
away.
Were it not for this replenishment, the abyss would soon go dry,
Were it not that the ten thousand creatures can bear their kind,
They would soon become extinct.
Were the barons and princes no longer directors of their people
and for that reason honoured and exalted, they would soon
be overthrown.
Truly 'the humble is the stem upon which the mighty grows,
The low is the foundation upon which the high is laid.'
That is why barons and princes refer to themselves as 'The
Orphan', 'The Needy', 'The Ill-provided'. Is this not indeed a
case of might rooting itself upon humility?[3]

1 Their *ling*, which is to spirits (or objects and animals 'possessed' by spirits)
what *tê* is to man. It is cognate to words meaning life, name, command, etc.

2 See additional notes.   3 From 'Truly' to 'humility' is quoted with
slight variants by the *Chan Kuo Ts'ê* (IV. 14 recto) as a saying of Lao Tzŭ. It
is probable that we have here an actual quotation of the *Tao Tê Ching*. For
the date of the *Chan Kuo Ts'ê*, see Appendix VI.

True indeed are the sayings:
'Enumerate the parts of a carriage, and you still have not explained what a carriage' is, and 'They[1] did not want themselves
to tinkle like jade-bells, while others resounded like stone-
chimes'.

Commentary

'Have understood the Whole'; literally 'Have got the
Whole'. But the parallel passage in *Chuang Tzŭ* (XXV. 10)
uses the expression 'getting a horse' in the sense of realiz-
ing what a horse is, as opposed to knowing what its parts
(ears, body, tail, etc.) are. 'Get' therefore here means 'get
the idea of'. Compare our colloquial expression 'Do you
get me?' Of the two sayings at the end of the chapter, the
first illustrates the theme of 'understanding the Whole'
with which the chapter opens; the second recapitulates
the latter part of the chapter, which deals with the reluctance of the wise ruler to put himself 'above' his subjects
and so spoil the unity of empire.

In line 8, the words 'It is the Whole' are accidentally
omitted in the Wang Pi text.

CHAPTER XL

In Tao the only motion is returning;[2]
The only useful quality, weakness.
For though all creatures under heaven are the products of Being,
Being itself is the product of Not-being.

---

[1] The Sages of old.   [2] Compare Ch. XXV, line 12.

CHAPTER XLI

When the man of highest capacities hears Tao
He does his best to put it into practice.
When the man of middling capacity hears Tao
He is in two minds about it.
When the man of low capacity hears Tao
He laughs loudly at it.
If he did not laugh, it would not be worth the name of Tao.
Therefore the proverb has it:
'The way[1] out into the light often looks dark,
The way that goes ahead often looks as if it went back.'
The way that is least hilly often looks as if it went up and down,
The 'power' that is really loftiest looks like an abyss,
What is sheerest white looks blurred.
The 'power' that is most sufficing looks inadequate,
The 'power' that stands firmest looks flimsy.[2]
What is in its natural, pure state looks faded;[2]
The largest square has no corners,
The greatest vessel takes the longest to finish,[3]
Great music has the faintest[4] notes,
The Great Form[5] is without shape.
For Tao is hidden and nameless.
Yet Tao alone supports[6] all things and brings them to fulfilment.

---

[1] Tao.
[2] See additional notes.
[3] Metaphorical meaning, 'The greatest capacities develop latest'.
[4] 'Most rarefied.' Cf. Ch. 14.
[5] Cf. Ch. 35.
[6] A commercial metaphor. Literally 'backs financially'.

Tao Tê Ching

Commentary

'The largest vessel. . . .' When the great Han dynasty general Ma Yüan[1] was young, he was worried by the fact that he could not understand or get any pleasure from the *Book of Odes*, but preferred hunting. 'I am sure', his brother told him, 'you have "high capacities" that will "develop late". A good craftsman does not show his work while it is still in the rough. The best thing you can do for the present is to go off and have as much fun as you can.'

[1] *Hou Han Shu*, Ch. XXIV, fol. 1.

CHAPTER XLII

TAO GAVE birth to the One; the One gave birth successively to two things, three things, up to ten thousand.[1] These ten thousand creatures cannot turn their backs to the shade without having the sun on their bellies,[2] and it is on this blending of the breaths[3] that their harmony[4] depends. To be orphaned, needy, ill-provided is what men most hate; yet princes and dukes style themselves so. Truly, 'things are often increased by seeking to diminish them and diminished by seeking to increase them.' The maxims that others use in their teaching I too will use in mine. Show me a man of violence that came to a good end,[5] and I will take him for my teacher.

Commentary

To be a prince is a 'sunny' as opposed to a 'shady' thing. But a prince does not feel properly 'harmonized' unless he also has 'the shade at his back', which he obtains by humbling himself.

A proverb[6] says: 'The man of violence never yet came to a good end; nor did he that delights in victory fail to meet his match.' Another proverb[7] says: 'The best doctor

[1] i.e. everything.

[2] Which symbolizes the fact that they are themselves a mixture of light and dark, hard and soft, water and fire, etc.

[3] The warm 'breath' of the sun and the cold 'breath' of the shade. Hence 'breath' comes to mean a 'state of the atmosphere' in a wider sense.

[4] Or 'balance', as we should say.   [5] See textual notes.

[6] See additional notes.   [7] See *Hou Han Shu*, XXX. fol. 3.

195

cannot save one whose life-span has run out; nor can the man of violence strive with Heaven.' It is possible that *Ch'iang-liang*, 'man of violence', is in reality the name of a mythological figure, a sort of Titan who warred unsuccessfully against Heaven. *Ch'iang* means 'violent'; but *liang* means 'rafter', and though the two together are said to mean 'man of violence', no proof is adduced; and I suspect that this Titan was called 'Rafter' because his image was carved on the ends of rafters. This theory is borne out by a passage in *Chuang Tzŭ* (VI. 9) which speaks of a strong man called Chü-liang, 'holder of the rafters' who like Samson 'lost his strength'. In order to conform to a quotation by *Huai-nan Tzŭ*, many modern editors have tampered with the text at the beginning of the chapter.

CHAPTER XLIII

What is of all things most yielding[1]
Can overwhelm that which is of all things most hard.[2]
Being substanceless it can enter even where there is no space;
That is how I know the value of action that is actionless.
But that there can be teaching without words,
Value in action that is actionless,
Few indeed can understand.

CHAPTER XLIV

Fame or one's own self, which matters to one most?
One's own self or things bought, which should count most?
In the getting or the losing, which is worse?[3]
Hence he who grudges expense pays dearest in the end;
He who has hoarded most will suffer the heaviest loss.[4]
Be content with what you have and are, and no one can despoil
    you;
Who stops in time nothing can harm.
He is forever safe and secure.

[1] Water. [2] Rock.
[3] i.e. which is better, to get fame and wealth but injure oneself, or
to lack fame and wealth and save oneself?
[4] He drives people to such exasperation that they attack him and
help themselves. For *ai* in the sense 'grudge' compare *I Chou Shu* 54,
'He who is stingy about rewards and gifts is called *ai*'. The primary
meaning of *ai* is 'to want to keep to oneself'. Hence the commoner
meaning 'to love', which would here be out of place.

CHAPTER XLV

What is most perfect seems to have something missing;
Yet its use is unimpaired.[1]
What is most full seems empty;
Yet its use will never fail.[2]
What is most straight seems crooked;
The greatest skill seems like clumsiness,
The greatest eloquence like stuttering.[3]
Movement overcomes cold;
But staying still overcomes heat.
So he[4] by his limpid calm
Puts right everything under heaven.

[1] Metaphor of a pot or vessel; applied to Tao.
[2] It can be drawn upon indefinitely.
[3] Compare *Analects* IV, 24; and the stuttering of Moses (*Encyclopædia of Islam*, under Musa).   [4] The Sage.

CHAPTER XLVI

When there is Tao in the empire
The galloping[1] steeds are turned back to fertilize the
    ground by their droppings.
When there is not Tao in the empire
War horses will be reared even on the sacred mounds[2]
    below the city walls.
No lure[3] is greater than to possess what others want,
No disaster greater than not to be content with what one
    has,
No presage of evil greater than that men should be want-
    ing to get more.
Truly: 'He who has once known the contentment that
    comes simply through being content, will never again
    be otherwise than contented'.

---

[1] i.e. carriage-horses, used not for war but for travelling. Every one
will be contented where he is.

[2] See additional notes. They are reared, of course, as a preparation
for offensive war, i.e. for 'getting more'.

[3] i.e. incitement to evil doers. See additional notes.

CHAPTER XLVII

Without leaving his door
He knows everything under heaven.
Without looking out of his window
He knows all the ways of heaven.
For the further one travels[1]
The less one knows.
Therefore the Sage arrives without going,
Sees all[2] without looking,
Does nothing, yet achieves everything.

[1] Away from Tao; away from the Unity into the Multiplicity.
[2] Read *ming* 'illumined', not *ming* 'name'. The two characters are constantly interchanged in old texts.

CHAPTER XLVIII

Learning consists in adding to one's stock day by day;
The practice of Tao consists in 'subtracting day by day,
Subtracting and yet again subtracting
Till one has reached inactivity.
But by this very inactivity
Everything can be activated.'[1]
Those who of old won the adherence of all who live under
    heaven
All did so by not interfering.
Had they interfered,
They would never have won this adherence.

---

[1] Compare *Chuang Tzŭ* XXII. 1.

CHAPTER XLIX

The Sage has no heart[1] of his own;
He uses the heart of the people as his heart.
Of the good man I[2] approve,
But of the bad I also approve,
And thus he gets goodness.
The truthful man I believe, but the liar I also believe,
And thus he gets truthfulness.[3]
The Sage, in his dealings with the world, seems like one
    dazed with fright;[4]
For the world's sake he dulls his wits.
The Hundred Families all the time strain their eyes and
    ears,[5]
The Sage all the time sees and hears no more than an in-
    fant sees and hears.

---

[1] Makes no judgments of his own.
[2] i.e. the Sage.
[3] Cf. Ch. 17 and 23.
[4] Read 'heart' beside 'leaf'.
[5] This line is accidentally omitted by the Wang Pi text.

CHAPTER L

HE WHO aims at life achieves death. If the 'companions of life'[1] are thirteen, so likewise are the 'companions of death' thirteen. How is it that the 'death-spots'[2] in man's life and activity are also thirteen? It is because men feed life too grossly. It is said that he who has a true hold on life, when he walks on land[3] does not meet tigers or wild buffaloes; in battle he is not touched by weapons of war. Indeed, a buffalo that attacked him would find nothing for its horns to butt, a tiger would find nothing for its claws to tear, a weapon would find no place for its point to enter in.[4] And why? Because such men have no 'death-spot' in them.

Commentary

In military language 'he who *ch'u ssŭ*[5] "goes out prepared to die" comes back alive and victorious'. Conversely, he who 'goes for' (aims at) life, achieves death. This is here adapted as an attack on the Hedonists, who maintained that the aim of life consists in giving satis-

1 The four limbs and nine apertures that constitute the human apparatus.

2 A military expression.

3 One would expect this to balance a clause about what happens when he is on the water.

4 Compare *Chuang Tzŭ* XVII. 1, end.

5 Cf. *Han Fei Tzŭ* P'ien 50: How can soldiers be expected to 'go out prepared to die', when at home admiration is accorded to those whose consciences (*i*) forbid them to enter endangered towns, dwell in camps, or in fact give one hair of their bodies, even if it would benefit the whole world?

faction to every constituent part of the human apparatus. But excessive 'feeding of life', says our author, defeats its own end, creating 'death-spots' (as I have said, this too is a military term). Ordinary people by 'fostering life' convert their thirteen constituent parts, which might be 'companions of life', into 'companions of death'.

We attribute the fact that some people do not meet tigers or get killed in battle to a thing we call 'chance'. The Taoist attributed such immunity to qualities in the 'lucky' person himself. Their view has perhaps as much to be said for it as ours. All efforts to make *shih yu san* mean anything but 'thirteen' do violence both to idiom and sense.

CHAPTER LI

Tao gave them birth;
The 'power' of Tao reared them,
Shaped them according to their kinds,
Perfected them, giving to each its strength.[1]
Therefore of the ten thousand things[2] there is not one that
does not worship Tao and do homage to its 'power'. No
mandate ever went forth that accorded to Tao the right to
be worshipped, nor to its 'power' the right to receive
homage.
It was always and of itself so.
Therefore as Tao bore them and the 'power' of Tao reared
them, made them grow, fostered them, harboured them,
brewed[3] for them, so you[4] must
'Rear them, but not lay claim to them,
Control them, but never lean upon them,
Be chief among them, but not manage them.
This is called the mysterious power.'[5]

[1] Its 'strong point', inborn capacity.
[2] Excepting Man?
[3] The word means a 'decoction', whether nutritive, medicinal or
(as always in modern Chinese) poisonous.
[4] The Sage.
[5] Cf. Chapter 10.

CHAPTER LII

That which was the beginning of all things under heaven
We may speak of as the 'mother' of all things.
He who apprehends the mother[1]
Thereby knows the sons.[2]
And he who has known the sons
Will hold all the tighter to the mother,
And to the end of his days suffer no harm:
'Block the passages, shut the doors,
And till the end your strength shall not fail.
Open up the passages, increase your doings,
And till your last day no help shall come to you.'
As good sight means seeing what is very small
So strength means holding on to what is weak.[3]
He who having used the outer-light[4] can return to the
    inner-light
Is thereby preserved from all harm.
This is called resorting to the always-so.

---

[1] Tao, the One, the Whole.
[2] The Many, the universe.
[3] i.e. Tao.
[4] This corresponds to 'knowing the sons'. *Ming* ('inner light') is self-knowledge.

CHAPTER LIII

HE WHO has the least scrap[1] of sense, once he has got
started on the great highway has nothing to fear so long as
he avoids turnings.   For great highways are safe and easy.
But men love by-paths.[2]
So long as the Court is in order
They are content to let their fields run to weed
And their granaries stand empty.
They wear patterns and embroideries,
Carry sharp swords, glut themselves with drink and food,
    have more possessions than they can use.
These are the riotous ways of brigandage;[3] they are not the
    Highway.

[1] See additional notes.
[2] All this is of course metaphorical. The highway is Tao; the by-
paths, the Confucian virtues. 'Loving by-paths' implies also neglecting
the essential and pursuing the secondary.
[3] Compare the riotous ways of the Robber Chê in *Chuang Tzŭ*.

CHAPTER LIV

What Tao[1] plants cannot be plucked,
What Tao clasps, cannot slip.
By its virtue alone can one generation after another carry on the
    ancestral sacrifice.[2]
Apply it to yourself and by its power you will be freed from dross.
Apply it to your household and your household shall thereby
    have abundance.
Apply it to the village, and the village will be made secure.
Apply it to the kingdom, and the kingdom shall thereby be
    made to flourish.
Apply it to an empire, and the empire shall thereby be extended.
Therefore just as through[3] oneself one may contemplate Oneself,
So through the household one may contemplate the Household,[4]
And through the village, one may contemplate the Village,
And through the kingdom, one may contemplate the Kingdom,
And through the empire, one may contemplate the Empire.
How do I know that the empire is so?
By this.[5]

[1] Literally 'what is well planted', i.e. planted by Tao.
[2] The 'power' of the ancestor's Tao carries the family on.
[3] By delving back through the successive stages of one's own conscious one gets back to the Unity of the Whole which is one's Tao.
Cf. the Maitri Upanishad (Hume, p. 435) 'having seen the Self through
oneself one becomes selfless'.
[4] i.e. the Tao of the household. When one has had vision of the
Tao (underlying essence) of a thing, one can control it. This catena
(self-household-village, etc.) is found in every branch of Chinese
philosophy, applied in a variety of ways. It originated I think with
the Yang Chu theory that to perfect a family one must perfect the
individual members of it, to perfect a village one must perfect each
several family, etc.   [5] What is inside me.

CHAPTER LV

The impunity of things fraught with the 'power'
May be likened to that of an infant.
Poisonous insects do not sting it,
Nor fierce beasts seize it,
Nor clawing birds maul it.
Its bones are soft, its sinews weak; but its grip is strong.
Not yet to have known the union of male and female, but to be
    completely formed,
Means that the vital force is at its height;
To be able to scream all day without getting hoarse
Means that harmony[1] is at its perfection.
To understand such harmony[2] is to understand the always-so.
To understand the always-so is to be illumined.
But to fill life to the brim is to invite omens.[3]
If the heart makes calls upon the life-breath,[4] rigidity follows.
Whatever has a time of vigour also has a time of decay.
Such[5] things are against Tao,
And whatever is against Tao is soon destroyed.

    1 Of hot and cold, soft and hard, etc. For the state of infancy as a
Taoist ideal, see Introduction, p. 55
    2 Compare *Analects*, I. 12.
    3 Here, as in the Short Preface to the *Book of History* (Legge, p. 6)
and *Shih Chi*, Ch. III, fol. 6, *hsiang* means a bad omen. It originally
meant a portent of any kind, whether good or bad. In current Chinese
it is, of course, only used in the favourable sense.
    4 The emotions were thought by the Chinese to make call upon and
use up the original supply of breath which was allotted to a man at
birth and constituted his life-spirit.
    5 Filling to the brim, calling upon the life-breath, having a time of
'vigour'. Cf. Ch. 30.

CHAPTER LVI

Those who know do not speak;
Those who speak do not know.
Block the passages,
Shut the doors,
Let all sharpness be blunted,
All tangles untied,
All glare tempered.
All dust smoothed.[1]
This is called the mysterious levelling.[2]
He who has achieved it cannot either be drawn into
    friendship or repelled,
Cannot be benefited, cannot be harmed,
Cannot either be raised or humbled,
And for that very reason is highest of all creatures under
    heaven.

---

[1] Cf. Ch. 4.
[2] In which there is a general perception not effected through particular senses. See *Lieh Tzǔ*, II. 3. 'Henceforward my eyes were one
with my ears, my ears with my nose, my nose with my mouth. . . .'

CHAPTER LVII

'Kingdoms can only be governed if rules are kept;
Battles can only be won if rules are broken.'[1]
But the adherence of all under heaven can only be won by
    letting-alone.
How do I know that it is so?
By this.[2]
The more prohibitions there are, the more ritual avoidances,
The poorer the people will be.
The more 'sharp weapons'[3] there are,
The more benighted will the whole land grow.
The more cunning craftsmen there are,
The more pernicious contrivances[4] will be invented.
The more laws are promulgated,
The more thieves and bandits there will be.
Therefore a sage has said:
So long as I 'do nothing' the people will of themselves be trans-
    formed.
So long as I love quietude, the people will of themselves go
    straight.
So long as I act only by inactivity the people will of themselves
    become prosperous.
So long as I have no wants the people will of themselves return
to the 'state of the Uncarved Block'.

---

[1] A military maxim, to the pattern of which the author proceeds to fit his Taoist formula. Cf. Lionel Giles, *Sun Tzŭ* pp. 34, 35. *Ch'i* means unexpected manœuvres. *Chêng* 'rules kept' is not here used in its technical military sense of 'open attack'.

[2] See Ch. 12. Through what I have found inside myself, 'in the belly'; through the light of my inner vision.   [3] i.e. clever people.

[4] Cf. the story in *Chuang Tzŭ* (XII. 11) about the man in whom the idea of a simple labour-saving contrivance inspired feelings similar to those aroused in Wordsworth by the sight of a railway train.

CHAPTER LVIII

When the ruler looks depressed[1] the people will be happy
    and satisfied;
When the ruler looks lively and self-assured[2] the people
    will be carping and discontented.
'It is upon bad fortune that good fortune leans, upon good
    fortune that bad fortune rests.'[3]
But though few know it, there is a bourn where there is
    neither right nor wrong;[4]
In a realm where every straight is doubled by a crooked,
    and every good by an ill, surely mankind has gone
    long enough astray?
Therefore the Sage
Squares without cutting,
Shapes the corners without lopping,
Straightens without stretching,
Gives forth light without shining.[5]

[1] As the Taoist is described as doing in Ch. 20.

[2] Like the people of the world in Ch. 20.

[3] Such are the maxims that pass as wisdom. The author is here
manifestly satirizing a passage in the *Lü Shih Ch'un Ch'iu* (P'ien 29,
beginning): 'It is upon bad fortune that good fortune leans, upon good
fortune that bad fortune rests. The Sage alone perceives this. How
should ordinary men reach such a bourn (of wisdom)?' To the Taoist
the real 'bourn of wisdom' lies far beyond the world of contraries
and antinomies.

[4] *Hsieh*, omitted by some versions of the Wang Pi text, should be
retained.

[5] Through Tao he reaches his *ends* without use of *means*. To translate
'shines without dazzling' is to misunderstand the whole sequence.
The Confucians as their 'means' use the virtues of 'squareness', i.e.
rectitude, and 'angularity' i.e. incorruptibility.

CHAPTER LIX

You cannot rule men nor serve heaven unless you have laid up a
    store;
This 'laying up a store' means quickly absorbing,[1]
And 'quickly absorbing' means doubling one's garnered 'power'.
Double your garnered power and it acquires a strength that
    nothing can overcome.
If there is nothing it cannot overcome, it knows no bounds,
And only what knows no bounds
Is huge enough to keep a whole kingdom in its grasp.
But only he who having the kingdom goes to the Mother
Can keep it long.
This[2] is called the art of making the roots strike deep by fencing
the trunk, of making life long by fixed staring.

Commentary

There is a common saying, which takes a variety of
different forms, 'With but one year's store, a land is a
land no more'. In order that the food of the living and of
the dead[3] may be assured in case of a failure of the crops
or an invasion, part of last year's grain must be retained in
the barns as a basis for the new store. This 'laying of the
new upon the old' is here used as a symbol for the rein-
forcing of one's stock of vital-energy (*ch'i*, 'breath') by
Quietist practices. Compare Mencius's famous *hao-jan
chih ch'i* 'welling breath' which issuing from such a

1 See textual notes.
2 i.e. going to Tao the Mother.
3 i.e. sacrifices to the Ancestors (Heaven).

'garnered store' as our author here describes was so great and strong 'that it would fill heaven, earth and all that is in between'. There is little reason to doubt that 'fixed staring' was used by the Taoists, as it was by Indians and by Byzantine Quietists, as a method of trance induction. Non-Taoists used the phrase without understanding it, imagining apparently that it was synonymous with *ch'ang-shêng*, 'long life'. Cf. *Hsün Tzŭ* 4, middle, and *Lü Shih Ch'un Ch'iu* 3, fol. 2.

CHAPTER LX

RULING A large kingdom is indeed like cooking small fish.[1] They who by Tao ruled all that is under heaven did not let an evil spirit[2] within them display its powers. Nay, it was not only that the evil spirit did not display its powers; neither was the Sage's good spirit[3] used to the hurt of other men. Nor was it only that his good spirit was not used to harm other men, the Sage himself was thus saved from harm.[4] And so, each being saved from harm, their 'powers' could converge towards a common end.

Commentary

A number of parallel passages, which the author quite certainly had in mind, make it evident that both *kuei* and *shên* are here used in a subjective sense: 'The enlightened (i.e. Realist) monarch in the carrying out of his institutes is a god (*t'ien*); in his use of men he is a demon (*kuei*).[5] He is a god, in that he cannot be gainsaid; a demon, in that he is subject to no restraint.'[6] 'The Sages of old did not damage their souls (*shên*)' by evil passions.[7] Another parallel passage, containing both a reference to *kuei* and the

---

[1] The less one handles them the better.   [2] *Kuei*.   [3] *Shên*.

[4] Omit *jên*, which has crept in under the influence of *Han Fei Tzŭ* who is, I think, simply adapting a traditional text to his own purposes. (P'ien 20, fol. 9.)

[5] A *kuei* is not of course necessarily bad. It is simply the spirit of a commoner as opposed to that of a dweller in heaven (*t'ien*) i.e. a Former King. But 'possession' by a *kuei* was always evil.

[6] *Han Fei Tzŭ*, 48. 1.   [7] *Lü Shih Ch'un Ch'iu*, 119.

curious sequence of a statement followed by 'Nay, it was not so . . .' was certainly also in the author's mind: 'If with the whole essence of your being you ponder on a question, the *kuei* will give you the answer. Nay, it is not that the *kuei* answer you, it is simply that you have pondered with the whole essence of your being.'[1]

The general meaning is that if the ruler follows the Realist's advice and is a 'demon' in his dealings with the people, he will do as much harm to his own soul as to them.

---

1 *Lü Shih Ch'un Ch'iu*, 147.

CHAPTER LXI

A LARGE kingdom must be like the low ground towards which all streams flow down. It must be a point towards which all things under heaven converge. Its part must be that of the female in its dealings with all things under heaven. The female by quiescence conquers the male; by quiescence gets underneath.[1] If a large kingdom can in the same way succeed in getting underneath a small kingdom then it will win the adherence of the small kingdom; and it is because small kingdoms are by nature in this way underneath large kingdoms that they win the adherence of large kingdoms. The one must get underneath in order to do it; the other is underneath and therefore does it. What large countries really need is more inhabitants; and what small countries need is some place where their surplus inhabitants can go and get employment. Thus[2] each gets what it needs. That is why I say the large kingdom must 'get underneath'.

---

[1] Literally 'becomes underneath', i.e. induces the male to mount her.

[2] i.e. if the large kingdom 'gets underneath'. It is assumed that the population of the large kingdom will be relatively sparse; that of the small kingdom relatively dense.

CHAPTER LXII

Tao in the Universe is like the south-west corner[1] in the
    house.
It is the treasure of the good man,
The support of the bad.
There is a traffic in speakers of fine words;
Persons of grave demeanour are accepted as gifts;
Even the bad let slip no opportunity to acquire them.
Therefore[2] on the day of an Emperor's enthronement
Or at the installation of the three officers of State
Rather than send a team of four horses, preceded by a disc
    of jade,
Better were it, as can be done without moving from one's
    seat, to send this Tao.
For what did the ancients say of this Tao, how did they
prize it? Did they not say of those that have it 'Pursuing,
they shall catch; pursued, they shall escape?' They thought
it, indeed, most precious of all things under heaven.

Commentary

The 'speakers of fine words' and 'persons of grave demeanour' were the itinerant sophists and sages who at
that time went round from capital to capital, selling their
services to the ruler who offered them the highest induce-
ments.

[1] Where family worship was carried on; the pivotal point round
which the household centred.

[2] i.e. if things other than presents in kind are not only accepted as
gifts, but even purchased at high price.

CHAPTER LXIII

It acts without action, does without doing, finds flavour in
    what is flavourless,[1]
Can make the small great and the few many,
'Requites injuries with good deeds,
Deals with the hard while it is still easy,
With the great while it is still small.'[2]
In the governance of empire everything difficult must be
    dealt with while it is still easy,
Everything great must be dealt with while it is still small.
Therefore the Sage never has to deal with the great; and
    so achieves greatness.
But again 'Light assent inspires little confidence
And "many easies" means many a hard.'
Therefore the Sage knows too how to make the easy diffi-
cult, and by doing so avoid all difficulties!

Commentary

The author first appropriates the maxim 'Requite
injuries with good deeds, etc.',[3] and shows how perfectly it
fits in with his own teaching. He then, as a *tour de force*,
appropriates a second and apparently contradictory proverb, with equal success.

The word *tê* ('good deeds' in the proverb) is the same as

[1] In Ch. 35 Tao itself is said to be 'flavourless'.

[2] Compare *Han Fei Tzŭ*, 38. The saying originally merely meant
'attend to troubles in time, before they get out of hand'.

[3] Confucius (*Analects* XIV. 36) criticizes this proverb and says if you
repay injuries with good deeds, how are you going to repay good
deeds?

219

that by which Taoists denoted the mysterious 'power' of Tao. The world laughs at Tao, the author says, and we requite this injury with the gift of *tê*. In what follows the 'easy' and 'small' is the Primal Unity underlying the apparent diversity of things. The Taoist passes as easily from the 'easy' aspect of things to their 'hard' aspect as he does from the 'hard' to the 'easy'; that is to say he is capable of seeing things as parts or as a unity, according to what the occasion requires.

CHAPTER LXIV

'What stays still is easy to hold;
Before there has been an omen it is easy to lay plans.
What is tender is easily torn,[1]
What is minute is easy to scatter.'
Deal with things in their state of not-yet-being,
Put them in order before they have got into confusion.
For 'the tree big as a man's embrace began as a tiny sprout,
The tower nine storeys high began with a heap of earth,
The journey of a thousand leagues began with what was under
 the feet'.
He who acts, harms; he who grabs, lets slip.
Therefore the Sage does not act, and so does not harm;
Does not grab, and so does not let slip.
Whereas the people of the world, at their tasks,
Constantly spoil things when within an ace of completing
 them.
'Heed the end no less than the beginning,'[2]
And your work will not be spoiled.
Therefore[3] the Sage wants only things that are unwanted,
Sets no store by products difficult to get,

---

 [1] Reading *p'an* with the 'knife' determinative; or 'What is soft is easily melted', if we keep the 'water' determinative.
 [2] For similar sayings see *Book of History*, Legge, pp. 183 and 211.
 [3] Because the 'end' (the world around us) is as important as the 'beginning' (the primal state, the One, the Whole). The Sage does not only work through Tao; he also shows the world the degree to which ordinary life can be moulded to the pattern of Tao.

And so teaches things untaught,
Turning all men back to the things they have left behind,[1]
That the ten thousand creatures may be restored to their Self-
so.[2]
This he does; but dare not act.

---

[1] Such as walking instead of riding, used knotted ropes instead of writing, etc. See Ch. 80.

[2] To what they are of themselves, as opposed to what they are in relation to other things.

CHAPTER LXV

IN THE days of old those who practised Tao with success
did not, by means of it, enlighten the people, but on the
contrary sought to make them ignorant.
The more knowledge people have, the harder they are to
    rule.
Those who seek to rule by giving knowledge
Are like bandits preying on the land.
Those who rule without giving knowledge
Bring a stock of good fortune to the land.
To have understood the difference between these two
    things is to have a test and standard.
To be always able to apply this test and standard
Is called the mysterious 'power',
The mysterious 'power', so deep-penetrating,
So far-reaching,
That can follow things back——
All the way back to the Great Concordance.[1]

---

[1] Cf. *Chuang Tzŭ*, XII, 8.

CHAPTER LXVI

How did the great rivers and seas get their kingship over
 the hundred lesser streams?
Through the merit of being lower than they; that was how
 they got their kingship.
Therefore the Sage
In order to be above the people
Must speak as though he were lower than the people.
In order to guide them
He must put himself behind them.
Only thus can the Sage be on top and the people not be
 crushed by his weight.
Only thus can he guide, and the people not be led into
harm.
Indeed in this way everything under heaven will be glad
to be pushed by[1] him and will not find his guidance irk-
some. This he does by not striving; and because he does
not strive, none can contend with him.

[1] 'From behind'.

CHAPTER LXVII

EVERY ONE under heaven says that our Way is greatly like folly. But it is just because it is great, that it seems like folly. As for things that do not seem like folly[1]—well, there can be no question about *their* smallness!

Here are my three treasures.[2] Guard and keep them! The first is pity; the second, frugality; the third: refusal to be 'foremost of all things under heaven'.

For only he that pities is truly able to be brave;

Only he that is frugal is truly able to be profuse.

Only he that refuses to be foremost of all things

Is truly able to become chief of all Ministers.[3]

At present your bravery is not based on pity, nor your profusion on frugality, nor your vanguard on your rear;[4] and this is death. But pity cannot fight without conquering or guard without saving. Heaven arms with pity those whom it would not see destroyed.[5]

---

[1] Literally 'that seem normal'.

[2] The three rules that formed the practical, political side of the author's teaching (1) abstention from aggressive war and capital punishment, (2) absolute simplicity of living, (3) refusal to assert active authority.

[3] The phrase has exactly the same meaning as the *kuan-ch'ang* of Ch. 28.

[4] i.e. your eminence on self-effacement. This is as perilous as to leave one's line of communication undefended.

[5] Such is the sense that our author gives to the saying. It is probable, however, that it is simply a couplet from some old ritual-song (like those in the last part of the *Book of Odes*) and means 'Heaven deigned to help them; in its pity it protected them'.

Tao Tê Ching

Commentary

The opening passage cannot be rendered satisfactorily, for it depends on a series of plays on words. *Ta* (1) greatly, (2) great. *Pu-hsiao* 'below the average in capacity'; the opposite of *hsien* 'above the average in capacity'. But there is a play on *hsiao* 'average', 'normal' and *hsiao* 'small' which is sometimes written with this same character.

CHAPTER LXVIII

The best charioteers do not rush ahead;[1]
The best fighters do not make displays of wrath.[2]
The greatest conqueror wins without joining issue;
The best user of men acts as though he were their inferior.
This is called the power that comes of not contending,
Is called the capacity to use men,
The secret of being mated to heaven, to what was of old.

---

[1] Wang Pi says quite rightly that *Shih* is a 'leader' of foot-soldiers. The leaders rode in war-chariots. He also says that *wu* means 'rushing in front of the others'. Cf. *Sun Tzŭ* P'ien 9, end. The usual translation ('The best soldiers are not warlike') misses the point.

[2] *Nu* is anger shown outwardly, as by glaring, grimacing or the like.

CHAPTER LXIX

The strategists have the sayings: 'When you doubt your ability to meet the enemy's attack, take the offensive yourself', and 'If you doubt your ability to advance an inch, then retreat a foot'.

This latter is what we call to march without moving,
To roll the sleeve, but present no bare arm,
The hand that seems to hold, yet has no weapon in it,
A host that can confront, yet presents no battle-front.[1]
Now the greatest of all calamities is to attack and find no
    enemy.
I can have no enemy only at the price of losing my treasure.[2]
Therefore when armies are raised and issues joined it is he
    who does not delight in war that wins.

Commentary

In the scramble for empire that marked the final phase of the feudal period in China the watchword was 'No enemy under heaven', i.e. each State looked forward to a time when it should have crushed all the other States. The Realists used this watchword in an extended application, applying it also to internal polities: the State can tolerate no criticism or opposition. That this maxim, in either of its senses, can only be fulfilled at the expense of 'pity' is obvious. Later editors, no longer understanding

[1] The Wang Pi commentary shows the order in which these clauses should come.

[2] i.e. pity. Secondary sense: 'He whose enemy presents no front, loses his booty'. For this sense of *pao* see *Kuan Tzŭ*, P'ien 17, middle.

228

the connotations of the phrase 'no enemy' altered the text to 'despising one's enemy'; but Wang Pi's commentary makes it clear that he read 'no enemy' and perfectly understood what the phrase denoted.

The two strategists quoted at the beginning of the chapter would appear to be Wang Liao and I Liang, cf. *Lü Shih Ch'un Ch'iu*, 99. A book by the latter still survived at the beginning of the Christian era, see *Han Shu* XXX, fol. 26.

CHAPTER LXX

MY WORDS are very easy to understand and very easy to put into practice. Yet no one under heaven understands them; no one puts them into practice. But my words have an ancestry, my deeds have a lord;[1] and it is precisely because men do not understand this that they are unable to understand me.

Few then understand me; but it is upon this very fact that my value depends. It is indeed in this sense[2] that 'the Sage wears hair-cloth on top, but carries jade underneath his dress'.

[1] To have 'neither ancestors nor lord' was to be a wild man, a savage. This is a metaphorical way of saying that all the Sage did and said was related to a definite system of thought.

[2] In this sense, and not in the sense that he flies in panic from the horrors of the world. Rich people, in times of tumult, dressed up as peasants and hid their jade treasures under their clothes. Metaphorically 'to wear haircloth' etc., came to mean 'to hide one's light under a bushel', 'to keep one's knowledge to oneself'.

CHAPTER LXXI

'To know when one does not know is best.
To think one knows when one does not know is a dire
    disease.
Only he who recognizes this disease as a disease
Can cure himself of the disease.'
The Sage's way of curing disease
Also consists in making people recognize their diseases as
diseases and thus ceasing to be diseased.

Commentary

The best way to explain this chapter is to paraphrase it.
The people of the world, the author says, have a saying
to the effect that it is best of all never to think that one
knows when one doesn't know, for to think one knows
when in reality one is ignorant is a dire disease; most
people, however, are bound to suffer to some extent from
this disease, and if they will only recognize the fact that
they suffer from it, they will take steps to extend their
knowledge and so protect themselves from the 'disease'.

'Well, the whole of my teaching', he replies, 'consists simply in making people recognize that what they
mistake for conditions of health are really conditions of
disease; that their virtues (humanity, morality, observance
of etiquette, etc.) are really vices, that what they prize
(luxury, fame, power, etc.) is really worthless.

In the last chapter the author says that his style seems
obscure, yet to anyone possessing the clue is perfectly
lucid. In this chapter he supplies the classic example of
this 'enigmatic lucidity'.

CHAPTER LXXII

NEVER MIND if the people are not intimidated by your authority. A Mightier Authority[1] will deal with them in the end. Do not narrow their dwellings[2] or harass their lives;[3] and for the very reason that you do not harrass them, they will cease to turn from[4] you. Therefore the Sage knows himself[5] but does not show himself. Knows his own value, but does not put himself on high. Truly, 'he rejects that but takes this'.[6]

[1] Heaven. Cf. *I Chou Shu*, P'ien 67.
[2] i.e. put them in prison. See textual notes.
[3] Literally, 'that whereby they live', their livelihoods. The author is thinking of heavy taxation and the like.
[4] There is a pun on 'harass' and 'turn from'; see textual notes. The root means originally 'to press down from above'. Hence (1) to oppress (2) to have food crammed into one, to be 'fed up', to turn away in disgust.
[5] i.e. knows his own power, but does not display it.
[6] See Ch. 12.

CHAPTER LXXIII

He whose braveness lies in daring, slays.

He whose braveness lies in not daring,[1] gives life.

Of these two, either may be profitable or unprofitable.

But 'Heaven hates what it hates;

None can know the reason why'.[2]

Wherefore the Sage, too, disallows it.

For it is the way of Heaven not to strive but none the less
    to conquer,

Not to speak, but none the less to get an answer,

Not to beckon; yet things come to it of themselves.

Heaven is like one who says little,[3] yet none the less has
    laid his plans.

Heaven's net is wide;

Coarse are the meshes, yet nothing slips through.

[1] i.e. in not daring to slay.

[2] Heaven hates the shedding of blood (i.e. it is 'against nature'),
and those who ignore the will of Heaven are bound to be trapped at
last in the meshes of Fate. This is the traditional pacifist argument of
the Mo Tzŭ school, which our author is here able to utilize by
identifying Heaven with Tao. For 'Heaven hates what it hates. . . .'
Cf. *Lieh Tzŭ*, VI. 5.

[3] See textual notes.

CHAPTER LXXIV

THE PEOPLE are not frightened of death. What then is the use of trying to intimidate them with the death-penalty? And even supposing people were generally frightened of death and did not regard it as an everyday thing, which of us would dare to seize them and slay them?[1] There is the Lord of Slaughter[2] always ready for this task, and to do it in his stead is like thrusting oneself into the master-carpenter's place and doing his chipping for him. Now 'he who tries to do the master-carpenter's chipping for him is lucky if he does not cut his hand'.[3]

[1] i.e. even supposing the death-penalty really had the effect of scaring people and keeping down crime, is it fair to ask anyone to undertake such a task?

[2] i.e. Heaven, or its agents (pestilence, famine, lightning, earthquake, etc.).

[3] Adaptation of a proverb meaning 'let every man stick to his task'.

CHAPTER LXXV

THE PEOPLE starve because those above them eat too
much tax-grain. That is the only reason why they starve.
The people are difficult to keep in order because those
above them interfere. That is the only reason why they
are so difficult to keep in order. The people attach no
importance to death, because those above them are too
grossly absorbed in the pursuit of life. That is why they[1]
attach no importance to death. And indeed, in that their
hearts are so little set on life they are superior to those
who set store by life.[2]

---

[1] The people.
[2] i.e. are superior to their rulers; so that there is no chance of the
state being well governed.

CHAPTER LXXVI

WHEN HE is born, man is soft and weak; in death he becomes stiff and hard. The ten thousand creatures and all plants and trees while they are alive are supple and soft, but when they are dead they become brittle and dry. Truly, what is stiff and hard is a 'companion of death'; what is soft and weak is a 'companion of life'.[1] Therefore 'the weapon that is too hard[2] will be broken, the tree that has the hardest wood will be cut down'. Truly, the hard and mighty are cast down; the soft and weak set on high.

[1] Cf. Ch. 50.

[2] The proverb exists in several forms, and the text has been tampered with, so that the exact reading is uncertain. But the general sense is quite clear. Cf. *Lieh Tzŭ* II. 16.

CHAPTER LXXVII

HEAVEN'S WAY is like the bending of a bow.[1] When a bow is bent the top comes down and the bottom-end comes up. So too does Heaven take away from those who have too much, and give to those that have not enough. But if it is Heaven's way to take from those who have too much and give to those who have not enough, this is far from being man's way. He takes away from those that have not enough in order to make offering to those who already have too much. One there is and one only, so rich that he can afford to make offerings to all under heaven. Who is this? It is the possessor of Tao. If, then, the Sage 'though he controls does not lean, and when he has achieved his aim does not linger',[2] it is because he does not wish to reveal himself as better than others.

---

[1] Not in the act of stringing it, but in the act of shooting an arrow from it. There is no reason at all to suppose with Wilhelm that the composite, double-bending bow is meant.

[2] Over the scene of his triumph.   Cf. Ch. 2. If he leaned, the people would know who it was that was controlling them; if he lingered, they would recognize who it was that had done the work. They would regard him as 'better', 'superior'; and to allow oneself to be so regarded is to sin against 'Heaven's way' and so lose one's power.

CHAPTER LXXVIII

NOTHING UNDER heaven is softer or more yielding than water;[1] but when it attacks things hard and resistant there is not one of them that can prevail. For they can find no way of altering[2] it. That the yielding conquers the resistant and the soft conquers the hard is a fact known by all men, yet utilized by none. Yet it is in reference to this that the Sage[3] said 'Only he who has accepted the dirt of the country can be lord of its soil-shrines;[4] only he who takes upon himself the evils of the country can become a king among those what dwell under heaven.' Straight words seem crooked.[5]

---

[1] Cf. Ch. 12; also 43.

[2] i.e. damaging.

[3] Lao Tan. Cf. *Chuang Tzŭ*, XXXIII. 5.

[4] Reference to a custom similar to the 'seizin' of medieval Europe, whereby a new tenant took a clod of earth in his hand to symbolize possession of the soil. The Chinese expression *han hou*, generally used in this connexion, suggests that the clod was originally held by the new feudal lord or tenant between his teeth—a sort of symbolic eating. Thus he absorbed the 'virtue' of the soil.

[5] Seem, as we should say, to be paradoxes.

CHAPTER LXXIX

To ALLAY the main discontent, but only in a manner that will certainly produce further discontents can hardly be called successful. Therefore the Sage behaves like the holder of the left-hand tally, who stays where he is and does not go round making claims on people. For he who has the 'power' of Tao is the Grand Almoner; he who has not the 'power' is the Grand Perquisitor. 'It is Heaven's way, without distinction of persons, to keep the good perpetually supplied.'

Commentary

The meaning of this chapter, which exemplifies the author's literary procedure at its subtlest, can best be made clear by a paraphrase.

It is no use trying to govern in the ordinary way, by laws and restrictions, penalties and rewards. For at any given moment (see Ch. XXIX) some of your subjects will be 'blowing hot while others are blowing cold. Some will be loading while others are tilting'. You will only be able to content some by discontenting others. In fact it is no use trying to *ho* (fit together, harmonize). Thus the Sage is like the holder of the left-hand half of a tally, who is ready to give out what is due (i.e. is ready to vouchsafe the bounties of Tao), but does not go round trying to fit (*ho*) his half of the tally to someone else's half, as the creditor does. He is indeed like the officer who gives public assistance (pun on *ch'i* 'tally' and *ch'ieh* 'help', 'assist')[1] to

[1] See textual notes.

the needy and aged; whereas the ordinary ruler is a sort of Grand Tithe-Collector. In the author's application of the proverb which he quotes at the end of the chapter, 'the good' of course means the Taoist Sage, whom Heaven supplies with the inexhaustible treasures of Tao, so that, though a debtor, the Sage is in a position to be always 'giving out', to be always 'meeting claims'. For the origin of the terms employed, see additional notes.

CHAPTER LXXX

GIVEN A small country with few inhabitants,[1] he could bring it about that though there should be among the people contrivances requiring ten times, a hundred times less labour,[2] they would not use them. He could bring it about that the people would be ready to lay down their lives and lay them down again[3] in defence of their homes, rather than emigrate.[4] There might still be boats and carriages, but no one would go in them; there might still be weapons of war but no one would drill with them. He could bring it about that 'the people should have no use for any form of writing save knotted ropes,[5] should be contented with their food, pleased with their clothing, satisfied with their homes, should take pleasure in their rustic tasks. The next place might be so near at hand that one could hear the cocks crowing in it, the dogs

[1] i.e. no need for a large country and many inhabitants, which was what the princes of the world pined for.

[2] Cf. *Shang Tzŭ*, I. I, and *Chan Kuo Ts'ê* VI. 26, where the principle is laid down that new mechanical contrivances may be accepted if they are ten times more efficient than the old. For the Taoist objection to mechanical contrivances see *Chuang Tzŭ* XII. II, already quoted.

[3] For *ch'ung-ssŭ* in the sense of 'die twice over' compare *Lü Shih Ch'un Ch'iu*, 131, end: 'Every one has to die once, but it may be truly said that Ch'ing Fêng died twice over'.

[4] Cf. Introduction, p. 80.

[5] One knots ropes as an aid to one's *own* memory (compare our 'tying a knot in one's handkerchief'); whereas one writes contracts down in order to make other people fulfil them. That, I think, is why 'knotting' belongs to the Golden Age. I doubt whether the *quipus* of South American Indians are relevant.

barking; but the people would grow old and die without
ever having been there'.[1]

---

[1] The passage in inverted commas occurs (with trifling differences)
in *Chuang Tzŭ* (X. 3) as a description of life under the rule of the
legendary agricultural Sage Shên-nung. The whole chapter can be
understood in the past, present or future tense, as the reader desires.

CHAPTER LXXXI

True words are not fine-sounding;
Fine-sounding words are not true.
The good man does not prove by argument;
And he who proves by argument[1] is not good.
True wisdom is different from much learning;
Much learning means little wisdom.
The Sage has no need to hoard;
When his own last scrap has been used up on behalf of others,
Lo, he has more than before!
When his own last scrap has been used up in giving to others,
Lo, his stock is even greater than before![2]
For Heaven's way is to sharpen without cutting,[3]
And the Sage's way is to act without striving.

[1] i.e. the 'sophist'; see Introduction, p. 64.
[2] Adaptation of a saying that occurs in several forms. Cf. *Chuang Tzŭ*, XXI, end.
[3] To achieve the end without using the material means.

ADDITIONAL NOTE ON INTRODUCTION

P. 26 The 'shih' (medium)

The question of the *shih* is one of considerable interest to the anthropologist. It appears that such an institution, though familiar enough in funerary ritual and indeed still surviving even in remote parts of Europe, has seldom save in China been extended to sacrificial ritual. My authority for saying this is E. O. James's very careful and scholarly work, *Origins of Sacrifice*, where there is no mention of such an institution. I do not mean of course that it is rare for anyone taking part in sacrifice to be 'possessed' by a spirit. The *shaman* is a common enough feature at sacrificial ceremonies. But the typical characteristic of the *shaman* is that he dances; whereas the typical characteristic of the *shih* is that he remains immobile.[1] It follows from this that field-workers in anthropology could not fail to notice a *shaman*; but might easily fail to notice or at any rate understand the significance of a *shih*. It would surprise me if it did not turn out that the *shih* is a much less unique institution than one might at first sight suppose. Some account of this custom may be found in Maspero's *La Chine Antique*. See also Kano Naoyoshi's *Shinagaku Bunso*, pp. 94-128 (in Japanese).

[1] Not, of course, during the whole ceremony, but during the major part of it.

ADDITIONAL NOTES ON
TRANSLATION

Chapter I

The original meaning of *ku* is 'old'. Hence 'well-established'; hence 'true'. It is put in front of a proverb or accepted maxim after a demonstration that what is propounded does not conflict with this proverb. It often has a sense transitional between 'Truly' and 'therefore'. But it would be possible to quote many passages in early Chinese literature where 'therefore', in such contents, is an impossible rendering; and this is often the case in the *Tao Tê Ching*. In later times *ku* with determinative 31 was reserved for the sense 'truly' and *ku* with determinative 66 always meant 'therefore'. For the characters, see textual notes.

'Ultimate results': *chiao*. The character is exceedingly common in early texts in the sense 'to seek' (almost always 'to seek a blessing from Heaven'). It does not occur in the quite different sense which it has here till *Lieh Tzŭ*, which is, at the earliest, a work of the late 3rd century B.C. This fact is important in connection with the dating of the *Tao Tê Ching*. See my article in the *Bulletin of the School of Oriental Studies*, 1934.

Chapter XIII

For *ching* in the sense 'beside oneself' cf. the story (*Kuo Yü*, 18) of Ho-lü, famous for his moral zest. On hearing of one good deed this monarch would become so excited that he was *jo ching* 'as it were beside himself'.

Tao Tê Ching

In Chinese the word *shên* 'body' also means 'self', and as this word was used to translate the Sanskrit *ātman* ('self'). Many Buddhist texts which deal with *Atman* ('personality') and not with the physical body look in their Chinese dress uncommonly like this passage of the *Tao Tê Ching*. Thus the Chinese version of the Sutra of Dharmapada Parables[1] says: 'Of all evils under heaven none is worse than having a *shên*.' It was natural that the Chinese (and Western writers in their wake) should take *shên* not in its real sense of *Ātman*, 'self', but as meaning body. Thus Tao-shih[2] in 659 A.D., commenting on this Dharmapada passage, explains it by quoting *Tao Tê Ching*, Ch. XIII, a reference which is in reality quite irrelevant.

Chapter XX

Line 12. Literally 'going up to the Spring Terrace'. This is generally taken merely to mean going up on to a terrace to admire the view. But 'Spring Terrace' balances 'Great Sacrificial-banquet', and must also be the name of a religious ceremony. Now we know from the *Ch'ing Chia Lu*[3] of Ku Lu that 'in the second or third month the richer and more public-spirited among the local gentry pile up a terrace on some open piece of unused ground and provide money for a play. Men and women look on together. It is called the Spring Terrace Play, and is intended to ensure fertility of the crops'. The terrace was of course not intended as a stage, but was a raised bank for the audience to sit on. The fact that men and women, contrary to Chinese custom, sat together indicates that the Spring

1 Takakusu, IV, 595a   2 *Ibidem*, LIV, p. 63.
3 I know this book only in quotation.

Terrace was originally the scene of a kind of carnival, a period of authorized license intended, as such festivals always are, to promote the fertility of the fields. It is of course a far cry from the 18th century (Ku Lu's period) to the 3rd century B.C.; but I think it may in any case be taken as certain that some kind of carnival is referred to.

Chapter XXI

A 'charge' (*ming*) consists of the 'life-giving words' that a general addresses to troops before a battle or the instructions that a king gives to a new feudal lord or minister. The object of this charge is to 'animate' the troops, lord, or minister, with a particular purpose. For this reason he speaks 'words of good cheer', which is the root meaning of the character I have translated 'cheers onward'. The 'ten thousand things are compared to troops in whose ears the general's (i.e. Tao's) orders of the day' still ring.

Of the three characters given for *fu* in the textual notes, the first simply means 'a big (i.e. adult) man'. The second, 'the hand with the stick', i.e. the person who beats one at one's tribal initiation, and so (at a later stage of society when fatherhood began to take its place beside motherhood as a known and recognized relationship) 'the father'. The third character ('use' plus 'hand with stick') means 'the name given to an adult for ordinary use', and it is only as a phonetic equivalent that it stands for 'grown man'. The most accurate way to write 'men' in the sense of 'soldiers' would be to use the first of the three characters.

[1] There is no evidence of violent initiation in China and I now (1948) feel doubtful about this explanation of the character.

249

Tao Tê Ching

Chapter XXVII

Hsi, 'to resort to'.

This character has two distinct sets of usages, which do not seem to be etymologically akin. (1) fold, double, repeat, imitate. With this series we are not here concerned. (2) It serves as an intensive to *ju* 'to go into', with the meanings 'go into and stay there', 'establish oneself in', 'put oneself under the protection of'; with a hostile sense, 'invade'. For parallels, see *Chuang Tzŭ*, XV, 2, 'Evil humours cannot *establish* themselves (in such a man)'; balances *ju*, to enter. *Ibidem*, VI. 4. 'It was by getting Tao that 'K'an-p'i *established* himself on Mt. K'un-lun.' *Ibidem*, XX. 7. 'The swallow though afraid of men *establishes* itself among them. . . .' *Huai-nan Tzŭ* VI. 'The bears slink into their mountain caverns, the tiger and leopard *establish* themselves (i.e. ensconce themselves) in their lairs, and dare not so much as utter a sound.' *Kuo Yü*, 8, 'When a large country is well ruled and a small country resorts to the large one for protection. . . .'

From the basic sense 'going in and stopping in' is derived, I think, that of 'adopting' a new form of attire. Cf. *Chan Kuo Ts'ê*, VI. 19.

Chapter XXXI

'In peace the left-hand side is the place of honour. . . .' We know too that circumambulatory rites were in civil life performed clockwise; but in war, anti-clockwise. The distinction is a very important one in all primitive ritual, cf. *I Chou Shu* 32. 'It is the way of Heaven to prefer the right; the sun and moon travel westward. It is the way of earth to prefer the left; the watercourses flow to the east[1] . . . In rites of good omen, circumambulation is to the left; it follows the way of earth, in order that the performers themselves may be benefited. In ceremonies of war, circumambulation is to the right; it follows the way of Heaven, in order that the weapons may gain in sharpness.'

Chapter XXXVIII

The *tao* (doctrine) of which foreknowledge was the flower is of course not Taoism, but may well be the branch of Confucianism represented, for example, by the *Doctrine of the Mean* (paragraph 24): 'The way of complete fulfilment (of one's own nature) leads to knowledge of what is to come.' Support for the idea of the Sage as prophet was found in *Analects* II. 23.[2] See also *Lü Shih Ch'un Ch'iu*, P'ien 85, where a whole section is devoted to foreknowledge. The Dualists and systematizers of theories based on the Five Elements also went in for prophecy. It is unlikely that diviners by the *Book of Changes* are meant, for this work is seldom alluded to by writers of the third century, and did not become part of the Confucian curriculum till the Han dynasty. As the clauses which go before are directed against Confucianism, it seems likely that it is a Confucian doctrine that is here condemned.

Chapter XXXIX

'Direct their people.'

Chêng ('cowry-shell' underneath 'to divine') passes in a particularly interesting manner from an auguristic to a

---

1 Read *tung*, not *chung*.
2 'Can ten generations hence be foreknown?'

moral meaning. In the Honan Oracle-records (12th-11th century B.C.), where it occurs thousands of times, it means to ask for an oracular response. When the *Book of Changes* began to be used as a text in conjunction with divination by the yarrow-stalks, the term *chêng* took on a number of technical significations, still purely auguristic. When however (perhaps in the 4th century B.C.) the *Book of Changes* was reinterpreted in a metaphysical and ethical sense, *chêng* was by a play upon words[1] taken in the sense 'straight', as opposed to crooked, and so (in a moral sense) 'upright', In the 3rd century B.C. the old auguristic meaning was practically obsolete, and the character simply means 'straight' or 'to straighten' morally or meta-phorically as opposed to straightening physically.

'Enumerate the parts of a carriage. . . .'

Buddhist writers[2] frequently use a parable which at first sight looks as though it were closely connected with this passage, and the late Sir Charles Eliot[3] went so far as to believe that the *Tao Tê Ching* was here influenced by Buddhism. There is however no real connection. The Buddhist argument runs: just as when the various parts of a carriage have been removed one by one, there is no carriage left, so when the various component parts of the human aggregate have been removed one by one, there is no *sat* ('being') left. Whereas here the argument (like

---

[1] i.e. by identifying it with *chêng*, 'straight', originally written with quite a different character. For the two characters, see textual notes.

[2] *Samyutta Nikāya*, V. 10. 6. *Samyuktāgama*, Takakusu, II. 327 b. *Milinda Questions*, Sacred Books of the East XXXV, 43-45, *Mahāparinir-vāna Sūtra*, Ch. 27, *Prajñāpāramitā Sāstra*, Ch. 31.

[3] *Hinduism and Buddhism*, III. 246.

that of *Chuang Tzŭ* XXV. 10) is that the whole cannot be known by separately knowing the parts.

Chapter XLI

'. . . Looks flimsy.' The original meaning of *t'ou* is to pull, to force (of doors, etc.). Hence (1) 'a forcer of doors', a thief. (2) (as here) 'able to be forced', flimsy.[1]

For *yü* (here translated 'faded') applied to colours, see *Huai-nan Tzŭ*, 20, par. 6. For *chih* applied to substances of natural as opposed to artificial colour, see *Ta Tai Li Chi*, P'ien 72, fol. 4 verso.

Chapter XLII

The saying 'The man of violence never yet came to a good end . . .' occurs in the so-called Inscription on the Statue, known to us in various forms. I here combine the versions in *K'ung Tzŭ Chia Yü*, XI, and *Shuo Yüan* X, neither of which is satisfactory in itself. The mouth of the statue (which is supposed to have stood in the Great Ancestral Hall of the Chous) was sealed with a triple seal. On its back was an inscription in homely, countryside language, the burden of which was 'least said soonest mended'. But at the end comes a series of maxims for the Quietist ruler: 'The man of violence never yet came to a good end. He that delights in victory meets his match at last. As surely as bandits hate their chief, so do the people of a country resent whatever is over them. The man of discernment, knowing that a kingdom cannot be mounted, gets under it; knowing that the people cannot be led he keeps behind them. . . . Play obstinately the female's part,

[1] In this sense sometimes written with the 'woman' determinative.

cling to the under place; and no one will be able to contend with you. All men turn to *that*; I only keep *this*. All men vainly stray; I alone am unmoved. I keep my knowledge to myself; I discuss the mysteries of my craft with none. . . . If the Yang-tzŭ and the Yellow River have mastery over the hundred streams, it is because they humble themselves and take the low ground. It is heaven's way to show no partiality,[1] but ever to side with the good[2] man.'

There is some reason to suppose that the Inscription on the Statue is one of the 'Six Inscriptions of the Yellow Ancestor', a work still current in the Han dynasty. See Ku Chieh-kang, *Ku Shih Pien*, Vol. IV, p. 501.

Chapter XLVI

Chiao means here not the 'outskirts' of the kingdom, but the mound on the outskirts of the capital, scene of the Great Sacrifice (cf. Maspero, *La Chine Antique*, p. 225 seq.) which inaugurated the season's agriculture. To let weeds grow on this mound was a sacrilege;[3] and to breed warhorses upon it, a double profanation. For the Great Sacrifice is essentially connected with peace.

'Lure.' The root means 'fluttering' like a bird. Hence (1) to set a trap, to lure. (2) to be caught in meshes (of the law), a criminal. (3) that which involves one in such meshes, a crime.

Chapter LIII

Chieh-jan, 'the least scrap of'. Cf. *Lieh Tzŭ*, IV. 2.

[1] No personal favour.   [2] i.e. with the Quietist.

[3] Compare *Hsün Tzŭ*, P'ien 16, end: 'He who does not sweep the droppings at home is not likely to notice that weeds run riot on the *chiao* mound.'

'The least scrap of any existing thing, the least whisper of
sound. . . .' It can also be used of time: 'A hill-way used
only for the least little while turns into a well-defined
path. . . . (*Mencius* VII. Part II, 21.)

Chapter LVIII

The phrase translated 'shapes the corners without lopping' has a long history, and has been put to a variety of
different uses. It primarily describes jade, which is 'cor-
nered without being jagged' (see *K'ung Tzŭ Chia Yü*,
P'ien 36) and thus becomes the symbol of morality, which
is scrupulous without being prickly', or of conduct (*hsing*),
as in *Kuan Tzŭ*, 39. For other applications see *Hsün Tzŭ*,
3, and 30 which is a variant on the *Chia Yü* passage.

Chapter LXXIX

It was believed[1] that in the time of the ancient Sages a
certain proportion of land in each village had been set aside
as 'common land' and its produce handed over to officials
to be used for communal purposes, such as (1) the support
of the aged and needy, (2) the support of officials. Under
the Yin dynasty, it was said, this system was known as
'labour-loaning', because the villagers lent their labour to
the community. This term came to have the meaning
'assistance', because the needy were 'helped' out of the
fund so established. But it also came to mean 'taxation',
because the produce was handed over to and in part used
by officials. The author here uses the term assistance
('Almoner', literally 'Assister') in the first sense. In the

[1] What relation these beliefs bear to any actual, ancient system of
tithe it is hard to say.

Chou dynasty, it was said, various local systems of tithe were replaced by a 'general' system, and the word 'general' (*ch'ê*) came to mean tithing, tax-exaction. This is the word here used in the phrase *ssǔ-ch'ê*, 'controller of taxes, perquisitor'. The saying quoted in the end of the chapter (It is Heaven's way . . .) is from the Inscription on the Statue (see Ch. XLII, additional notes); but it occurs elsewhere, in a variety of forms.

Tallies played in the life of the early Chinese the same part that tickets, cheques, etc., do in Europe to-day. They were used as 'passes' of admission to fortified places, as 'tickets' entitling the owners to a share in sacrificial meat, as 'cheques' in commerce. The importance of the tally in actual life is attested by the great variety of metaphorical senses in which the expression 'fitting the tallies' is used by early writers. Thus Mencius (IV. 2. 1) says that the methods of all the Sages, both former and latter, 'fit like tallies'. The Codifiers said that if everything helpful and everything inimical to the State were defined, the ruler would merely have to 'fit the tallies' by allotting rewards and punishments according to the Code. It is used of deeds that are 'as good as' words, of theories that work in practice, and finally at a later date, of the successful 'fitting together' of ingredients in alchemy.

TEXTUAL NOTES

Ch. 1 故; 固. 徹. Ch. 2 較. 形 was merely substituted to secure an extra rhyme. Ch. 10 營 for 熒, as frequently in old texts, with the meaning 惑 'astray'. Ch. 13 omit 寵 before 爲; it is a gloss on 之. Ch. 21 'warriors'. 夫, 甫 and 父 are all etymologically the same, coming from a root meaning 'adult man'. Its 'charge'. . . . 名 in the sense of 命. 令 is cognate; the original root was *mling*. Ch. 25. Play on 大 and 達, which were both pronounced approximately *d'ât*. 域 in sense of 或, logical 'divisions' (?). Ch. 32 read 道常而無名. Ch. 34 read 而不有. 衣被 . . . Ch. 39 貞 and 正. Ch. 42 read 者得, omitting 不, which has crept in owing to the negative in the original proverb. Ch. 59 read 服, in the same sense as in 服藥, etc. Ch. 72 壓 and 厭. 狎 in the sense of 狹. The two words are however etymologically the same; see Karlgren, *Anal. Dict*, p. 123, Ch. 73 繟 in sense of 嘽.

Ch. 79: Pun on 契 and 挈. The original of course facilitated the play on words by merely writing 㓞.

INDEX

Index

Index

Index

Wadsworth
Belmont, CA
94002

Expl. Rel.
Roger Schmidt